What's Wrong with Microfinance?

Praise for *What's Wrong with Microfinance?*

'*What's Wrong With Microfinance?* unapologetically asks questions that others have been too polite, complacent, or uncritical to ask. Each chapter challenges received wisdom about banking the world's poor. You don't have to agree with everything here, or even most of it, to learn a great deal. Creating the next generation of inclusive banks will require tough-minded appraisals of what we know and what we don't. By tackling hype, *What's Wrong With Microfinance?* provides hope for achieving the real promise of microfinance.'

Jonathan Morduch, Professor of Public Policy and Economics, New York University and co-author of *The Economics of Microfinance*

'A timely collection of expert treaties questioning the scope of and rationales for microfinance. Specifically aimed at giving a reality check at a time when hype around microfinance's potential has never been greater, the book's uniquely well-informed authors success in debunking key myths that have arisen in the mushrooming of this global industry.'

Dr Ben Rogaly, Senior Lecturer in Human Geography, University of Sussex, UK

'During a stampede it's useful for someone to ride apart from the herd and speculate about where the multitude is going. The Harper and Dichter book does this for the widely promoted and highly praised microfinance industry...'

Dr Dale W. Adams, Professor Emeritus, The Ohio State University

'This book by Microfinance insiders will be invaluable to the enthusiasts as well as the critics of Microfinance...'

Sukhwinder Arora, Microfinance Professional

What's Wrong with Microfinance?

Edited by
Thomas Dichter and Malcolm Harper

PRACTICAL ACTION
Publishing

Intermediate Technology Publications Ltd
trading as Practical Action Publishing
Schumacher Centre for Technology and Development
Bourton on Dunsmore, Rugby,
Warwickshire CV23 9QZ, UK
www.practicalactionpublishing.org

© Intermediate Technology Publications Ltd, 2007

ISBN 978 1 85339 667 0

Since 1974, Practical Action Publishing has published and disseminated
books and information in support of international development work
throughout the world. Practical Action Publishing (formerly ITDG
Publishing) is a trading name of Intermediate Technology Publications Ltd
(Company Reg. No. 1159018), the wholly owned publishing company of
Intermediate Technology Development Group Ltd (working name Practical
Action). Practical Action Publishing trades only in support of its parent
charity objectives and any profits are covenanted back to Practical Action
(Charity Reg. No. 247257, Group VAT Registration No. 880 9924 76).

Cover design by Mercer Design
Indexed by Indexing Specialists (UK) Ltd
Typeset by SJI Typesetting
Printed by CPI Antony Rowe, Eastbourne, UK

Contents

Part One: Clients

List of figures

List of tables

Acronyms and abbreviations

AMFI	Association of Microfinance Institutions
AP	Andhra Pradesh
ASCA	accumulating savings and credit association
ATM	aggravation, time and money
B&H	Bosnia and Herzegovina
BAAC	Bank for Agriculture and Agriculture Cooperatives
BRI	Bank Rakhyat Indonesia
CFPR/TUP	Challenging the Frontiers of Poverty Reduction: Targeting the Ultra Poor
CGAP	Consultative Group to Assist the Poor
CIPE	Centre for International Private Enterprise
COB	Central Obrera Boliviana
CRS	Catholic Relief Services
DFID	Department for International Development
DRDA	District Rural Development Agency
EIR	effective interest rate
GCS	Grameen classic system
GGS	Grameen generalized system
HYV	high yielding variety
IFI	international financial institution
IGA	income generating activity
IGVGD	Income Generation for Vulnerable Group Development
ILO	International Labour Organization
LAIW	livestock artificial insemination worker
LIP	Local Initiatives Project
MFI	microfinance institution
MFRC	Microfinance Regulatory Council

MIX	Microfinance Information Exchange
MSME	micro, small and medium enterprise
NABARD	National Bank for Agriculture and Rural Development
NBFC	non-banking finance company
NSUP	not selected ultra poor
OPM	other people's money
PfP	Partnership for Productivity
PKSF	Palli Karma-Sahayak Foundation
RBI	Reserve Bank of India
RD-12	Rural Development Project-12
ROSCA	rotating savings and credit association
SED	small enterprise development
SEWA	Self-Employed Women's Association
SFRY	Socialist Federal Republic of Yugoslavia
SHDF	Self-help Development Foundation
SHG	self-help group
SHPA	self-help promotion agency
SME	small and medium enterprise
SPM	social performance management
SUP	selected ultra poor
VGD	vulnerable group development
VO	village organization
VSLA	village saving and loan association
WFP	World Food Program

Contributors

Irina Aliaga (email irinaaliaga@hotmail.com) is a microfinance consultant in La Paz, Bolivia. From January 2007 she will be working for the Ford Foundation IMPACT consortium on measuring social performance in the microfinance NGO ProMujer Bolivia.

Hugh Allen (email hugh@vsla.net) has focused for the last 36 years on microfinance and market development activities. He is on the faculty of the Boulder Microfinance Training Program and Southern New Hampshire University's Microenterprise Development Institute. He is the founder of VSL Associates and writes extensively on community-based microfinance.

Milford Bateman (email milfordbateman@yahoo.com) is a freelance consultant specializing in sustainable local economic development policy and programming and community development strategies, focusing mainly on the Western Balkans. Since November 2005, he has been Visiting Professor of Economics at the University of Pula, Croatia.

Thomas Dichter (email tspdich@gmail.com) has spent half of his 40-year career in international development working in microfinance on three continents. He has published on microfinance and other development issues and is the author of *'Despite Good Intentions: Why Development Assistance to the Third World has Failed'*. He has a Ph.D. in anthropology from the University of Chicago.

David Ellerman (email david@ellerman.org) is visiting scholar at the University of California/Riverside after 10 years at the World Bank (advisor to Chief Economist Joseph Stiglitz) and has recently published: *'Helping People Help Themselves: From the World Bank to an Alternative Philosophy of Development Assistance'*.

Prabhu Ghate (email pghate@airtelbroadband.in) was formerly a Senior Economist with the Asian Development Bank and is now an independent researcher and consultant based in New Delhi. He was the lead author of *Informal Finance: Some Findings from Asia*. He has a Ph.D. in public policy from Princeton University.

Malcolm Harper (email Malcolm.harper@btinternet.com) taught at Cranfield School of Management until 1995, and since then has worked mainly in India. He has published on enterprise development and microfinance. He was Chairman of Basix Finance from 1996 until 2006, and is Chairman of M-CRIL, the microfinance credit rating agency.

Mary Houghton and *Ronald Grzywinski* are chairman and president of ShoreBank Corporation, a US$1.9 billion asset regulated commercial bank holding company, operating banks and NGOs in low- and moderate-income African-American neighbourhoods and two rural regions in the USA, and providing advisory and investment services in Africa, Asia and Eastern Europe. ShoreCap International is the equity investment company it has managed since 2003 for regulated financial institutions specializing in lending to the self-employed and small firms.

David Hulme is Professor of Development Studies, Institute for Development Policy and Management, University of Manchester, UK.

Susan Johnson has a background in economics and agricultural economics and has a Ph.D. in development studies from the University of Bath where she is lecturer. She has undertaken a range of research on microfinance and local financial markets particularly investigating their gender dimensions and impact.

Vijay Mahajan, a graduate of the Indian Institute of Management (Ahmedabad), was the founder chief executive and is now chairman of the Basix Finance group of companies in India. He is on the board of numerous livelihood promotion and other institutions. He is a charter member of the Development Finance Forum.

Imran Matin and *Munshi Sulaiman* work at BRAC's Research and Evaluation Division, and *M. A. Saleque* works in BRAC's Development Programme.

Richard L. Meyer (email meyer.19@osu.edu) is emeritus professor in the Department of Agricultural, Environmental and Development Economics in the Ohio State University. He is the former director of the Rural Finance Program.

Paul Mosley (email p.mosley@sheffield.ac.uk) is professor of Economics at the University of Sheffield. He has worked on microfinance and microinsurance in Asia, Africa and Latin America and is co-author of *'Finance Against Poverty'* (Routledge, 2 vols.,1996).

J. D. Von Pischke (email, jdvp@erols.com) is president of Frontier Finance International, the Washington office of IPC and ProCredit Holding. He was a World Bank staff member from 1976 to 1995, specializing in financial sector policy, and rural and small-scale industry finance

S. M. Rahman (email smr@bangla.net) was educated in business administration and statistics. He has worked in development banking, microenterprise and microfinance. He has reviewed microenterprise and governance issues of MFIs for joint donor strategy, and has authored articles on microfinance regulation and a book on client satisfaction in microfinance programs for CARE Bangladesh and co-authored a book on the commercialization of microfinance for the Asian Development Bank.

Paul Rippey (email paul@rippey.org) has worked in MFI management and as a technical donor in Africa over two decades. He is doing penance for past sins of debt-mongering by working with village savings and loans associations and consumer education, and as a climate change activist.

Namrata Sharma is currently a freelance consultant. She was the founding managing director of the Center for Microfinance Nepal and then director of the Indian School of Microfinance for Women, Ahmedabad. She has also been a visiting research fellow at the University of Bath, and is a board member of Microfinance Opportunities, USA and other organizations in Nepal.

Frances Sinha (email francessinha@edarural.com) is co-founder and executive director of EDA Rural Systems Pvt. Ltd, a development consultancy for microfinance and livelihoods. A graduate from Oxford University and the London School of Economics, Frances has over 20 years' development experience based in India.

Kim Wilson (email Kimberley.Wilson@Tufts.edu) is lecturer in international business at the Fletcher School, Tufts University. Previously, she was director of the Microfinance Unit at CRS. At varied points in her career she has been a microfinance client, microloan officer, manager, board member, consultant, investor, donor and evaluator.

Introduction

Thomas Dichter

> To halt the momentum of an accepted idea, to re-examine assumptions, is a
> disturbing process.
>
> Barbara Tuchman, 1970[1]

Microfinance has been an accepted idea with a longer run than most in the
realm of third world poverty reduction. If one counts the time from the advent
of microcredit (still the bulk of the practice), it has been around for about half
the six-decade-long lifespan of official development assistance. But it is only in
the last decade that its momentum has picked up dramatically, beginning with
the huge attendance at the first Microcredit Summit in Washington in 1997 and
reaching a glorious peak in 2005 and 2006 that few would have predicted a
decade earlier. 2005 was declared the Year of Microcredit by the UN and in
2006, Mohamed Yunus and the Grameen Bank he founded in 1983 won the
Nobel Peace Prize. Suddenly microfinance (and in particular microcredit) was a
subject of discussion where it had never been before – at dinner tables, cocktail
parties and in the lofty heights of publications like *The New Yorker*.

Asked in an interview what she thought the results of the UN's Year of
Microcredit were, Christina Barrineau, senior technical advisor to the Year of
Microcredit said:

> people stopped seeing microcredit only as a ten-dollar loan to a woman
> buying a goat, and started seeing the poor as masterful business people,
> tremendously entrepreneurial – people who have fundamental business skills
> and really warrant access to financial services that will help them grow their
> wealth.

This view of the poor as budding entrepreneurs, who, with access to formal
financial services, would pull themselves out of poverty through business
development, asset accumulation and wealth creation lies at the core of the new
high profile of microfinance. It is this view that has inspired a new breed of
philanthropists, like Pierre Omidyar who created a US$100 million microfinance
fund, the ultimate goal of which is 'to unleash the entrepreneurial instinct' of
the poor.

This book is aimed at the microfinance industry itself, but also, and perhaps
more importantly, at the growing numbers of policy makers, politicians and

especially new money philanthropists who have become enthusiasts of such views of the power of microfinance. It is not meant 'to halt the momentum of an accepted idea' – we could not do that even if we tried – but to raise questions about it, indeed reexamine certain assumptions, and deflate the least warranted of the growing number of over-inflated expectations.

The book's authors are 22 microfinance 'insiders', who together have over 300 years of experience practicing, evaluating and studying microfinance. If we are mustering any courage here, it is no more than the willingness to step off a large boat that we helped build and propel, at least long enough to slow it down a bit, so that some space for sober reflection on the future might be created.

Why bother? After all, over-inflated expectations are nothing new when it comes to trying to improve the lot of the poor, and some may even argue that they play a positive role in raising the bar of achievement higher than it otherwise would be.

But in this case over-inflated expectations are unhelpful for several reasons. First, there is an opportunity cost involved when so much attention is paid to one sector – inevitably other possible answers to poverty reduction get less attention, especially if they seem more complex or difficult. Second, they propel more organizations to get involved in microfinance, some because that is where the limelight is shining. The proliferation of more and more players, while perhaps creating healthy competition, is also likely to add amateurishness where we need more professionalism, to add noise to a field that right now may need a bit of quiet time, and to raise the possibility of distortions in the microfinance marketplace as players vie for the same markets or client territory. Finally, over-inflated expectations make it more likely that in the excitement to do more of what appears to be such a good thing, more money will be attracted to microfinance. Hence the chances of some harm being done – collateral damage, if you like – become greater, if only because there are absorptive capacity limits on both the part of lenders and borrowers (despite a statistical basis for concluding that there exists huge unmet 'demand', it remains to be seen whether or not that demand is 'effective demand').

How did we get here?

Microcredit evolved slowly. From the 1950s through to the early 1970s, the development endeavour focused much on economic development and still toyed with the notion of industrial development, a kind of catching-up with the west by replication and imitation. Other efforts were being made of course, especially in agriculture where a mix of crop improvement technologies and small farmer credit was tried, with little long-term success. As development thinking focused more on the intractable nature of poverty in the early 1970s, the poor and their immediate needs became paramount. The emphasis on industrial development shifted downward to small business development, or what came to be called 'small-scale industry promotion', and then 'small enterprise development' (SED).

It wasn't long before the shift to direct aid to the poor brought us from small to 'micro enterprises'. The assistance tool kit accordingly became a reduced version of business school – marketing, bookkeeping, inventory control, production skills and the like. Capital was not really a part of the mix. But by the 1970s, experiments in supplying capital were being undertaken, not just by Yunus in Bangladesh in 1976 (when he first began), but by the Self-Employed Women's Association (SEWA) in India and in Latin America.

In 1972, in an International Labour Organization (ILO) report by Hans Singer (ILO, 1972) and his colleagues, the term 'informal sector' was coined and by the 1980s it was growing rapidly in many of the poorest countries. The informal sector became a magnet for development thinking and funding. Because so many poor were trying to generate income in it, loans for the poor to develop the activities they were engaged in, seemed a logical step.

The Committee of Donor Agencies for Small Enterprise Development gave impetus and legitimacy to the joining of microenterprise development and credit, and in turn their marriage to NGOs. Mohamed Yunus of Grameen Bank was the principal speaker at the committee's June 1988 international meeting in Washington, where a large number of issues were debated. It was there that the debate on technical assistance versus credit became more pronounced. Judith Tendler reported on projects that only provided loans, and she and others used the term 'minimalist' to advocate a credit-only approach to microenterprise assistance. And it was there that NGOs were called upon as naturals to provide credit to the microenterprises run by the very poor. NGOs could do it, it was assumed, because they were both ideologically motivated and, as grassroots practitioners, appropriately positioned. Banks and governments, it was claimed, could not be counted upon to reach the poor effectively. A new kind of financial intermediary, a microfinance institution (MFI) was now being discussed more widely.

As more and more microcredit projects were undertaken, many were led by NGOs, some quite specialized, but some also large and venerable ones like CARE or Catholic Relief Services, which added microcredit projects to what they were already doing. There was much to learn and much experimentation went on. The reasons why formal banks did not lend to the poor supplied the challenges to the new movement. What could substitute for collateral? How could the loan product be made more accessible? How could the lender become efficient when the loan size was so small? Could other services, or other messages to the poor (about health, nutrition, etc.) be combined with microcredit? Should not women become the main clientele because they are better repayers and invest more in their families' welfare?

Out of these questions grew experiments with joint liability or 'solidarity' groups, village banking, bicycle bankers, door-to-door service, and so on. Accounting systems, and later software specifically designed for microlending evolved, as did training programmes for the staff of microcredit operations.

Microcredit also began to be taken more seriously by more agencies and policy makers. The World Bank began looking at it, studying and funding it.

And eventually, as the excitement grew, the demand to be seen as 'involved in microcredit' also grew and all manner of projects and programmes began identifying themselves as such. Credit unions, which have been around for a century, claimed (sometimes legitimately so) to be doing microcredit, as did others.

A new generation of issues and questions took shape. With some data under its belt, the field began to note some operational problems such as drop-outs and certain inefficiencies. The intention of reaching the poorest began to run up against the growing demand to become more business-like and to be successful as a financial institution. The outreach versus sustainability debate was on. And below the surface a debate on subsidized microfinance (which has characterized most programmes to date) versus commercially viable microfinance began forming. A few began questioning why the field did not focus more on savings and one of the answers was that savings deposit mobilization was not something anyone could do, since in most places bank regulations were involved and NGOs and other non-bank financial intermediaries were not qualified to take deposits under existing laws. A debate on impact began and some began studying borrower behaviour. Female empowerment and consumption smoothing began to appear as effects that were not originally predicted. Some also began to ask more trenchant questions about the almost universally reported high repayment rates of 96–99 per cent. Weren't there other measures that said more about performance such as arrears rates? The question of how and whether success could be had in rural agricultural lending, where the constraints were very different than in high cash flow urban markets, kept popping up periodically. All the while the field grew at a strong pace, with more and more operators and more and more donors getting involved.

By the 1990s, an inevitable effort to make microfinance more professional took place. CGAP (whose original name was the Consultative Group to Assist the Poorest) was formed in 1995 by a group of major donors and created a secretariat housed at the World Bank. A corpus of 'best practices' had evolved and was now being promoted. A series of exhaustive manuals was produced, and some academics became interested in studying microfinance. Within the industry, the focus began to be as much on the lender as on the beneficiary.

Almost as a sign of legitimacy was the coming to prominence of a number of writers and organizations whose main aim is not to practice microfinance but to promote it, such as the Grameen Foundation and Results, Inc., which evolved into the MicroSummit Campaign. Yet notwithstanding this exciting history of a field 'coming into its own', in some important ways microfinance is an immature and unproven field. It is significant that we don't really know where we stand. We have no reliable aggregate numbers on clients, active or inactive, and continue to assume that the gap between those reached and those not reached automatically means a demand for our services (without taking debt capacity into account). Nor do we have even a rough sense of who has moved out of poverty and who has not. With so many different operators and types of projects and programmes all finding common ground under the rubric of microfinance, we have instead a babel of claims, some based on anecdote, others more rigorously based on solid research, but still with methodological differences needing to be unpacked very carefully in order to sort them out. One result is that anyone can say almost anything, and with the public relations surrounding the field, much of it goes unquestioned. The Microcredit Summit campaign not surprisingly claims that its 1997 goal of outreach to 100 million poor families has come close to being reached, whereas Microfinance Information Exchange (MIX) data suggest that specialist microfinance institutions have reached about 30 million.

Yet in 2005, the Year of Microcredit, according to CGAP, 55,000 staff days and US$30 million were spent on 120 microfinance conferences, many of them in celebration of microfinance as an accepted idea and an accomplished set of practices. Despite the fact that there continue to be some lively debates within the field, it is undeniable that a degree of self-satisfaction has set in.

Perhaps because of all the publicity, there is now some 'push back', on the part of the poor, on the part of some large players who have decided to quit the field, and on the part of governments, who raise questions about transparency and about whether some of the players have gone beyond the bounds of their legal status. And the old debate about interest rates is back.

The time is ripe to look again, to raise some new questions as well as some old ones in new ways. Is microfinance in some sense a temporary, perhaps even second rate kind of intervention, promising at best to be a short-term palliative? Is it really a step on the road to business development and economic growth, and if it is not, what else needs to be done to make it so (business advisory services, crop insurance, health insurance, remittance transfer services, etc.)? Can an MFI really work if it embraces the 'double bottom line' of both profit and social good? Does the issue of who reaches (or whether we ought to reach) the poorest, or the just plain poor, or the not-so-poor, still have resonance? (Note that in 2003, CGAP somewhat quietly substituted the word 'Poor' for 'Poorest' in its name.) Has the level just above the poor been neglected – the so-called 'missing middle', who might make productive use of a loan that is not quite 'micro'?

Savings is back on the table and many who were once the solid backbone of the credit movement have abandoned credit as misguided. Village-level savings associations, sustainable almost by definition, requiring little outside help and no funding, are now much discussed; an ironic comment perhaps on a long history of rotating savings and credit associations (ROSCAs) in the developing world, indigenous (and informal) savings and loan systems that ran pretty well on their own.

Is microfinance, especially credit, harmful? Ought we not to talk more openly about its flip side – debt? Are too many players creating a supply-driven phenomenon, where borrowers are being in some sense forced to take the money? What does microfinance's emphasis on groups mean? Do people like being in groups? Is this form for our benefit or theirs? Can communities really run formal financial services on their own, over time and sustainably? What does microfinance do to social norms? Is women's empowerment perhaps an even better outcome of microfinance than any other because it creates a genuinely revolutionary foundation for development?

And of course we are ready now to see that much gamesmanship goes on in the field, where politicians, the elite and governments take advantage of microfinance programmes, using them for ends other than helping the poor.

All of these topics and questions are touched upon in the book, which is organized in three sections: Part One – Clients, Part Two – Institutions, and Part Three – Expectations. We have put clients first, in part because in some quarters they have taken second position to the MFIs themselves. And we have placed expectations as a rubric for the questions of impact and a hopefully sober reflection of what microfinance does and cannot, and perhaps ought not, do.

However limited an effort our book may be (we know much has been left out) we hope it will stimulate a more reflective microfinance in the future than we have witnessed thus far.

Note

1   Barbara Tuchman is describing American 'misapprehension' of the reality of China's mismanagement by the Kuomintang, in *Stilwell and the American Experience in China, 1911–1945*, Macmillan, New York, 1970, p. 354.

Reference

International Labour Office (ILO) (1972) *Employment, Incomes and Equality*, ILO, Geneva.

PART ONE

Clients

CHAPTER ONE

Can microcredit make an already slippery slope more slippery?
Some lessons from the social meaning of debt

Thomas Dichter

Neither a borrower nor a lender be. For loan oft loses both itself and friend, and borrowing dulls the edge of husbandry.

> William Shakespeare (Polonius in *Hamlet*, 1603)

Kupopa harusi kulipa matanga!
(It's merry to borrow money but paying back is a sad affair – more like milking a stone!)

> Swahili proverb

Abstract

This chapter looks at the complex and often contradictory symbolism behind the concept of debt, and raises questions about the extent to which the microfinance industry, with its recent tendencies to promote microcredit for all, may be ignoring these subtle meanings and their functions. By better understanding the deeper meanings surrounding debt, the microfinance industry might better understand such issues as the role of moneylenders, or the problem of client drop-out. The chapter also discusses the social cohesion roles of pre-existing informal safety nets and mutual aid systems, and suggests that by pushing more formal microcredit, we are hastening the demise of such systems. The industry ought to give more careful thought to what pitfalls and social costs it may be abetting by pushing credit as if it were a natural 'right', and ignoring the darker side of credit-debt.

For years the microfinance industry has swept the issue of debt under the carpet. Microcredit, seen as a poverty alleviation tool, could only have one side, the good side. But if microcredit providers have been myopic about debt, the poor of the developing world have not. They get it. Borrowing money means being in debt and their attitudes about this fact have generally been neglected. Perhaps more important, the mechanisms that kept people out of debt in traditional societies – mutual aid, family exchanges and other reciprocal forms of economic safety nets – may well be threatened by the growing tendency to democratize credit for the poor as a natural 'right'. There is – and this is the point of this chapter – hidden beneath the surface of microcredit, a dark and slippery slope that begins with the simple fact of debt.

But first, a couple of caveats. I argue elsewhere in this book (Chapter 15) that mass credit aimed at the poor was historically consumer credit and not enterprise credit. In current microfinance (as argued by others in this book), while there is evidence of some microcredit use as working capital for income generation, large amounts of microcredit go to consumption, even if that consumption is not 'consumerist' but necessary 'consumption smoothing'. I do not want, in this chapter, either to demonize microcredit as being a step on the way to a cold capitalistic consumerism in which all other values recede in importance, nor, in some nostalgic paean to the past, to romanticize social capital and social cohesion in traditional societies. What I want to do is show that somewhere between the hopes surrounding more accessible credit, and the dangers surrounding debt, there is a multi-layered grey area, filled with rich symbols and often conflicted meanings. Microfinance institutions ought to pay more attention to them.

A brief foray into the symbology of debt

There are levels and nuances of meaning surrounding debt, and these change with time, place and context. But generally speaking, debt has almost always carried a heavy load of largely negative symbols as well an emotional 'charge' for the debtor. The basis for that richness is probably money itself, which has a universally powerful emotional and symbolic magnetic 'field'. Money is clearly much more than just an efficient means of exchange. Money has been associated with magic, with male virility and female fertility, with power and dominance and more. We all know that having lots of money is seen as enabling freedom and independence, and even conveying authority (we tend to listen to people who have lots of money, as if that gives them special access to knowledge). Money can carry negative imagery, as for example a 'drug' or a 'poison', and it can be characterized positively, as for example, a great leveler, erasing the lines between 'classes'. And money's 'charge' can be different depending on whose money it is. If it is perceived as 'my money', it is likely to be used, cared for and categorized differently than if it is other people's money (OPM). If my travel is being reimbursed by a client I'll take a taxi to the airport. If I'm using my own money, I'll take the bus. There is 'cold' money and 'hot'. And the categorization process, the symbolization process, can be further parsed depending upon whether OPM is being lent to me as a credit, or given to me as a gift. And if the OPM is being lent to me as a credit, how I perceive it (and even how quickly I pay it back) may depend on who the other people are, whether they are a bank, a moneylender, a relative or an NGO, and even on whether the lender is seen as 'near', or 'far away'.

Given how such symbols and meanings cling to money like thousands of iron filings drawn to a magnet, it should not be surprising that debt is also fraught with complex meanings in different times and places, and even that people might play mind games with the subject, telling themselves that what is really a debt is not.

In an oral history of credit in Northern Ireland's working class, the author notes the role that community networks have played '…in producing frequently complex and often ambiguous attitudes to various forms of credit' (O'Connell, 2004). The study goes on to note a fair amount of denial in beliefs about credit. Many people do not call certain kinds of arrangements credit, especially informal ones, for example, 'for those women a system involving weekly payments… did not represent credit as they understood it' (O'Connell, 2004).

Debt, obligation and power: A complex relationship

To be in debt can mean a loss of respectability, to be seen by others as less independent, less self-reliant, or in the power or control of others. To be in debt can mean weakness, or being dominated by or 'beholden' to others.

Debt etymology is revealing. To 'owe' is related to 'to own' and in medieval times had the sense of to 'keep something away from'. In French the word *devoir* means both to be in debt and to have a duty. To pay off the debt is, in current slang, to be *quitte*, the sense of which is 'we're even', or we are once again equals. For in French culture (the land of *liberté, égalité et fraternité*) to be in debt has less to do with a loss of self-reliance and more with a sense that one is 'less' than the other, unequal.

When a debt is incurred between a borrower and a creditor who know each other, or who are relatives or friends, a subtle change in the relationship is involved. That change can be complicated, involving other shifts in power or shifts in self-image. Even cancelling or forgiving a debt can involve a subtle change in power – the creditor may exercise even more power by saying 'forget it', than when the debt was still outstanding. Ironically, even though the debt is now gone, at some level the debtor and creditor are likely to feel it still lives on. And if debt involves a loss of power on the part of the debtors, debt can be a burden on credit-givers too, especially when it is something they perceive as having little choice about.

In 1950, American anthropologist Laurence Wylie installed himself and his family in a southern French village. They stayed there a year, penetrating as much as they could the inner workings of the community. Here are some of Wylie's observations about credit:

'Ah, Monsieur, credit is a festering sore on the body of commerce!' says Monsieur Reynard. This is a favorite phrase of all the merchants of Peyrane… A request for credit makes the merchant uneasy, though he may smile and say, 'Why, of course. Pay whenever you like.' An unpaid account is an account that despite the best intentions may, through some unforeseen accident, never be paid. (Wylie, 1964)

Wylie tells the story of a Madame Malitourne who has a myriad of financial problems, including a husband who has gone to Marseille in a futile search for work. She is the classic case of what Wylie calls a 'credit attack' when she goes from grocer to grocer, having been refused by Monsieur Reynard (above), who apparently had certain limits after all.

> Fortunately for Madame Malitourne, there are four other groceries in Peyrane, too many... for so small a town, but each of them continues to struggle along, hoping that the others will fail first. Of these four Arène's is the least secure, so it is there that the poorest families shop. When Arène fails, as he inevitably will, they will turn to the next most insecure grocer. In effect, the credit system amounts to a poor tax on the merchant who is least able to afford it. (Wylie, 1964)

The debt burden affects the creditor in other ways too. In a situation where the debt is incurred by a relative or friend, and the payment is not made when expected, the relationship can easily deteriorate. But for the creditor especially there is an emotional burden of how and when to begin to ask for the money back. Confronting late borrowers is also a burden in formal credit arrangements. NGOs in microcredit do not like the role of hounding clients. There is a cost to this, not just in terms of time and money, but in terms of one's view of who one is and what kind of organization one is.

The complexity of the debtor–creditor relationship in traditional societies shows itself when the formal part of the relationship (such as a promissory note) gets into direct conflict with prevailing attitudes or values, thus making the formal arrangement moot or ineffective. So even though legally a debtor can by law be forced to pay, few creditors are willing to take this course, not only because it might be bad for future business, but, in the case of Wylie's village, simply because it's just not done; to go to the law is seen as a traitorous act: '...people of Peyrane have the utmost distrust of the Law and anyone connected with it. ("*Homme de loi, homme de merde,*" the men say)' (Wylie, 1964).

Complex attitudes towards debt are more likely to prevail in village or other traditional settings

In the microfinance context of today, it is important to see how much the symbology of debt and credit is likely still to remain alive, given how similar are the conditions of many of today's microfinance targets to the peasants, villagers and 'little men' of Europe, the US or Canada in the 19th and early 20th centuries. The attitudes of Wylie's French villagers in 1950 have their roots in peasant life in Europe, a life that was agricultural, based on subsistence, with little surplus; a life in isolation, lacking in mobility, a family economy, often using very little cash.

Another anthropologist, Conrad Arensberg studied rural life in Ireland in the 1930s. He points out that in the census of 1926, 63 per cent of Ireland's people lived in rural areas, and the vast majority of these were farmers, with a landholding of 30 to 50 acres, with small farmers being the single largest group.

> He works a small farm with the help of his family. He raises a small garden of potatoes and a few other foodstuffs which feed both himself and his beasts. He need go to town only for clothing and sundries, for flour and tea, and to sell at the fairs the calves and yearlings which bring in his principal monetary income... and with the sale his participation in trade and commerce, in 'business', is finished except for his account with the shopkeeper... it is a livelihood little connected with the outside world. (Arensberg, 1959)

In a world of relative isolation, based on a family economy, lack of familiarity with the outside world and hence distrust and fear of it, are somewhat inevitable. Whatever is 'outside' is alien. Trust can only exist among known and familiar entities. Thus the law, and formal institutions such as banks, are distant abstract strangers. To be in debt to such outsiders is thus fundamentally different from being in debt to a friend, a family member or even a landlord. With these creditors one understands the rules of the game and thus, even though one gives up a degree of control, it is better than the total loss of control involved in a debt to a large, formal, far away institution such as a bank.

Microfinance today makes a mistake in thinking that it is about financial services, plain and simple, with the main concerns being the technical ones surrounding operating costs, transaction costs for both the MFI and the borrower, innovations in collateral substitutions, repayment discipline, interest rates and the like. Those MFIs that work especially close to the poorest borrowers and do so in a 'close' relational way, as is the case with many non-bank MFIs like NGOs, need to be especially aware of the symbols and layers of what is going on behind the mere transaction. Looking at the deeper social meaning of debt can provide insight, for example, into why joint liability works or does not work, give more depth to the issue of drop-outs, help explain misunderstandings about interest rates, uncover unexpressed hopes about further larger loans, or about what happens when women give their loans to their husbands.

Thinking about debt in this socio-cultural way might also reveal, for example, that moneylenders are not the villains they seem, at least not to those they are presumed to 'exploit'. The insight one might gain is that moneylenders are often viewed benignly because they combine several things at once. They are near and distant, known entities but not 'friends'. As a result there is less loss of face incurred in dealing with a moneylender, less ambiguity, less ambivalence. Most important, they give fast service and are available. In an emergency, moneylenders may even lend needed cash in the middle of the night.

Reflecting on the symbology of debt may also provide a better understanding of the willingness-to-pay reasoning. Willingness to pay may not be simply a proxy for a presumed 'good' use of the funds, nor may it be proof that the borrower is afraid of sanctions. It can also be a way to create, maintain or further a relationship, even when in fact there isn't one.

Debt and morality

Beneath the surface of the concept of debt, almost everywhere in the world, are moral implications. And almost everywhere debt has been seen as bad; bad for society, bad for the individual, bad for religion, bad for the family. A debtor was everything from lacking in strong moral fibre and character, to a costly burden on society. Debtors' prisons were widespread in Europe and were only outlawed in the USA in 1833. In the late 18th century in some areas of the state of New Jersey, the publicly supported pauper – one who lived off the charity of the state or who was in debtors' prison – was stigmatized by being required to wear a blue or red letter 'P'.

Debt was trouble and the trouble was associated very often with alcohol or gambling, thus further deepening the stigma – a drinker or a gambler was intemperate and so was a debtor. Debt, like gambling and alcohol, can be addictive; once you begin, it's hard to stop, as expressed in the commonly used metaphor 'the treadmill of debt', or this Somali proverb: 'Don't dig a hole, and if you do, don't dig it deep, you don't know if you might fall into it'.

The first reform movements in the USA, Scotland and elsewhere were an interesting conflation of this symbolism of the poor as tending to intemperate behaviour and as potential debtors. The early savings movement was associated with the teaching of a moral code to the poor, so that they would stop 'wasting' their money (the subtext often was) 'on drink'. In the early 1730s, reformism took root in the American state of Georgia when 'the well meaning founders... hoping to create a moral climate to turn the victims of debtors' prisons into sound pioneers, barred from the new Colony both slavery and strong drink' (Furnas, 1969).

The obvious first association that debt seems to conjure up almost everywhere is shame, not just a private shame, but one that is reinforced by the opinions of one's peers. In the Belfast study mentioned earlier, 'all the interviewees had a preference for cash purchases wherever possible... They were almost universally critical of those who got themselves into debt' (O'Connell, 2004). Debt was a sign of bad management, to be sure, but the moral opprobrium was perhaps more important, since if you were in debt you were at the least, imprudent, perhaps even extravagant, and extravagance is the opposite of thrift.

Debt and guilt

Besides the social stigma carried by the opinions of others in one's social circle, the debtor's own psychology can and could become implicated in an even more complex set of twists. Nietzsche claimed that the indebted person internalizes the guilt imposed by the debt. That is to say that the indebted person could end up feeling, depending on the constructs available in a particular culture, unequal in stature, unempowered, diminished, and could even undergo a loss of identity. One possible result of this is suicide. Chapter 14 in this book on the Andhra Pradesh crisis in 2006 notes the large numbers of debtor suicides. We have seen similar but less dramatic phenomena in other countries including the UK, Canada, the USA and Japan, where it has recently been estimated that 30 Japanese per day kill themselves because of economic problems, including debt (West, 2003).

Suicide seems to be carrying the internalization of guilt (or shame) to an extreme of irrationality. But such extremes can also occur at the other end of the psychological spectrum, when feelings of guilt or shame become *externalized* as anger, resentment and even violence towards others.

One might seek to find the origins of this guilt in some sort of primal tension between good and evil or between savage and civilized. The American psychologist Edward L. Thorndike was thinking along those lines when he talked about the essential conflict between the 'potency of the sensory appetites' and 'thrift'. To borrow in order to spend is to give in to those sensory appetites; to give in to one's primal (uncivilized) side (Thorndike, 1920).

Encouraging credit can help the poor, but it can also be a slippery slope, not just towards debt, but to a loss of certain values

In 1950, the attitude towards credit in Laurence Wylie's French village was probably similar to what it had been in 1850. Wylie reports what the local blacksmith, Monsieur Prayal, had said to him: 'No one here will ask for credit if he can avoid it. No one wants to be obligated to anyone' (Wylie, 1964). But ten years later, after television (and the instalment plan) had come to Peyrane, attitudes had changed drastically. Emile, a mason, bought a TV and paid for it on the instalment plan. 'This sort of transaction was new to him and contrary to his family training... Now, however, he is convinced that he has been foolish all these years to stay out of debt. "The way prices keep going up," he said, "it's stupid not to get what you want when you want it – within reason, of course"' (Wylie, 1964).

My own experience may help highlight the changes in developed country attitudes towards debt. I grew up in a small rural town in the eastern USA. In 1955 at the age of 14, I opened a savings account at a local bank. I had no further interaction with banks until after college when I opened a checking account. In my early 30s, I took a mortgage when I purchased my first house. I am now in my 60s and have paid off my mortgages and have no debt at all. My only relationship with a bank is a checking account. My savings are now in the form of stocks and bonds and the equity in my property. I have one credit card and I take advantage of the 30-day 'float' between when I purchase and when the credit card amount is due, at which time I pay in full. The credit card company doesn't like people like me since they are in effect paying *me* interest. And while, in a sense, I am no longer an 'average person' (my education and my modest net worth have to my surprise moved me into a higher than average category), I am in many ways still fairly representative of the mind set of most people of my generation. Debt is still not a nice word, credit is not something I want or need, and the best thing one can do with money is to save it.

On the other hand, I am a part of a dwindling group.

We see today in most affluent countries a growing tendency to accept debt as OK, in fact in some quarters being in debt is not only OK but even 'cool'. Led by the USA, with its enormous load of credit card debt, many other countries are following the same path. And the youngest generations are on the road to what is in effect instant gratification, through debt. This seems to have replaced delayed gratification through savings, and the USA in 2005 reached a 0 per cent savings rate, the lowest in 75 years. Some societies resist this, such as Japan that continues to have a high savings rate, and France that encourages debit cards rather than credit cards, though the latter are catching up fast. But the movement in the affluent developed world is fairly clear – more and more, there is less and less a negative association with debt. Certainly the social stigma is gone.

For the most part, microfinance has failed to see the slippery slope towards consumerism, and the loss of certain values (embodied in indigenous ways of coping based on reciprocity or mutual aid) that may occur as the result of even partly encouraging widespread formal credit use. Historically valuable mechanisms of reciprocity, exchange, and mutual trust constituted what Durkheim called *'gemeinschaft'* (community). This was the original 'social capital'. And Durkheim's student, Marcel Mauss, studying gifts and exchange in primitive society, concluded that gift exchange formed the entire basis of solidarity – exchanges held people together.

In Tswana society, principles of reciprocity are linked to a central principle of civility (*Botho*) with its implication of being well-mannered, courteous and disciplined. These principles and their associations in personality and character are being actively encouraged in Botswana today, in part as a way of coping with the spread of HIV/Aids. Tswana burial societies, for examples, are a resurrected form of savings-based mutual aid and take off from traditional principles of reciprocity and indigenous definitions of character.

The historical shift from *gemeinschaft* to *gesellschaft*, from community to formal, contractual, more abstract connections (society in the coldest sense of the term), is in some sense what the encouragement of widespread formal credit can hasten, especially since there is evidence that a significant portion of microcredit goes to consumption.

In South Korea, for decades the government promoted a policy of consumer nationalism, in which frugality and savings were put forth as fundamental values. Consumption was to be modest for the sake of social solidarity and an appeal was made to sacrifice for the sake of one's children and for the future of the nation. But by the 1990s, 'with the rapid rise of consumer credit, the nation no longer has a monopoly on the promise of a better tomorrow' (Loberg, 2003).

In Japan, historically a country with a very high savings rate and a culture in which economic security played a central role, there is now widespread agreement that the these traditional tendencies are weaker as a result of a growing consumption of 'western' goods and a rise in the use of credit cards.

Many microfinance practitioners, especially those who are credit evangelists, need to ask themselves if they want to be part of hastening an erosion of informal mechanisms based on, or contributing to, social cohesion. But on a more practical level, the clear implication of any examination of the deeper meaning of debt is that, as several of the pieces in this book emphasize, microfinance ought to shift wholesale into the encouragement of savings. It may be time to entertain the possibility that our emphasis on credit, indeed, in some instance credit-only (note the continuing priorities of the Microcredit Summit process), has been misguided.

References

Arensberg, C. M. (1959) *The Irish Countryman: An Anthropological Study*, Peter Smith, Gloucester, MA.

Furnas, J. C. (1969) *A Social History of the United States, 1587–1914*, G. P. Putnam's Sons, New York.

Loberg, M. (2003) *Consumer Culture and its Discontents*, conference report of CGP-SSRC Seminar, 9–11 April, http://ssrc.org

O'Connell, S. (2004) *Credit, Class and Community: Working Class Belfast 1930–2000*, University of Ulster, School of History and International Affairs, Ulster.

Thorndike, E. L. (1920) 'Psychological notes on the motives of thrift', *Annals of the American Academy of Political and Social Science* 87: 212–18.

West, M. D. (2003) 'Dying to get out of debt: Consumer insolvency law and suicide in Japan', *Michigan Law and Economic Research Paper No. 03–015*, University of Michigan Law School, Michigan.

Wylie, L. (1964) *Village in the Vaucluse, An Account of Life in a French Village*, Harper and Row, New York.

CHAPTER TWO

Is microdebt good for poor people? A note on the dark side of microfinance[1]

David Hulme

Abstract

This short chapter focuses on the 'downside' of microfinance: on the way in which some microfinance activities can damage the prospects of poor people. It is not a polemic that argues that microfinance has failed – there is much evidence, not least from my work with colleagues, that it can help many poor people improve their lives. Rather, it is a reminder that those who provide microfinancial services (referred to here as MFIs, but recognizing that many institutions also provide enterprise development or social development services) need to monitor carefully not only their positive impacts but also their negative effects, look to the future and not rest 'on their laurels'. The 'microfinance industry' needs to practice more humility about what it has achieved (outside of Bangladesh it has not even scratched the surface of poverty, for example in Kenya less than 70,000 people out of an estimated 9–10 million poor people have access to microfinance) and deepen its understanding of the financial service needs of poor people.

Microfinance, microcredit or microdebt?

Most MFIs focus on disbursing loans. Their savings services are designed as a means of collateralizing loans and providing low-cost capital; they are not designed to meet the poor's need for savings mechanisms. Such loans are usually referred to as 'microcredit' and MFIs have created the myth that poor people always manage to repay their loans because of their ability to exploit business opportunities. This is nonsense, and Von Pischke's dictum that we should call microcredit 'microdebt' can help us be more realistic about the different ways in which loans can impact on the livelihoods of poor people.

Microdebt can create considerable opportunities for people to utilize 'lumps' of money so that they can improve incomes and reduce vulnerability. But not all microdebt produces favourable results, especially for poor people working in low-return activities in saturated markets that are poorly developed and where environmental and economic shocks are common. Because of circumstances beyond their control (sickness, flood, drought, theft and so on), lack of skills and knowledge or taking bad decisions, a proportion of poor borrowers encounter great difficulties in repaying loans. While MFIs suggest that such problems are overcome through 'social support' in some painless way, this is often not the case – talk to the drop-outs of MFIs! Many (though presently we have little understanding of exactly what proportion) report being threatened by group members and MFI staff or having their possessions (pots and pans, roofing iron) seized. In Bangladesh, MFI debtors have been arrested by the police (this came to light in 1997 when a police vehicle carrying such debtors crashed and the individuals concerned were killed), are threatened with physical violence (Montgomery, 1996), and the press regularly report female suicides resulting from problems of repaying loans. Many poor people are very frightened about getting into debt; this is a rational response to the dangers that arise from indebtedness to MFIs and not a 'misunderstanding'.

Microcredit and microfinance

The emphasis that most MFIs place on microenterprise lending has led to the evolution of a microfinance industry in which services have a poor match with client needs. Clients have to pretend that they want microenterprise loans (when they need to pay school fees, cope with a medical emergency, buy food, etc.) and do not have access to the types of microsavings services that they desire (Rutherford, 2000). In extreme cases, such as the Kenya Women's Finance Trust and several other East African MFIs, clients who wish to stop taking loans and only wish to make savings are 'balanced out' (namely, they have to leave the MFI). Whereas most banking services aimed at individuals find that demand for savings accounts is much greater than for loan accounts, the microfinance industry tries to force every saver also to be a borrower. This is often because of product design through which MFI institutional viability is dependent on expanding the loan portfolio while savings products are not designed to cover costs.

MFIs do not work with the poor and the poorest

Effective MFIs – such as those in Bangladesh – provide services that help poor people improve their prospects and reduce their vulnerability. However, the claims that microfinance assists 'the poorest' and 'the poorest of the poor' are unfounded within national contexts. MFIs virtually never work with the poorest – the mentally and physically disabled, the elderly, street children, the destitute and refugees – and many MFIs (for example, virtually all of those in Kenya and Uganda) have high proportions of clients who are non-poor, if one takes official national levels of the poverty line as the criteria. (In Nyeri, Kenya, for example, I was amazed to find that 13 out of 13 group members I interviewed in 1999 of a 'poverty-focused' MFI owned cars!)

The common assumption that microfinance is automatically about working with the poor and poorest needs to be dropped, unless MFIs can provide clear evidence that this is the case. Donors also need to be more circumspect. The grandly named Consultative Group to Assist the Poorest (through disseminating microfinance best practice) has spent its first three years as the Consultative Group to Assist the Not Very Well-Off if one examines its portfolio. (To its credit, CGAP is now making serious efforts to incorporate a poverty focus into its work.)

There is no moral requirement that MFIs need to work with the poor. However, if they seek access to aid funds targeted on poverty reduction then they do need to explain what they are doing for poor people, rather than hide behind rhetoric and anecdote.

Microfinance and poverty reduction policy

MFI and donor hype has created the impression that microfinance is a cure for poverty. This is encapsulated in the work of the Microcredit Summit and the thousands of well-intentioned but misguided supporters who believe that microcredit is the answer to the problems of poverty. This is a potentially dangerous line of argument as it distracts attention from the fact that poverty reduction requires action on many fronts: social safety nets for the poorest and most vulnerable, an effective education system, low-cost and reliable health services, governments that can provide social inclusion (and thus maintain law and order) and sound macroeconomic policies, and many other issues.

Providing effective microfinance services to poor people is part of a poverty-reduction strategy, but only a part. Those who present microfinance as a magic bullet to reduce poverty provide such a simple message for policy formulation that they encourage it to be simple-minded.

Microfinance in the future

The microcredit breakthroughs of the 1970s and 1980s contributed greatly to the understanding of poverty reduction by illustrating the feasibility of creating MFIs that can approach sustainability and provide valued financial services to poor people. However, this contribution is now being undermined by unproven claims about microfinance always helping poor people and the exaggeration of the role of microfinance within poverty reduction policies. Worse still, the microfinance industry has ossified! It promotes group-based microenterprise loan products and is obstructing the development of the full range of services and products that poor people want and need: flexible savings, contractual savings, loans for education and health, microinsurance and lines of credit.

The 1990s have been the 'Decade of Microcredit Complacency'. It is time to stocktake, to stop recycling myths, to stop copying the initial breakthrough products and to focus on the real job in hand: developing institutions that can create and provide the broad range of microfinancial services that will support poor people in their efforts to improve their own and their children's prospects.

Note

1 This chapter was previously published in *Small Enterprise Development* XI (1).

References

Montgomery, R. (1996) 'Disciplining or protecting the poor: Avoiding the social costs of peer pressure in microcredit schemes', *Journal of International Development* 8(2): 289–305.

Rutherford, S. (2000) 'Raising the curtain on the "microfinancial services era"', *Small Enterprise Development* XI (1).

CHAPTER THREE

Imagining microfinance more boldly: Unleashing the true potential of microfinance

Imran Matin, Munshi Sulaiman and M. A. Saleque

Abstract

In this chapter we argue that the potential of microfinance as a tool of poverty alleviation is both underimagined and overimagined. It is overimagined as a near panacea of poverty alleviation in its financial service characteristics. And it is underimagined and underharnessed in using its process characteristics as a lever to deliver a bolder attack on poverty.

We argue that the processes and methodologies of providing microfinance, especially those that are more social intermediation grounded, create other forms of capital: social, network and institutional. These 'process capitals' are generally underharnessed. We describe some cases from BRAC's experiences of how such hidden forms of capital can be creatively used to deliver a bolder attack on the different dimensions of poverty and categories of the poor.

The current microfinance discourse with its exclusive focus on innovations in the financial space of microfinance not only fails to make better use of such process capital, but also underinvests in its creation. We conclude that the dominant microfinance discourse needs to accommodate the imagining of a different brave new world of microfinance that can and should be also bolder in its social promise of attacking poverty better and deeper.

Introduction

The greatest power of microfinance lies in the social, network and institutional capital that is unleashed in the processes of providing microfinance. Getting women to form groups of their own choosing to engage with a formal institution is itself a redefinition of a contract that has been traditionally patriarchic. The act of staff who are socio-economically of a higher status going to the door steps of these women to transact with them, seeking their help in solving problems, carries significant meaning and is the beginning of a redefined relationship among socio-economic hierarchies, and between formal institutions and the poor women. In an institutional environment that is generally exclusionary, uncertain, unpredictable and at times hostile to the poor, the clockwork-like, almost ritualistic, rule-bound process followed by microfinance opens up the possibility of a new culture of expectation from engagement between the poor and external institutions.

For the institution, learning the art and science of managing large-scale microfinance operations, engaging with the details of developing systems and procedures, understanding incentives, psychology and motivations of staff and clients, getting to grips with the details of developing a performance-driven management culture and system, constant vigilance, all create strong institutional foundations.

In brief, the processes of microfinance provision create different forms of 'process capital' that we divide into three broad types:

- *Social capital* emerges from the new trust-based social contract between formal institutions and the women in their groups;
- *Network capital* emerges from the network of producers, consumers and citizens, sharing similar socio-economic background, hopes, aspirations and constraints, brought together within a new culture of responsibilities and reciprocities;
- *Institutional capital* emerges from the ability of microfinance providing institutions in managing large scale delivery systems.

However, the dominant microfinance discourse chooses to focus on the output component of microfinance, the provision of financial services, black boxing its process components, which makes the process components valuable only to the extent that it serves the output component. This undermines the possibility of understanding the dimensions and dynamics of these process contents of microfinance provision and using them to creatively deliver a bolder and more comprehensive attack on poverty. This is a waste that development practice, which is starved of good institutions, can ill afford.

Harnessing the process capital of microfinance: Some cases from BRAC

The poor are a diverse group with diverse livelihoods, needs and potential, which change over time due to lifecycle, new opportunities and external shocks. This diverse and dynamic reality of poor peoples' lives and livelihoods forms the canvas within which BRAC conceptualizes and designs its repertoire of development programmes, in which microfinance is a core element. More important for the arguments in this paper, BRAC uses the process capital of microfinance as an entry point to address other constraints and open up new opportunities for the poor. We provide some examples in this section.

Developing poultry as a viable enterprise for the poor

Poultry have been traditionally reared by women in rural Bangladesh mostly as a subsistence activity and for managing small crises. In order to develop poultry rearing as an income-generating enterprise for poor rural women, a number of constraints had to be addressed. In 1983, BRAC realized that access to microfinance would have to be complemented by measures that would also increase returns to existing activities in which the poor rural women were engaged. Poultry seemed to a good place to start and BRAC initiated a series of consultations with villagers to identify major constraints. High poultry mortality, which villagers often took as unavoidable, emerged as a main constraint. BRAC assessed the existing government services and found them to be limited in outreach and effectiveness.

Initially BRAC used its own staff to increase the outreach of poultry vaccination services. Soon, it was realized that the vast outreach that was needed to systematically serve the poultry vaccination needs of an area could not be addressed through this approach, and its sustainability was also an issue. BRAC then developed the community-based volunteer approach. The idea is simple. A suitable member from its village organization would be trained in poultry a vaccination along with treatment of basic poultry diseases. This cost would be borne by BRAC. Trained vaccinators would then get a flask to carry the vaccine, a syringe to apply the vaccination, and a bag with the BRAC logo. They would buy the vaccine from BRAC or government facilities and sell the service to poultry rearers in the community. In order to start the process off, BRAC gives a small loan to the vaccinator. Today BRAC has over 20,000 poultry vaccinators working in villages throughout the country, serving a very important need of micro poultry rearers.

Initially, BRAC began with male volunteers from its male village organizations (VOs) and husbands or relatives of female members. A number of problems emerged. Drop-out was high as the income from selling the service was low. This was mostly because poultry was predominantly an activity that belonged within the women's domain and it was not easy for male vaccinators to enter. They also tended to be more literate and had other job options. BRAC then changed its policy and focused on developing women VO members as poultry vaccinators, lowering the level of literacy required and adjusting its curriculum and training methods. Recently, in order to increase the earning of the poultry vaccinators, they are also being trained to provide livestock vaccination.

Once poultry mortality was lowered significantly through the introduction of these vaccinators, the next bottleneck that was identified was yield. The average yield of local varieties of poultry is 40–60 eggs a year while it is 250–300 eggs a year for high yielding variety (HYV) poultry. The government was the main supplier of these birds. BRAC sourced most of the HYV chicks from the government to distribute among its VO members on a pilot basis. However, a major constraint emerged. Rearing HYV poultry is different from rearing local varieties, requiring feed, clean water and maintenance of basic poultry hygiene.

BRAC started training its VO members on these issues so that the maximum yield could be achieved from rearing HYV poultry. In order to facilitate feed distribution, BRAC used a model very similar to that for creating poultry vaccinators, and developed a new cadre called 'feed sellers', who were trained in preparing good quality poultry feed to be sold to poultry rearers. As HYV poultry rearing expanded, traditional middlemen started exploiting the women, who due to their isolation did not have good information about local market prices. BRAC then developed a cadre of egg collectors, again from its VO membership base. When the local market price of eggs was discussed in the weekly VO meetings, it was difficult for middlemen to continue to exploit the women.

Milking more

Livestock rearing is another popular activity for poor households in Bangladesh. Women also play a key role in this. Many BRAC members were using their loans to invest in livestock. Yet local breeds on average produce 1–1.5 litres of milk a day with 250 days of milking days in a year, while a 25 per cent improved variety will typically yield 1–8 litres a day with a total of 270 milking days in a year. Clearly, livestock breed improvement could hold significant opportunities. In 1985 BRAC piloted an approach similar to its poultry worker model to develop a cadre of livestock artificial insemination workers.

The government was the main insemination provider through 1,100 Livestock Artificial Insemination Centres. However, these centres were distant from many rural households rearing livestock. This led to two problems: first, the expense and inconvenience of bringing livestock to these centres; and second, the problem of timing. A cow is usually 'in heat' for 24 hours, and the optimal 'heat period' only lasts about six hours. Many rural livestock rearers did not know about government services due to lack of outreach. The government facilities relied predominantly on liquid livestock semen that had to be refrigerated and used within three days. This meant that centres had to be located in areas with electricity and there was high wastage. Frequently, out-of-date liquid semen was used leading to low conception rates. This led to a vicious cycle of dissatisfaction and lower demand.

After some research, BRAC developed a model of recruiting husbands or male relatives of VO members with secondary education, and training them in modern methods of livestock rearing and artificial insemination in partnership with Bangladesh Agricultural University and Bangladesh Livestock Research Institute, which had excellent technical knowledge in this area. Men were found to be more appropriate for this work. Initially, a few women were also trained, but the work involved travelling long distances on bicycles, and administering the artificial insemination. It was more suitable for men.

BRAC used frozen semen that did not have any expiry date but needed liquid nitrogen for storage. BRAC currently sources liquid nitrogen from Bangladesh Oxygen Limited and distributes this in cylinders to its 55 Livestock Artificial

Insemination Centres across the country. The trained livestock artificial insemination workers (LAIWs) come to these centres on fixed days of the week to buy the frozen semen.

The LAIWs buy a single shot of frozen semen for Tk70 (US$1) and provide on-farm service to the livestock rearers for Tk100 (US$1.40). BRAC provides regular training and the basic equipment that is needed. The average income of an LAIW is around Tk2,500 (US$35) per month. The conception rate is over 65 per cent, which is higher than the internationally acceptable standard of 50 per cent. This is leading to rapidly increasing demand of the services of the LAIWs, which also means greater income for them.

BRAC publicized the services of the LAIWs and the importance of modern methods of livestock rearing through posters, popular theatres and 'miking'. Miking is a very popular method of publicizing different types of information in Bangladesh, especially in the rural areas. A rickshaw, bicycle or scooter is decorated with posters and a mike is placed in the front for announcement, and moves around the villages. The microfinance VO meetings and networks are also used to inform people about improved breeds and the opportunities they offer.

Initially, to facilitate service delivery at the community level, BRAC used 'post boxes' that were placed in villages so that clients who needed the service could leave a note. With the massive expansion of cell phones in Bangladesh, BRAC is now providing loans to the LAIWs to buy phones. The name and number of the relevant village LAIW is displayed throughout the village and in the BRAC area office, and is publicized through the microfinance VO network.

Getting basic health services to reach the poor

Many of the costly health problems faced by the poor can be reduced if basic information and prevention services are available in villages. One of the main reasons for increased poverty and microfinance defaults is illness. The traditional MFI response to this issue has been insurance, which addresses the demand-side financial constraint. However, there are other demand-side constraints beside finance, such as knowledge of prevention methods that the household can use. There are also significant supply-side constraints that cannot be addressed through addressing only the financial aspects of the demand side.

BRAC approached this problem by making basic health services available at the community level. Again, the microfinance VO structure played an important role. A suitable VO member was selected and trained in essential health care. These health volunteers are assigned a work area covering around 300 households each, within which they provide basic health information, advise and sell non-prescription medicine for basic illnesses, take pregnant mothers for ante-natal checkups, help mothers to immunize their children at government facilities, and mobilize communities for national immunization days. BRAC's annual expenditure on training is Tk285 (US$4) per volunteer. The health volunteers' income sources consist of selling medicine at retail rate, and referral to health facilities. In this way, the health volunteers can on average earn Tk200–250 (US$2.80–3.50) per month.

Harnessing the 'process capital' of microfinance

The fact that these cadres of volunteer workers are recruited from the VO members helped in many ways. The VOs are the focus of BRAC's delivery structure, including microfinance. Typically, a VO consists of 35–40 members who are formed into smaller groups of five. This provides a ready market for services, arising from the initial access to microfinance. Because the workers are members of the VOs and are trained and certified by BRAC, and despite their low education and socio-economic standing, their services are trusted by fellow VO members, as they would not be by villagers outside VOs. They can also be held to account for their services by their fellow members more effectively than could an external actor.

Initial entry into the service markets was greatly facilitated because the workers were members of existing VOs. As their services became established within the secure and controlled environment of the VO, they could then be extended to market beyond the VO membership.

This model of 'frontier market development' using the 'process capital' generated through microfinance also increases the likelihood of success in scaling up, as shown in figure 3.1. Financial sustainability has been achieved in the poultry and livestock services. In 2005, net earnings from sale of different agro-based commodities were Tk106 million (US$1,484,000). Total expenses on training and monitoring all the volunteers and awareness building among the community members were Tk94 million (US$1,316,000). The net surplus from these sectors was equivalent to US$166,000.

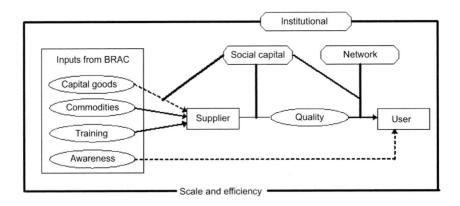

Figure 3.1 'Process capital' in action

Building opportunity ladders for the extreme poor: 'From graduating out to nowhere to crafting a graduation pathway into microfinance'[1]

BRAC long realized the difficulties of addressing the needs of the extreme poor using conventional microfinance. In Bangladesh, where outreach to the poor and the poorest had the greatest influence in shaping the microfinance discourse, evidence suggests that about 15 per cent of all microfinance clients are among the poorest. This is not an insignificant outreach, and mainly came as microfinance expanded with the support of the Palli Karma-Sahayak Foundation (PKSF), the government-sponsored and donor-funded wholesale institution. However, research finds that a significant portion of these poorest clients tend to be relatively inactive as participants – they borrow far lower amounts, less frequently and tend to have long-overdue debts that they cannot repay (Matin, 2005). They are also more likely to drop out from one MFI and not join other MFIs, a trend that is quite common among general microfinance members. All this suggests that the focus of discussion on microfinance and the extreme poor should go beyond whether or not the poorest are joining MFIs, to examining the quality of their MFI participation and how it can be improved.

For BRAC, the challenge was to develop mechanisms through which the extreme poor could be included in the programmes in a way that were cost-effective and yet went beyond grants.

IGVGD programme: Including those left out

In 1985, BRAC approached the World Food Program (WFP), which at that time was providing time-bound food assistance to the extreme poor living in vulnerable areas under its Vulnerable Group Feeding programme, to implement a new sustainable model for the vulnerable group. The Income Generation for Vulnerable Group Development (IGVGD) programme was designed to link extremely vulnerable women to mainstream development activities. Under this initiative, extremely poor women were organized into groups and provided with skill development training in sectors, such as poultry, where large-scale self-employment could be created.

During the programme period, these extremely poor women received food transfers. A savings scheme was developed and later, small amounts of programme credit were provided, so that the training they received could be more meaningfully used for more secure livelihoods. The whole programme aimed to develop a systematic approach to take advantage of the window of opportunity in the lives of these extremely poor women while they were receiving food transfers and had some short-term security. It provided support so that the women could stand on more solid ground once the transfer period was over. An independent study by WFP found that through this strategic linkage, more than three quarters of those who received the VGD card became regular clients of BRAC's microfinance programme.

A CGAP study found that the subsidy per VGD women is about US$135, which is fairly small, given that the overwhelming majority of IGVGD women graduated out of their need for continuous hand-outs. The greater the proportion of the VGD women who graduate to BRAC's microfinance programme and the better the quality of graduation, the more the possibility that over a period of time this subsidy will be recouped.

CFPRP/TUP: Building more solid opportunity ladders

BRAC's IGVGD experiences demonstrated the possibility of creating opportunity ladders from safety nets for those who are left behind by conventional microfinance. This made BRAC even bolder in carrying out further experiments with this concept.

BRAC noticed that though for a great majority, the IGVGD approach led to increased ability to benefit from regular microfinance programmes, a significant minority still failed to reach this stage. More worryingly, those who failed to 'make it' were among the poorest of the poor. There were several reasons for this. The local representatives sometimes selected participants based on political and other self-interested motives. More importantly, the VGD women often failed to get the full benefits of the window of opportunity provided by the food transfer. This is because one VGD card was often unofficially shared between two or more. Sometimes, VGD cards had to be 'bought' and more often than not, this would mean advance selling of VGD cards to wheat dealers to raise the money for the 'payment'.

BRAC felt the need for a programme where the organization would have more control over the processes and one where the window of opportunity would be specifically designed to build solid ground from which the extreme poor could move forward. In January 2002, BRAC started a new experimental programme to deal with these challenges. This was called, 'Challenging the Frontiers of Poverty Reduction: Targeting the Ultra Poor' (CFPR/TUP). The programme seeks to 'push down' the reach of development programmes through specific targeting of the ultra-poor by using a careful targeting methodology that combines participatory approaches with simple survey based tools. The programme covered 100,000 ultra-poor women during 2002–06.

The whole idea behind the CFPR/TUP approach is to enable the ultra-poor to develop better options for sustainable livelihoods. This requires a combination of approaches – promotional, such as asset grants and skills training, and protective, such as stipends and health care services, as well as attacking constraints at various levels such as households and the wider environments of institutions, structures and policies. The CFPR/TUP approach aims to deliver on all these fronts and the hope is that the initial subsidy that this approach entails, which will be heavier than the IGVGD, will reap benefits by building a more solid and comprehensive base from which the extreme poor can move ahead.

Does the approach work?

We collected longitudinal data on over 5,000 ultra-poor households who joined the programme in 2002 along with a comparable group that did not and carried out a repeat survey on these households in 2005. As the programme cycle is two years, we also collected consumption data on a sub-sample of these households in 2002, 2004 and 2005 to examine the sustainability of consumption change after the two-year grant phase of the programme. Separate studies on targeting effectiveness and microfinance participation of the 2002 cohort of CFPR/TUP programme members were also carried out. We shall draw on these studies in this section on the impact of the CFPR/TUP approach.

The local knowledge of BRAC programmes, especially of its microfinance staff, played a very important role in selecting areas within its operating area where the poorest tend to be more concentrated. A series of meetings with local-level microfinance staff to identify such areas was an important part of the targeting process followed by the CFPR/TUP programme. Research on targeting effectiveness of the methodology followed by the programme was found to be more than satisfactory, as suggested by Figure 3.2 (Suleiman and Matin, 2006a).

The results from the 2002–05 repeat survey find that though at baseline in 2002, the not selected ultra-poor (NSUP) (the comparison group) were better off compared to the selected ultra-poor (SUP) (the CFPR/TUP programme participating group) in most dimensions, in 2005 the picture was reversed (Rabbain et al, 2006). Some of the key dimensions of change include:
- Better access to land;
- Diversification and more physical assets;
- Reduced illness, but taking more days off, spending more on illness, and better health-seeking behaviour;
- Better access to formal and informal credit market;

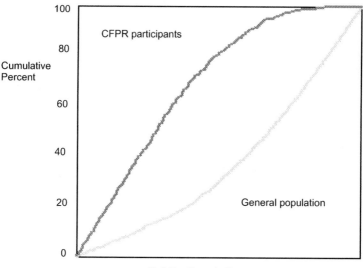

Figure 3.2 Targeting effectiveness of CFPR using the relative poverty assessment tool

- Greater social and legal awareness;
- Improved nutrition and calorie intake.

Figure 3.3 shows how the income distribution of the programme participants (SUP) and the comparison group (NSUP) have changed over time suggesting a significant positive shift in favour of the programme participants.

Indices of different types of assets (viz. natural, physical, human, financial and social) were formulated to test the dimensions of changes. A general pattern in the indices is that the SUP were worse off than the NSUP in all the five types of assets in 2002. However, the scenario has reversed in three years after the SUP joined the programme. The asset type in which there is little change is human assets, consisting mainly of education and health. Both these variables are more systems performance-oriented and take longer to change. However, the fact that primary school enrolment, continuation and consumption and nutrition for children under five years old have not increased is something that the CFPR/TUP programme is looking into carefully and will focus on during the next phase of the programme from 2007.

Crafting a graduation pathway for the poorest: Implications for microfinance discourse and practice

Microfinance through financial innovations can achieve deeper poverty outreach, and through better management can reach many more poor people. However, there will always be a group of the poor who are trapped in multiple constraints, for whom microfinance on its own cannot unleash the small

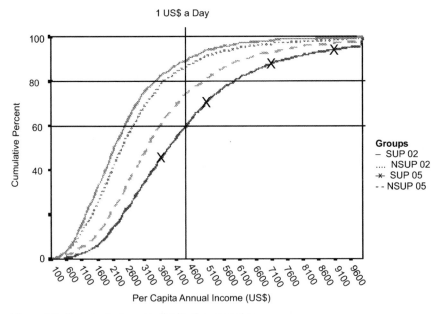

Figure 3.3 Changes in income distribution over time

beginnings of the virtuous cycle that takes place for the moderate poor. As one of the CFPR/TUP participants narrated so vividly, 'We are caught up in a complex knot. Other poor people also get caught up in knots, but those are simpler. You can find the source and hopefully unknot slowly. Not the knots we are in – often pulling on one carelessly only creates another'.

Current microfinance discourse is correct in pointing out that unknotting these constraints needs interventions that go beyond microfinance. But what it does not emphasize is that microfinance can and needs to be made a part and parcel of the package so that the poorest too can craft their way out of extreme poverty. Here the role microfinance plays is that of a rung in the ladder and it cannot do so effectively without being a part of the ladder. This is not about incentive distortion, or softening of the hard incentives that makes good microfinance work, it is about designing deliberate policies and strategies to link and align with lower rungs of the ladder. The management and the incentives that make the lower rungs of the ladder effective are clearly different from that of microfinance.

This is why in the CFPR/TUP programme, BRAC has a completely distinct management structure for the 'grant phase' of the approach. However, it is closely coordinated with microfinance to prepare it to include the 'grant-phase graduated' ultra poor members. The ultra poor members are themselves gradually assisted to prepare themselves to engage with the higher rung in the ladder, microfinance, through confidence building, group formation and financial education. This consultation has made BRAC realize that the 'grant-phase graduated' CFPR/TUP members do not want to be immediately integrated within the existing microfinance groups, but to form their own. We also find that they have carefully planned and clearly understand the process of taking microcredit (Sulaiman et al, 2006b).

Such an approach could also be undertaken with different institutions playing the key role at different rungs of the ladder based on their comparative advantage, although the complexity of coordination and alignment would be more demanding. This is particularly so as there is no immediate direct financial gain for the microfinance institutions from such partnerships. However, we hope that MFIs have larger social objectives that can inspire such partnerships, and CGAP is indeed experimenting with such arrangements in several countries.

Needed: A bolder microfinance vision to fight poverty

Globally, given the huge unserved and underserved demand for microfinance and the lack of solid institutions, there is still a large unfinished agenda to ensure that the largest number of the poor get reliable and reasonably priced access to different kinds of financial services. However, there should also be room for finding innovative ways of doing more. What we have argued in this chapter is that the process of microfinancing, through social intermediation, creates valuable forms of capital that remain unharnessed. We have provided some examples from BRAC's experiences of how the process capital of microfinancing can be harnessed to address other constraints that the poor face in their fight against poverty. In doing so, new forms of exchanges are created, new forms of service-based employment are created, and new techniques are adopted that increase the returns to the enterprises of the poor. The modalities of such a model, whether it should be carried out by a single institution or in partnership, and its sequencing will evolve depending on institutional characteristics, incentive structures and other contextual variables. The purpose of this chapter is not to prescribe, but rather to draw attention to the possibilities of using the microfinance structure and processes to be bolder in the social performance mission.

The current microfinance discourse with its exclusive focus on innovations in microfinance not only fails to make better use of such process capital, but also underinvests in its creation. The dominant microfinance discourse needs to accommodate the imagining of a different brave new world of microfinance that can and should be also bolder in its social promise of attacking poverty better and deeper.

Note

1   Our thanks go to Anton Simanovitz for this phrase.

References

Mabin, I. (2005) *Delivering Inclusive Microfinance with a Poverty Focus: Experiences of a Bangladesh Rural Advancement Committee (BRAC)*. Presentation given at the ADB Microfinance Week, 14–18 March. Available at http://www.adb.org/Documents/Events/2005/ADB-microfinance-week/presentation-day1-03-matin.pdf

Rabbani, M., Prakash, V. and Sulaiman, M. (2006) *Impact Assessment of CFPR: Descriptive Analysis Based on 2002–05 Panel Data*, CFPR Working Paper 12, Research and Evaluation Division, BRAC, Dhaka, http://www.bracresearch.org/workingpapers/impact_tup.pdf

Sulaiman, M. and Matin, I. (2006a) *Targeting Effectiveness of CFPR in a Scaled Up Environment*, CFPR Working Paper 8, Research and Evaluation Division, BRAC, Dhaka, http://www.bracresearch.org/workingpapers/scaletargeting.pdf

Sulaiman, M., Matin, I., Shahadat Hossain Siddiquee, M., Barua, P., Alarakhaia, S. and Iyer, V. (2006b) *Microfinance Engagements of the 'Graduated' TUP Members*, CFPR Working Paper 9, Research and Evaluation Division, BRAC, Dhaka, http://www.bracresearch.org/workingpapers/mftup.pdf

The Holy Bible, King James version (1944), Oxford University Press, p. 886.

CHAPTER FOUR
What's wrong with groups?

Malcolm Harper

Abstract

Most microfinance institutions outsource a substantial part of their transaction tasks to their clients through some form of group intermediation. The groups are not remunerated for providing these services, and the interest cost for loans taken through groups is usually higher than for individual microcredit. Group membership also imposes heavy burdens on members in terms of time, risk and loss of privacy. A few institutions are beginning to offer individual services, but group intermediation is still the norm in spite of customers' expressed preference for alternatives. Groups should be regarded as a regrettable short-term second-rate expedient, and microfinance institutions should work towards offering individual services as rapidly as is possible.

Groups: A low quality service

Sometimes I start seminars on microfinance by asking:

> How would you like a new kind of bank account? You will be required to join a group and attend a meeting with a dozen or so other new account holders every week, you will have to take a fixed weekly savings deposit to every meeting, and if you fail to show up you will be fined. You will be responsible for repaying other group members' loans if they default. If you decide to close the account you will only get back your savings, without interest. The interest rate on any loans you take will be two or three times the usual commercial rate in your country. Are you interested?

Not surprisingly, they laugh and say they would reject such an offer outright. Some realise why I have asked such an absurd question, and start to mutter about village people and poverty. I then ask them to explain, or excuse, the fact that so many MFIs are proud to supply such a service to their clients, when their management would not chose it for themselves. Some embarrassment follows, but the response can usually be summarized as 'because they are poor'. This may be true, there may be no other way of providing financial services to poor people in some places, and the disadvantages that are clear from the above description may be outweighed by the advantage of being able to access formal financial services for the first time. Unlike the seminar participants, or the readers of this book, these people open accounts of this kind because they have no alternative.

My purpose in this chapter is not to deny that group microfinance methodologies may sometimes be the best available option for some people. I aim merely to point out that we should not fool ourselves, and still less our supporters and our clients, that such accounts are ideal. We are not doing our clients a favour by providing them with a second-rate service of this kind. It is a temporary stop-gap, from which we should hope we can help them to 'graduate' as soon as possible to the kind of financial services that we ourselves enjoy.

Group-based microfinance delivery systems are temporary low-quality expedients, like shared toilets, primary school classes of 60 children, or clinics without doctors. These are the best that can be provided at the present time for some people in some places, but they are recognized as fundamentally unsatisfactory. Microfinance groups are the same.

The varieties and origins of groups

No exact figures are available for the proportion of microfinance clients who are reached through groups, rather than individually, and the dividing line is in any case unclear. Nevertheless, such figures as are available show that group methods dominate the microfinance marketplace.

The *Micro-Banking Bulletin* (MBB, 2005) provides data from a sample of 302 institutions. About a third of these institutions work directly with individual clients, but their clients are only about 12 per cent of the 36 million clients served by the sample institutions. The remaining 88 per cent are serviced through some form of group. Another report (M-Cril, 2003) includes data for a sample of 110 MFIs and similar institutions in South, South-East and Central Asia. They cover 2.65 million clients, of which 94 per cent are reached through groups.

The figures in these reports do not include the 30 million individual customers of the village units of Bank Rakhyat Indonesia, by some standards the world's largest and most profitable microfinance operation, which does not use any form of group intermediation. They also exclude the approximately 30 million members of the self-help groups serviced by Indian commercial banks.

There are many different types of microfinance group systems, which make different levels of demands on their members. The best-known method is that pioneered by the Grameen Bank in Bangladesh. This requires its members to join groups of five, which in turn form larger 'centres' of about 30 members. The groups meet every week, although some Grameen replicators are moving to fortnightly or even monthly meetings in response to their members' complaints and competition. A bank worker runs the meeting. He or she (the members are almost always women, but most bank workers are men) collects the members' savings and repayments. Member loan proposals have usually been discussed by the group before the meeting. The proposals are presented to the bank worker, and if the member has reached the right stage on the loan ladder, her loan is approved and is disbursed from the branch. The bank maintains individual savings and loan accounts for each member, and the function of the group is to guarantee their fellow-members' loans, to exert pressure on defaulters and to attend meetings in order that cash can be conveniently collected at one place.

The self-help group (SHG), of which there are over two million with some 30 million members in India, as well as others under different names elsewhere, is more autonomous than a Grameen group. The MFI or bank does not select the members or have any veto over who joins, and the members are usually free to decide who should borrow, how much, for what term and even at what interest rate. The SHG is effectively a microbank, which can access funds from its members' savings and through bulk borrowing from a bank or MFI.

The members, who are almost always women, very busy and very often illiterate, are jointly and severally responsible for repaying any loans the group does take, and they are responsible for managing what is often quite a complex operation. They may or may not receive assistance with record keeping, but many of the more leisured and better-educated bankers, NGO staff or others who promote the SHG movement would find it quite challenging actually to run one. The bank or MFI acts as a wholesaler of funds to the SHG, and need not maintain separate accounts for each member.

There are a number of other types of groups, or sometimes groups of groups. Some, such as village savings and loan associations (VSLAs), which were initiated in Niger by CARE and have been successfully promoted elsewhere in Africa, do not include any external finance, from banks, MFIs or elsewhere. They are designed to help groups of women to intermediate between their own needs for saving and borrowing, and are effectively no more than a formal and improved version of traditional tontines, or ROSCAs. These are not promoted as a condition for obtaining formal financial services, however. They are a way by which poor people can marginally improve their condition without any such access.

Advocates of group-based microfinance claim with some justice that their methodologies are formalized and improved versions of traditional informal methods of financial intermediation. Ardener and Burman (1995) describe a large number of different kinds of women's traditional ROSCAs, from several different countries, but the only examples from rich countries are groups of alien women, such as Somalis in the UK, or Koreans in Los Angeles. The Japanese 'Kou' groups, which are used by indigenous women, are said to have more or less ceased to be used for financial intermediation as women can now access individual bank accounts.

Informal group-based financial systems are certainly a common phenomenon in poorer countries, and women in richer countries also organize 'kitty parties' and other quasi-social functions, but these complement rather than replace individual formal banking services. Formal services may be provided by cooperative banks or credit unions, but these institutions do not ask their member/customers to attend weekly meetings or to guarantee each other's loans.

Why do MFIs and banks use groups?

Group microfinance methodologies are very useful for MFIs and banks. First, and most obviously, they offer economies of scale. Grameen Bank replicators have to maintain separate accounts for every client, but their field staff can meet 30 customers in one place, and even the physical task of collecting the savings and handing them over to the bank worker is undertaken by the group.

The sub-groups of five sit in a line, and these lines sit in rows behind one another. The members insert their savings into their passbooks and hand them along the line to their sub-group leader, who then hands them forward to the group leader in the front row, who hands them over to the bank worker. Any missing members or savings can be observed at once.

SHGs do even more of what would normally be considered the bank's work. They are effectively full-service unremunerated retailers. They aggregate their members' savings and repayments and either redisburse them to new borrowers or deposit them in the group's bank account. They keep the records, possibly after some training or with assistance, which they usually pay for. In theory, and usually in fact, the bank branch has a record of the members' names from the initial savings account and loan documents, but the bank need know nothing of their individual savings or loans. So long as the bulk loan repayments are made on time, there is no need for the banker to know any more.

Group members in both systems have to perform much more than these mechanical tasks, however. They help to bridge the wide information gap between their members and the bankers or MFI staff, by appraising fellow members' loan proposals. They do this because they also have to guarantee their loans. This is no formality.

The livelihoods of the poor are uncertain, and even a woman who is well known to her fellow group members may be hit by ill-health or other misfortunes and have difficulty in repaying her loan. Her fellow members then have to perform what is probably the most difficult of the bankers' tasks, overdue loan recovery.

It might be expected that the use of groups as unremunerated distributors, appraisers, guarantors and recovery agents, with relatively inflexible loan products, often financed by subsidized on-lending funds, would make it possible for banks and MFIs to offer low cost loans. This is not the case. The Micro-Banking Bulletin database (MBB, 2005) of MFIs is not a suitable source of data for comparing interest rates across different types of lending method, since the sample does not include most Indian SHGs. These are financed by commercial banks and not by MFIs. It does, however, show that the average portfolio yield of MFIs that lend through groups of 10 or more members is 61 per cent. This approximates to the effective interest rate. Stated interest rates are often misleading because of the common use of the mendacious term 'flat' rates, up-front fees and other charges. This figure, which is usurious by most standards, drops to 37 per cent for MFIs lending to groups of nine or less members, and 34 per cent for MFIs lending to individuals. Not surprisingly, the average loan amounts also differ dramatically. They range from almost US$1,000 for individual lenders, to US$370 for the smaller groups and US$136 for the larger groups. About 90 per cent of the members of the larger groups are women, but over half the individual borrowers are men.

The institutions covered by the M-Cril (2003) are analysed according to the lending methodologies they use. The average portfolio yield for Grameen replicators is 36 per cent, for SHG lenders 13 per cent and for individual lenders 30 per cent. The SHGs are of course retailers, and their rates to their members are usually around 2 per cent per month. The sample is dominated by Indian MFIs, where interest rates are generally much lower than elsewhere, but opinions differ as to the actual transaction costs of lending to SHGs, and there is usually some element of cross-subsidy. The Indian banks are also constrained by public opinion and by the interest rate caps that still apply on smaller loans.

In general, however, the costs of promoting and training the groups, and the small scale of the members' individual loans, which are probably of short duration also, outweigh the cost advantages of no-cost outsourcing. It might be even more costly to lend such small sums to individuals, but there are other advantages for banks and MFIs that use groups.

The main attraction of microfinance to bankers and investors is the high quality of the loan portfolios, combined with the relative insensitivity to interest rates. Many Grameen replicators claim that they achieve 100 per cent on-time recoveries, year after year, and figures of under 95 per cent are considered unsatisfactory. Group intermediation provides a 'cushion' that can conceal the real rate of repayments. Members help one another when they are in difficulty, and one of the main purposes of groups is to spread the risk.

If one member's goat dies or is barren, a goat belonging to another woman in the same group may have twin kids. The group wants to preserve its repayment record, and the bank worker is judged and may in part be paid according to the recovery performance of the groups he serves. The members and the worker will encourage some sharing of fortune and misfortune, and the less fortunate member's default will never appear in the MFI's records. Group liability is often more a threat than a reality, but it can be a very powerful threat. It is hardly surprising that MFIs prefer to work with groups, and that recorded recovery rates are so high.

There are also some political advantages. It is clearly convenient for any institution to outsource to borrowers themselves the task of collecting debts from the poor, particularly when harsh methods may have to be used. Similarly, interest rates on smaller loans are still controlled at low levels in some countries, and it would in any case be a public relations disaster for a national or foreign commercial bank to be seen to be lending to poor people at much higher rates than are available for mortgages or other facilities for the rich. It is more acceptable to lend at a lower rate to a SHG whose members can then on-lend to one another at any rate they chose. The opprobrium and the work are both out-sourced.

There are other political aspects to groups. Politicians wish to be seen to be assisting the poor, but there are economies of scale in the delivery of political patronage as well as financial services. If a local politician can provide subsidies or other favours to a microfinance group, or even better to a group of groups, votes can be much more easily obtained than by working with individuals. There are obvious synergies and economies to be gained by MFIs and banks from working with political interests in this way, particularly if they are in the public sector or beholden to it.

Groups may also be more amenable to pressure, and less contentious, than individuals. Financial institutions, particularly those in the public sector, do not wish to be accused of favouring one individual; this danger can be avoided by working through groups. And group formation is one aspect of 'community development', which is the professed aim and the main justification for the existence of many NGOs. Donors and governments prefer to diffuse their assistance over large numbers of people, even if the cause of economic development would have been better served by helping a smaller number to create employment for the majority.

What do groups do for (and to) members?

Both the financial and social intermediation of the groups assist the institutions that use them. What benefits do their customers obtain from their membership? First, and most obviously, the group members get financial services that they would not otherwise have got. In SHGs and VSLAs they build a small fund with their savings, from which they can borrow without reference to a bank or MFI. The savings may not be as accessible as money saved with a 'money guard', but they are probably more secure and they may earn some interest. The loans are far from cheap, and not always available, but they are usually cheaper than from the local moneylender.

Microfinance loans are still costly, and microfinance services do not generally replace moneylenders or the ubiquitous 'friends and family', but they do complement them and enable their customers to spread their risks and access a wider range of services. Like all of us, the poor like to keep their options open.

Second, groups also provide the pressure to save, for which people everywhere are willing to pay. Overweight people pay Weight Watchers International to place them in groups and thus to pressure them into eating less. Similar strategies are used by smokers, alcoholics, drug addicts and others. People everywhere are prepared to pay to be pressured not to do things that are bad for them, or to do things that are good for them, including saving money. Daily savings collectors provide this service in another way, by coming every day at about the same time to a saver's home or place of work, and collecting a small sum. They often charge for this, perhaps one day's savings per month, but groups provide another source of motivation to save, and their members pay for this in terms of time, risk and low returns.

There is an extensive literature on impact assessment of microfinance (Copestake et al, 2005). The findings are mixed, but generally favourable. Most poor people benefit from access to formal financial services. Our concern here, however, is with group intermediation. Is it necessary that the financial service needs of the poor should be served through groups, and, even if it is, should this be viewed as permanent?

Empowerment

Much is made of 'empowerment', the unquantifiable but very important social achievements of microfinance group members. Some argue that these are more important than the financial benefits, and that regular saving, borrowing and group guarantees are a means of building and maintaining strong groups that can work towards changes in society.

This is of course particularly important for women, given their disadvantaged social and economic position in many places. It is a fortunate coincidence that women save and repay more reliably, and work better in groups, than men, because they are also the same people who can benefit most from social change. Annual reports, websites and the press are replete with heart-warming stories of how microfinance has changed women's lives, socially and economically. Women also say that groups give them a legitimate reason to be allowed to go out of their own homes. For many this is a major step forward, and they can also access services such as health care or literacy classes more easily once their routine absence from home has been accepted. There have, however, been few efforts rigorously to assess the scale, the prevalence or the permanence of the social changes that have been achieved by women through microfinance groups. In Chapter 7, Frances Sinha reports on the number and longevity, of Indian SHGs' social initiatives; the results are impressive but hardly represent a social revolution. Chapter 3 described some of the ways whereby BRAC in Bangladesh has used the 'process capital' of microfinance groups to assist extremely poor people to improve their lot, but these remarkable programmes go far beyond microfinance.

In a similar way, the Grameen Bank uses its groups as a means of introducing private for-profit provision of telecommunications, through its GrameenPhone business. Groups can be a means of outsourcing the distribution of non-financial as well as financial services.

This work is useful, and even unsuccessful attempts to improve social conditions are an achievement. Nevertheless, they do not indicate that microfinance groups are spearheading a social or economic revolution. It is obviously unrealistic to assume that millennia of oppression can be overcome within a few years. The problem is one of exaggerated expectations rather than with microfinance itself.

What does group membership cost the members?

We have seen that group intermediation does not lead to cheap money. The Grameen system in particular is very labour intensive, and the potential economies of scale from serving people through groups, rather than individually, are outweighed by the heavy costs of group formation and supervision.

The village banking and SHG systems are less expensive to operate, and commercial banks in India claim that they can profitably lend to SHGs at 12 per cent or less, even without the benefit of subsidized refinance. The groups themselves may or may not add a margin when they on-lend to their members, but spreads of a further 12 per cent are normal. The resulting rate of 24 per cent that the members pay is lower than the rates of most Grameen replicators, and is much lower than moneylender rates. The spread belongs in any case to the group of which the borrower is a member, rather than going to pay the expenses of an MFI or bank as with the Grameen method.

There are a number of other costs that are less quantifiable, but are nevertheless significant. Some are financial. Most groups pay their members nothing for the regular savings deposits that they have to make as a condition of membership. This would not matter if every member borrowed the same amounts for the same periods, but this is not what happens. Members who borrow less than the average, generally the poorest who are risk averse and have few opportunities for investment, are effectively providing free money for their colleagues who borrow more. They also receive no payment for guaranteeing their neighbours' loans.

The financial service they receive is highly inflexible. Most Grameen replicators, today not including Grameen Bank itself, still maintain strict weekly repayments and 12-month loans. Loan sizes and timing are fixed according to a loan 'ladder' that allows loans to increase year after year, not to suit client needs but to minimize the lender's risk and simplify the system. Many SHGs are kept on a similar system by conservative bankers who are reluctant to allow groups to decide who will borrow and how much.

Most institutions following the Grameen methodology require their clients to be in debt more or less continually, since both the group dynamics and the economics of the MFI depend on this. Two weeks 'dormancy' is the normal allowed maximum period; if this is exceeded, members have to leave (EDA, 2003). Group members also take social risks when they join a group. Only about 10 per cent of members drop out of groups, but they tend to be the poorer members. In addition to receiving no interest on their savings, failure can exacerbate their marginalization within their community.

The major cost, however, is time, for very busy people. Women everywhere are usually fully occupied, and poor rural women, the main 'beneficiaries' of microfinance, are busier than most. Membership of a microfinance group adds hours per month of non-remunerated work. One study of the impact of microfinance in India (EDA, 2003) addressed this question and obtained figures for the time members of SHGs and of Grameen groups estimated that they spent

Table 4.1 Time spent in microfinance meetings by members and leaders

	Grameen replicators	Self-help groups	Individual borrowers
Members	53 hours per year	17 hours per year	16 hours per year
Leaders	95 hours per year	102 hours per year	N/A

in microfinance meetings. Individual borrowers also estimated how long they spent getting loans. The findings are shown in Table 4.1

It is difficult to put a monetary value on this time. At the worst, the timing of a meeting might be such as to make a member lose a whole day's casual labour work, because she could not be there at the beginning of the day. At the other extreme, the meeting might take place during evening leisure time, or when no casual work was available, so the opportunity cost would be negligible.

If these times are valued at a sadly typical Indian female day labourer's wage rate of US$0.10 an hour, and if it is assumed that each member has a US$100 loan that is being repaid in weekly instalments so that the average amount outstanding at a given time is US$50, the costs of this time amounts to the increases in the effective interest rates shown in Table 4.2.

These are significant amounts, not only for the leaders. It is rightly claimed that interest rates are less important for poor people than access, and it may take even more time to access credit from a bank, as well as bribes. But time costs money, wherever it is spent.

Bank workers are responsible for several groups under the Grameen system, and they have to attend every meeting. The timing of meetings thus has to be at least partly at the bank worker's convenience, not the group members'. Hence it is reasonable to put some value on the time they occupy.

The costs for the leaders are very significant. They are in any case likely to be leaders in their communities, with better than average opportunities for investment, so they expect larger loans than their fellow members, or even demand inducements from other members in return for approving their loans.

There are of course some positive sides to group meetings. Many SHG members said that they enjoyed meeting other women, although this was not mentioned by members of Grameen groups. We must accept, however, that group membership is not a wholly positive nor cost-free experience. The women who make up some 90 per cent of the members of microfinance groups worldwide are surely not fundamentally different from 'us'. We do not have to attend meetings to obtain financial services, and if we did have to, we would probably regard this as a regrettable short-term necessity.

Table 4.2 Effective interest rates based on the value of time spent in microfinance meetings

	Grameen replicators	Self-help groups	Individual borrowers
Members	10.6%	3.4%	3.2%
Leaders	19.0%	20.4%	N/A

What do members think?

There have been few attempts to elicit group members' views about groups in principle, since the option of individual service is usually not available. There are few opportunities to shift to individual systems. One study of post-conflict microfinance in four countries in Africa posed the question as to whether group or individual services were preferred. It was found that groups were unpopular and clients stated a preference for individual products (Nagarajan and Wilson, 2004). An unpublished study in Morocco found that about one third of clients actively disliked groups, and it is believed that the proportion who dislike them in Uganda is higher (Rippey, 2006).

There has been some pressure to reduce the frequency of meetings, but the general consensus appears to be that higher repayment rates are directly associated with more frequent meetings. This is unsurprising, since group-based microfinance systems depend on meetings to secure recoveries.

There are signs, however, that members are starting to 'vote with their feet' when options are available. Vietnam Plus, an MFI serving some 6,000 women in Binh Thuan province through a group system similar to Grameen, has seen its meeting attendance rates drop from almost 100 per cent to about 20 per cent in two or three years (Kervyn, 2003).

This is partly the result of competition from other MFIs that offer individual services, and also because the women members have become more competent and independent, in part as a result of the services they have received from the MFI. They have been empowered, although not in a way that suits the MFI that has helped to empower them.

This experience is similar to that described by Shahin Yaqub (1995) where he shows that the repayment rates of long-term clients of BRAC were lower than those who had only borrowed once or twice. Perhaps group-based microfinance systems are actually nurturing within themselves the seeds of their own destruction.

The industry's response

There are the beginnings of movement away from group microfinance, or at least towards adding individual or quasi-individual options. By the end of 2004, about 8 per cent of loans from Indian MFIs were channelled through joint liability groups, which are a half-way house between group and individual loans. Around five or six potential borrowers agree to cross-guarantee each others' loans. No meetings are required, except at the outset when all the members assemble in the presence of an MFI staff member to sign the guarantee agreement. Indian banks are also starting to offer this facility, and a number of public sector regional rural banks, particularly in the more prosperous south of the country, have provided loans through several thousand such groups (Shankar, 2006; Thorat, 2006).

Arohan, a new Grameen replicator operating in Calcutta, has made some modifications to the Grameen model. The members still attend weekly meetings, but these take a maximum of 15 minutes. There are no songs, or sitting in lines, and the purpose is to get the business completed quickly and to leave (Shubhankar, 2006).

The Grameen Bank itself has also made some quite fundamental changes to its system, under the 'Grameen Generalised System'. The groups and their regular weekly meetings are still the fundamental unit for contact between the bank and the members, but loan terms and amounts are more flexible, as are the weekly savings requirements. The groups are also no longer held liable for fellow members' defaults (Yunus, 2002).

CARD, one of the largest MFIs in the Philippines, has also made some important modifications to its group system. The compulsory pre-membership training period has been shortened and the frequency of meetings has been reduced (Alip, 2002). However, the groups are still the basis of CARD's interaction with its clients, and this seems to be fundamental to the operating system and culture of the institution, as it is to so many MFIs elsewhere.

Spandana, one of India's fastest growing Grameen replicator MFIs, has recently launched a new individual loan product for small business owners and others with small but regular incomes. The loan limits are between US$500 and US$4,000, and only one personal guarantor is needed. The interest rate is 18 per cent with a 2 per cent up-front fee, and the organization anticipates that the outstandings will reach US$10 million by early 2007. A number of existing group members are apparently interested in this individual product.

Loans of this sort tend of course to be larger than those provided through group mechanisms, but the village units of Bank Rakhyat Indonesia (BRI) offer loans as low as US$3, and US$35 loans are very common. BRI does not use any sort of group intermediation (Seibel, 2005).

There are a number of MFIs in Indonesia that offer group-based services, and some of them serve people who are much poorer than most of BRI's customers. The BRI experience shows, however, that very small-scale borrowers, and savers, can be reached effectively and economically as individuals, without group intermediation.

Safesave is a far smaller MFI, working with very poor people in slums in Dhaka, Bangladesh. Safesave serves about 10,000 customers and covers its costs. It does not use any form of group intermediation.

What next?

There are some moves away from group-based intermediation, but they are still small by comparison with the dominant group-based methodologies, and they are mainly designed for larger borrowers, or occasionally for 'graduates' from groups. There do not seem to be any substantial efforts to push down the upper limits of group loans to allow poorer people the opportunity to escape from groups and to enjoy the same individual-based financial services as the readers of this chapter.

An authoritative recent forecast of the future of microfinance (Rhyne and Otero, 2006) has little to say on groups. The writers stress that the quality of services must be improved as well as their outreach:

> A person who receives only a single loan product in a rigid group format cannot be said to have the same quality of access as someone who has a tailored loan, savings services, insurance and money transfers, especially if these services are delivered in a flexible way, at a convenient location, and without absorbing too much of the client's time and trouble.

The implications of this are not followed through, however, and the report neither forecasts nor recommends a move towards individual services, except in a passing reference to a likely increase in individual provision of working capital for businesses, and a brief quotation from myself.

A basic change of attitude is required. No group-based mechanism should be considered as the ideal method; they should all be regarded as temporary second-rate expedients. Most microfinance institutions and practitioners adopt a competitive stance, arguing that their preferred method is the best. Competition is of course good for customers, and the pressure for 'sustainability', that is, profitability, encourages competitive attitudes. In order to avoid excessive client indebtedness, however, and to shield themselves from competition, many MFIs and banks adopt informal cartels or market sharing arrangements. This means that their customers do not have the luxury of choice.

There is already a 'ladder' of delivery methods. The Grameen method, which asks little of its members except obedience to the rules, is probably the most suitable approach for the poorest and least 'empowered'. The VSLA groups are more independent and self-managed, and are perhaps more suitable for very poor people with few investment opportunities and without access to or need for sources of funds beyond their own savings. Next above these two comes village banking and the self-help group on the Indian model, which require considerable management skills and can access formal finance. Members of these groups can then 'graduate' to joint liability groups of five or six members, then to individual products with one co-guarantor, and then, finally, to a 'proper' bank account.

It is unlikely that anyone would proceed through all these six stages, but I have met several customers of Basix finance who were initially customers of SHARE, India's largest Grameen replicator. They had then moved to self-help groups with Basix, and then to joint liability groups. Some institutions might prefer to operate one system only, as does SHARE, but it would be in their clients' interest, and ultimately in their own, if they were to segment the market and focus primarily on those for whom their product was the most suitable.

It should be possible to make mutually beneficial strategic alliances with other institutions operating lower 'rungs' on the ladder, from which new clients could be accepted. They could then in turn be recommended to institutions operating higher 'rungs' of the ladder. The relationships between MFIs and commercial banks are not always easy, but any enterprising banker should be delighted to acquire and even perhaps to pay for a customer with a consistent savings and repayment record over several years.

More fundamentally, the continuing focus on group delivery methods may be the result of the unstated belief that 'you have the poor always with you' (The Holy Bible (1944) St Mark's gospel, chapter 14, verse 7). Development has become an industry, whose continued existence depends on the perpetuation of poverty. Microfinance is an exciting and potentially profitable component of the development industry, and group methodologies are fundamental to the operations of most MFIs.

The development industry, and particularly microfinance, appear to be based on the assumption that they will never really 'work', and that the problem they are designed to cure can never be cured. It is implied that the poor can never really be like 'us', and that poverty is not like smallpox or polio, that can one day be eliminated, but is a condition that will always afflict large numbers of the world's population, so that there will be a permanent need for means to alleviate it. Many young people seek long-term careers in microfinance, as if it will be a permanent feature of the financial landscape.

Microfinance, on this basis, is like healthcare, the judiciary or defence, which humanity has always needed. Can we not be more optimistic and look for ways to put ourselves out of business?

References

Alip, J. A. (2002) *CARD's Transformation*, APRACA, Bangkok.

Ardener, S. and Burman, S. (eds) (1995) *Money-go-rounds*, Berg, Oxford.

Copestake, J., Greeley, M., Johnson, S., Kabeer, N. and Simanowitz, A. (2005) *Money with a Mission*, ITDG Publishing, Rugby.

EDA (EDA Rural Systems) (2003) *SFMC Impact Assessment*, Small Industries Development Bank of India, , EDA Rural Systems, Delhi.

Kervyn, B. (2003) *The Vietnam Plus Microfinance Programme at a Crossroads*,www.vietnamplus.org/en/doc/2004-01-28_vnp_microfinance_crossroads.doc

M-Cril (2003) *Microfinance Review*, M-Cril, Gurgaon.

MBB (Micro-Banking Bulletin) (2005) *Micro-Banking Bulletin* 11, CGAP, Washington DC.

Nagarajan, G. and Wilson, T. (2004) *Post-conflict Microfinance*, Concern, Dublin.

Rhyne, E. and Otero, M. (2006) *Microfinance though the Next Decade*, Accion, Boston.

Rippey, P. (2006) (Uganda Financial Deepening Project) personal communication, September.

Seibel, H. D. (2005) 'The micro-banking division of BRI', in Harper, M. H. and Arora, S. S. (eds) *Small Customers: Big Market*, ITDG Publishing, Rugby.

Shankar, S. (2006) *Business Line*, April 14.

Shubhankar, S. (2006) (CEO Arohan) personal communication, September.

Thorat, Y. P. S. (2006) *Indian Banking: Shaping an Economic Powerhouse*, FICCI, Calcutta.

Yaqub, S. (1995) 'Empowered to default', *Small Enterprise Development* IV (6): 16–23.

Yunus, M. (2002) *Grameen Dialogue*, Grameen Bank, Dhaka.

CHAPTER FIVE
Finance begins with savings, not loans

Hugh Allen

Abstract

Despite their growing visibility, MFIs have not been successful in reaching the very poor and, while innovating, are unlikely to reach the bottom of the pyramid. This is because their survival depends on significant scale and the management of large, low-cost loan portfolios. But the poor place much greater emphasis on savings and insurance services to manage their household cash flow, and their demand for credit is constrained by risk aversion and limited investment opportunity.

While small and medium enterprises (SMEs) need MFIs, because they need access to larger loans through institutions that can intermediate a large pool of capital, most of the very poor can adequately be served by access to smaller pools of capital that can satisfactorily – and cheaply – be intermediated by informal, community-based institutions. The author argues that the industry needs to adapt to this reality and, for the long term, embrace the difference, seeking relationships that play to the competitive advantage of each type of institution.

Why MFIs find it hard to reach the very poor

Of the 10,000 or so MFIs worldwide it is variously estimated that only 3–5 per cent have achieved full financial sustainability. This is an upper-end estimate. Citing Pralahad, Aneel Karnani (2004) states that of 7,000 microfinance institutions worldwide, fewer than 100 claim self-sufficiency. More recent reviews suggest that the number may lie between 300 and 500. This is distinctly at odds with the public perception of microfinance and the special exception claimed by the industry that it is somehow different because it is sustainable. It is also the case that more than 80 per cent of MFI clients receive services from fewer than 10 per cent of the largest MFIs and that sustainable MFIs tend to be large scale.

To be sustainable MFIs have to operate under favourable market conditions amongst which are the following:

- Easy, low-cost access to a very large number of potential clients, concentrated mostly in urban and peri-urban areas characterized by high levels of economic activity;
- Clients who, for the most part, work full time in their businesses, or for whom the enterprise is where they principally invest their capital;

- Clients with moderate work-site investment that has some degree of stability and permanence;
- A legal environment that favours low-cost debt recuperation;
- An emphasis on credit as the principal method of making money;
- Large average loan sizes.

The more successful MFIs propose solutions to reaching the very poor that can be delivered only by large-scale players. Maria Otero (Otero and Morduch, 2006) makes a powerful case for enlarging formal sector provision in the *Economic Self-Reliance Review*. Agreeing that only a small minority of MFIs worldwide are sustainable, the author advocates massive growth of the larger, more successful institutions, arguing that the application of technology, economies of scale and improved management practice will lead to many more of the poor being captured as MFI clients.

For the most successful MFIs the following trends are emerging:

- There is a move towards significant scale;
- They are headed towards regulated status so as to mobilize low-cost loan funds through savings;
- Their strategy for reaching the very poor is based on profitable market segments subsidizing the less profitable, where the very poor are concentrated;
- There is an increasing emphasis on technology as a way of managing costs while going down-market.

How far down towards the very poor this will take them is an open question, but no matter how clever, efficient and committed an MFI may be, it will be working against the natural tendency of capital to seek an optimal return, especially when it bears the costs and complexity of submitting to regulation. Despite such policies as internal cross-subsidy to provide pro-poor outreach, it is inevitable that a large percentage of the truly poor will be left out, with only the informal sector able to provide deposit and savings services of last resort – and it would be ingenuous to claim that this is not the case.

Thus, the larger MFIs use a number of technical strategies for trying to deepen outreach, but most of the smaller MFIs work under more difficult conditions. Frequently they try to target the very poor but, unable to exploit economies of scale, quickly realise that it is much too costly to create a rural clientele because roads are bad, qualified staff may be expensive and hard to find, markets may be scattered, and the legal system dysfunctional in terms of debt recuperation.

Setting aside the cost argument there are two additional factors that inhibit outreach. Most rural clients do not operate full-time growth-oriented enterprises and their need for credit is, accordingly, much less than for urban or peri-urban clients; as a result, the costs per unit of currency lent is likely to be high. At the same time, while the demand curve for credit quickly flattens out amongst the very poor, there is normally a robust demand for safe and reliable deposit and insurance facilities, involving very small sums and numerous transactions. But these are inherently less profitable for the MFI, no matter how vital to the client, unless loan demand is also robust. This realization is, increasingly, acknowledged across the industry and the result is steady retreat of the smaller MFIs from rural outreach, especially in Africa, while the industry waits for the technological development and investment capacity of the larger institutions slowly to take up the slack – a thoroughly unrealistic and limited prescription, even for the long term.

In the face of these realities voices are now being heard that advocate 'smart' subsidies for the smaller-scale MFIs that operate under fragmented and difficult market conditions, justified on cost-benefit rather than financial sustainability grounds. In a counterpoint to Otero's argument in the same issue of the *Economic Self-Reliance Review*, Jonathan Morduch believes that reaching the very poor will require these subsidies because, no matter how efficient an institution may be, there will always be a large number of people who live in hard-to-reach places, or whose needs are so small-scale that they cannot be served profitably.

So the solutions suggested by some of the best minds in the business appear to be that we should either wait for the large-scale institutions to figure out how to serve the very poor, especially in rural areas, or to subsidize the effort because it makes for good development economics. Neither proposal is pertinent to the very real problem of reaching the 50–60 per cent of people who, right now, have no access to formal sector financial services. The one solution will take too long and reach only a small extra percentage, while the other will, most likely, receive short shrift from donors who have bought in to the sustainability rhetoric.

What is common to these proposals is the implicit belief that the poor need to be connected to national capital markets to satisfy their needs for useful lump sums, mostly to invest in enterprise growth. This seems to me to be wrong and a major block to creative thinking. Also implicit is the assumption that this can only be done by formal sector institutions that are highly efficient and either large scale and profitable or smaller scale and subsidized. This, too, must be challenged, especially bearing in mind the origins of microfinance, which were guided initially by a respectful awareness of what informal providers were doing right and the formal sector might do better. Some of that early interest has been lost in the current rush to establish regulated institutions in national capital markets, but at least part of the solution to deepening outreach may lie in support to institutions that are less, not more, formal.

Who is 'the client'?

Microfinance clients are not an undifferentiated mass with the label 'poor' pinned to their collective chest. Being poor means being poorer than some people and better off than others. There is an obvious relationship between poverty and vulnerability: the poorer you are the more affected you will be by social and economic shocks and stress, and the better off you are the more you can cope.

This may seem self-evident, but is often ignored in the way MFIs have traditionally plied their trade. The rationale that drove early practice was to supply useful amounts of affordable capital so that poor people could invest their way out of poverty. It was assumed that by easing access to loans and increasing the amount you could invest productively, the better off you would be and the more economically and socially secure you would likely become. It was also assumed that the poor would find it hard to save useful amounts of money to invest in enterprise creation and growth, so credit was, clearly, the product of choice. This was convenient for MFIs, most of whom were legally prevented from mobilizing and managing savings, but was it really so convenient for clients?

The poor are risk averse. This unremarkable statement has profound implications for the way in which financial services need to be designed, configured and consumed. Because the livelihoods of the poor are poised almost constantly between just getting by and catastrophe, there is an abiding awareness in very poor households of the terrible consequences that follow economic loss, be it from crop failure, adverse market conditions, illness or the loss of a productive member of the family. Once a process of economic decline begins, the more it rapidly erodes the productive base of the household, ultimately leading to the sale of productive assets. This accelerates the rate of economic decay, with attendant ills of reduced health and nutrition, loss of educational opportunity, family disintegration and social stigma.

The poorer a person is, the more likely it is that she or he will be adversely affected by economic loss, even when very small amounts of money are involved. Thus, while an MFI may be convinced of the benefits of credit for productive investment, the very poor are much more likely to be frightened at the thought of what may go wrong, than respond excitedly to what may go right. In fact, the very poor react more powerfully to financial services that build and protect assets than they do to the chance to take on debt. In Zimbabwe in 1995, I carried out a review of microfinance provision for the UK's Department for International Development (DFID). I counted a number of highly visible MFIs whose total membership amounted to about 30,000 clients. Almost by chance, I came across the Self-help Development Foundation (SHDF), which, for 10 years, had been quietly setting up autonomous rural savings groups. There were more than 250,000 members. What was especially remarkable was that none of the major players had, at that time, even heard of SHDF and none offered savings services, other than forced savings to cover bad debt. Until recently, this has been largely ignored by most MFIs, whose own survival depends on large, low-cost loan portfolios. Even now it is given insufficient importance.

It should be no surprise that Grameen and many other MFIs have recently discovered that their loan portfolios can easily be supported by member savings, reducing dependence on money markets and donor funds, especially when savings products allow for easy, unconstrained withdrawal. Typically, in Africa, MFIs that offer savings services have many more savers than borrowers and, often, an excess of liquidity; it is the norm, not the exception, that deposits significantly exceed the value of loans outstanding.

It has long been known that the poor are ready to pay for the safe storage of their money. The need to have access to a useful lump sum, usually to meet a predictable expense such as school fees or the monthly rent, is so pressing that it is worth paying for. Women in the Maputo markets in Mozambique pay as much as 10 per cent a month on the closing balance of their monthly savings to a daily collector, so urgent is their need to reliably meet monthly lump-sum costs and protect their livelihoods from instability or the economic costs of emergency borrowing. Increasingly, also, experiments with insurance are well received.

By contrast, established full-time enterprises, already in the (usually urban) marketplace, owned by the not-so-poor and oriented for growth, benefit substantially from an MFI line of credit. People who fit this description tend to have multiple income streams and substantial reserves of liquid and semi-liquid assets. For them, credit represents no fundamental risk to their economic security and enables them to expand and consolidate their competitive position, create jobs at low cost and generate new capital.

What differentiates these categories of client, one from the other? There are two perspectives that count: the household itself and the type of economic enterprise. Let us first consider the enterprise(s). Figure 5.1 is a simplified schematic that illustrates a fundamental difference between types of enterprises. The rising line shows a different propensity to draw income for consumption from the enterprise, balanced against the propensity to reinvest. It posits that owners of income generating activities (IGAs) tend to maximize drawings from their enterprises and minimize the amount of money that is reinvested; usually sufficient to continue operations but not usually enough to finance significant growth. At the other end of the continuum are owners of small- and medium-scale enterprises. These are people who tend to minimize the amount of drawings from the business and reinvest for growth.

The enterprise

All economic activities/enterprises can be found at different positions along this continuum, but it is a fundamental mistake to believe that it is less desirable to be at the left-hand end and more desirable to be at the right-hand end. The position of the individual enterprise is largely determined by the circumstances of the owner and will be influenced by a number of different variables. A woman who runs a seasonal business selling surplus grain at a weekly market may only be engaged in the activity for a small part of the year. She may have many other duties that prevent her entering full time into business and may be managing multiple economic activities to ensure a stable flow of household income and to spread the risk of business failure. She is in no position to make the activity full time, large scale and specialized, and is likely more interested in moving marginally along the continuum so that she doesn't need to liquidate her stock every so often to meet expenses such as school fees or medical bills. *She is likely,*

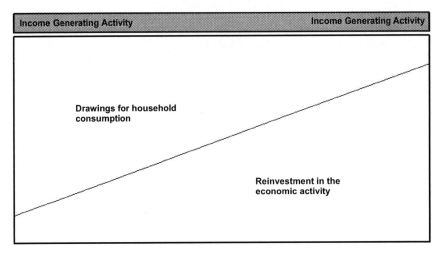

Figure 5.1 The IGA SME continuum
Source: with acknowledgments to Alex Brown of CARE.

then, to need access to very small lump sums to secure her livelihood and make her income more reliable.

Meanwhile, the SME owner may be interested in taking on extra employees, upgrading the workplace and buying some machines; she or he can do so because she or he is engaged in the activity full time, is already economically secure and can absorb the risks inherent in taking on debt to acquire other assets. *She or he needs access to much larger useful lump sums, probably for longer periods of time.* Table 5.1 suggests other differences.

Table 5.1 Key differences between IGAs and SMEs

Income generating activity	Small to medium enterprise
Little reinvestment: Maximum drawings	*Maximum reinvestment: Low drawings*
Strategy: Diversification	*Strategy: Specialization*
• Mixed with household economy	• Separated from household economy. Owner draws salary
• Family labour	
• Little or no investment in workplace	• Paid labour
• Traditional technology	• Extensive investment in work site
• Few fixed assets	• Modern technology
• Part time and seasonal. Owner engaged in multiple activities	• Extensive fixed assets
	• Full-time occupation
• Traditional, low-level skills	• Higher skill level
• Illiterate or semi-literate	• Literate
• Few, if any, written records	• Extensive records and systems
• Not legally registered and does not pay taxes	• Likely to be legally registered and pays some business-related taxes

Source: Waterfield et al, 1993.

It is simple to see that the types of financial services needed by an IGA are likely to be very different to those required by an SME. But apart from the fact that the amounts involved will be very different and for different periods of time, *it is also likely that the types of services needed will be different to suit the different types of enterprise.* SMEs are likely to be interested in long-term low-interest loans for fixed assets and working capital. They will be much less interested in savings, because they are likely to have reliable, multiple streams of income. Insurance services will likely be needed to cover fixed assets. An IGA owner, by contrast, will probably be more interested in short-term (usually high-cost) working capital loans and will look on savings services to guard against livelihood shocks and acquire assets without taking out a loan. Insurance services, such as burial societies and contributions to stretcher groups, as well as moneylenders where they are available, will mostly be directed at the household (such as to cover medical costs) and not the enterprise. IGAs will also be less interest-rate sensitive than SMEs, because, although the transaction sizes are small, the returns to most IGAs are very large – they have to be, so as to support a survival level of drawings.

If it follows that the IGA owner has a vulnerable livelihood, while the SME owner is likely to be more secure, the priority that they place on different types of financial service might look something like the description in Table 5.2. Both IGA and SME owners make use of savings and credit services, but for different purposes, at an entirely different scale and with a different degree of emphasis. Table 5.2 indicates the types of service most likely to be demanded by each type of client in descending order of preference (or at least the likelihood of use).

Table 5.2 Differing financial service needs: Vulnerable and less vulnerable

Vulnerable	Least vulnerable
Principal need: Household cash-flow management to meet 'lumpy' expenses, including IGA investment	*Principal need: Investment for enterprise growth*
• Maximize savings for meeting predictable expenses • Savings for productive investment • Savings for managing household cash-flow • Savings for recovering from unpredictable crises • Savings for IGA investment • Insurance for reducing impact of unexpected crises • Credit for managing household cash flow • Credit for IGA investment	• Large, long-term, low-interest credit for fixed assets in SME • Large, medium-term credit for enterprise working capital • Savings for collateral/loan guarantee • Insurance for asset protection • Savings for enterprise cash-flow management • Savings for consumption

Source: adapted from Waterfield et al, 1993.

It is clear that, given a choice, the IGA owner will be more inclined to use savings-based services to cover a wide variety of household and business contingencies than the SME owner. The preference of the poor to work with their assets rather than assume liabilities is frequently striking, but not as well catered for by MFIs, whose preference is to make their money from lending and who, in any case, may be legally unable to offer such services. This is not so important to an established and successful growth-oriented entrepreneur as it is to an impoverished farmer living on very tight and unstable margins.

The foregoing analysis seeks to illustrate that the limited debt capacity and risk aversion of poor people is best catered for by a set of services that are savings based, since they stress the accumulation and protection of assets rather than successfully managing liability-based risk. The breezy assumption that the best prescription for poverty and vulnerability is the immediate provision of debt for the poor needs to be carefully assessed (if not challenged) relative to the type of enterprise and household targeted.

The household

As we have implied above, savings and insurance services provided in preference to easy credit are attractive to poor people who are often afraid of the risks inherent in taking out a loan in an unpredictable economic environment. But another much more common assumption is that financial services are principally used by people to help them run small enterprises; this is absolutely not the case. Most people (rich, poor and not-so-poor alike) look on financial services as a way of managing domestic cash flow, and only a few are interested in investing their way out of poverty. Most of the commentators who enthusiastically propose increasing the debt burden of the poor as a way of creating economic security are curiously hesitant themselves to follow suit, preferring instead to use checking and savings accounts, overdrafts, consumption loans, insurance and lease purchase, to manage their livelihoods from a cash-flow perspective.

If we accept that cash-flow management may be a powerful reason why most of the poor are themselves attracted to the same type of financial services as anyone else, it is also necessary to recognize that the scale of their needs (and the priority) may differ from those of the not-so-poor and the rich. While the principal aim of the better-off may be to access large, credit-based lump sums to finance full-time growth-oriented enterprises, the poor are likely to need very small sums (less than US$20 and as little as US$1), derived from a mixture of savings, insurance and incremental amounts of credit to manage their combined business and household cash flow. Rural IGAs in central Zimbabwe, for example, have an average capitalization of US$13 and weekly turnovers of about US$20 and take out loans from local accumulating savings and credit associations (ASCAs) that average US$5. They wouldn't know what to do with typical entry-level MFI loans of US$50 and frequently fall into debt when they are provided. A very well-known international MFI development agency operating in Malawi with a rigorous approach to debt recovery has made it so easy to obtain credit in low-potential rural areas that they have become popularly known as 'the bank that takes away your furniture'. The poor tend, instead, to be much more interested in services that protect productive assets and reduce risks to their livelihoods.

Figure 5.2 suggests the range of uses to which different financial services may be applied, indicating that there is significant crossover between need (why) and the type of service (what) that is most appropriate. It suggests that savings, insurance and credit are all useful sources of useful lump sums to cover emergencies and planned investment, while savings services are also useful for planned investments (such as small asset acquisition or in education).

This conforms to Rutherford's (2000) concept of useful lump sums from different sources being applied to different needs and opportunities, in a manner that is unpredictable and best determined by the client. None of this is remarkable, but the 'preference by client for type of service' column suggests that the likely comparative use rate, or level of attraction to different services, may be influenced by the poverty level (and thus the risk profile) of the client, with poorer clients biased towards savings and the better-off clients towards credit.

Critically, it suggests that the very poor prefer low-risk savings-based services and require a myriad of very small transactions, both of which make it hard for MFIs to provide profitable service. This is not a new insight, but a reality that is being faced by most of the small to medium MFIs that struggle daily with the conundrum of providing services to the poorest, while seeking sustainability.

The industry response

To suggest that MFIs have a hard time reaching the very poor is not to conclude that there is anything wrong with MFIs; they may just not be the best type of

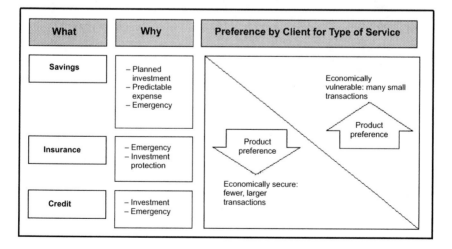

Figure 5.2 Product purpose and client service preference

institution to bring services to the *very* (especially rural) poor and there is no need to feel either guilt or dismay, or for the industry to bang its collective head against the challenge of making a myriad of small transactions affordable and attractive to retailer and client alike. It is especially important that they do not dismiss alternative approaches out of hand. Instead of attempting to make formal institutions capable of delivering an impossibly wide array of services to a heterogeneous clientele spread across town and country (at very high cost), new configurations need to be considered, in which small-scale institutions mobilize and intermediate small, local pools of capital for the poorest, while large-scale institutions mobilize and intermediate much larger pools of capital for growth-oriented entrepreneurs, all the time seeking synergies between them that enables each to do what it does best, at the optimal price.

Table 5.3 suggests the characteristics of institutions that can meet the needs of these two broad category of client. It suggests not only what may be desirable, but, in some cases, what is inherent to the type of institution.

Thus, the rural client with multiple, seasonal small-scale IGAs can likely be served quite adequately by a local community-based ASCA, while the market-based retailer/artisan who wants to buy a new machine and hire more workers is probably better served by an MFI. The IGA owner who has entrepreneurial ambition and is able to capture growing opportunities in the market can benefit from linkages between the two.

Having said this, it should be clear that community-based institutions do not need, as some believe, to 'grow up' and evolve into fully regulated institutions,

Table 5.3 Match of client type to service provider

Vulnerable	Least vulnerable
Strategy: Linkage to local pools of capital through community-based institutions	Strategy: Linkage to larger pools of capital through banks and MFIs
Key characteristic: Savings-led to build assets; quickly sustainable	Key characteristic: Credit-led to finance growth; takes time to reach sustainability
• Many small transactions • Local and informal • Social collateral • Quick, simple and transparent • Flexible • Frequent opportunities to save • Less frequent, but regular opportunities to borrow • Interest earnings retained within the community • Volunteer management, no staff • Very low cost structures	• Fewer, larger transactions • Formal and more distant • Physical and financial collateral • Slower and more complex • Fixed • Frequent opportunities to save • Less frequent, but regular opportunities to borrow • Interest earnings exported from the community • Professional management and staff • Moderate to high cost structures

Source: Waterfield et al, 1993.

integrated into national capital markets. The necessity for external regulation can substantially be replaced by systems whose transparency enhances internal oversight and renders external regulation much less important, while linkage to capital markets may only be needed for a minority. The two types of institution are different and serve different (although overlapping) market segments with different, complementary, products. *Linkages* between the two (and shared membership) may be feasible but they are not essential and the community-based institution is not necessarily constrained or diminished by its autonomy. There is no inherent good in linkage and a lot of well-documented risk and cost in making the effort, which only makes sense when a large proportion of members are engaged in full-time, growth-oriented economic activity and frustrated by the limitations imposed by intermediating only a small, local pool of capital.

The challenge for the industry as a whole is to recognize that there are limits to how far down MFIs can reach, which some are reluctant to accept, but there is no one-size-fits-all prescription. The amount of money at the bottom of the pyramid may be large, but it is dispersed and its flows are hard to estimate and capture. The very poor may, then, best be served by member-managed micro-institutions that can operate flexibly and profitably and can offer appropriate services at a smaller scale until such time as the economy grows to the extent that the pot of money and the scale of the average microenterprise are large enough to attract the regulated formal sector. The credit union movement in Germany started as we know it today in 1864, in response to the banks' unwillingness to serve the poor. Now that the German poor have become the not-so-poor, the banks are there to serve them too. We cannot wait for the same type of growth finally to deliver financial services to the rural poor in the developing world, but we need to be ready to consider that MFIs, increasingly headed towards regulated bank status, will (despite desktop computers, smart cards and a welcome trend towards more product flexibility) be limited in how far down they can go. Recognizing this and embracing and strengthening a wider array of institutions – especially informal institutions – and forging alliances based on competitive advantage are necessary next steps.

References

Karnani, A. (2004) *The Fortune at the Bottom of the Pyramid: A Mirage*, Ross School of Business, Michigan State University, Michigan.
Otero, M. and Morduch, J. (2006) 'Perspectives: Sustainable microfinance', *Economic Self-Reliance Review* 8.
Rutherford, D. (2000) *The Poor and their Money*, DFID and OUP, Oxford.
Waterfield, D., Watefield, S. and Duval, A. (1993) *CARE Savings and Credit Sourcebook*, PACT Publications, Washington DC.

CHAPTER SIX

'Institutionalizing suspicion': The management and governance challenge in user-owned microfinance groups[1]

Susan Johnson and Namrata Sharma

Abstract

One of the key failures of microfinance has been in its limited outreach to remoter areas and poorer people in them, especially in Africa. NGOs that have worked in these areas mobilizing community groups with savings and credit activities have often produced poor financial performance and run the risk of making people poorer. This chapter argues that this 'bottom-up' strategy is necessary but can be improved. These groups often perform poorly because of their internal power dynamics and it is necessary to 'institutionalize suspicion' by equipping groups with the means to hold powerful members accountable. While it is no doubt impossible to make these systems work perfectly, it is important to make them work better as they are a key means through which poor people can access financial services that help them manage their livelihoods.

Introduction

The pressure for financial sustainability of microfinance institutions over the last decade has meant that mainstream approaches to microfinance service provision have had limited outreach to more remote and rural areas, especially in Africa. The current vision of 'Access for all: Building inclusive financial systems' aims to increase depth of outreach to poorer people and remoter areas and to do this cost-effectively (Helms, 2006). This is, of course, a welcome vision but in turn raises the question of whether or not the microfinance sector can get there by simply doing more of what it is currently doing? The route to achieving the vision surely requires some careful consideration of the current situation and past mistakes if there is to be success in the face of past failures.

While mainstream MFIs have consolidated their approaches of scale and sustainability, savings and credit activities have also increasingly appealed to NGOs and CBOs, especially as an initial community mobilization strategy for developing various types of community development initiatives. Ironically, this interest has in part been promoted through campaigns such as the decade-long rallying call of the Microcredit Summit and the more recent 2005 UN designated International Year of Microcredit. However, there appears to have been relatively little attention paid to this use of savings and credit by the mainstream microfinance discussions that now emphasize commercialization, tranformation into licensed deposit takers and banks, and engagement with the mainstream financial sector.

There is thus an increasing rift between those interested in employing savings and credit groups within wider development strategies and the mainstream microfinance approach, and this in part also reflects a rural–urban divide. This fissure is particularly apparent in Kenya and has resulted in a serious lack of engagement between the two sides of the industry. Consequently little is known about the performance of these NGO initiatives. Figures from the Association of Microfinance Institutions (AMFI) in Kenya suggest that membership in mainstream MFIs is approximately 2.1 million savers and 0.5 million borrowers. This includes the Post Office Savings Bank and Equity Bank, as well as K-REP Bank and institutions such as Faulu Kenya and Kenya Women Finance Trust. Estimates also suggest that there may be approximately 0.5 million members in groups operated by NGOs not registered with AMFI. Unsurprisingly, these NGOs are often operating in the poorer and more remote parts of the country that MFIs are not reaching. The performance of the groups they work with is often – if not usually – poor, with repayment performance levels similar to those experienced before the apparent 'break through' of group-based solidarity approaches. Some would argue that this poor performance is because microfinance is being done badly. Many of these NGOs lack specialist microfinance advisers to develop their approaches. The worst aspect of this situation is that it can make people worse off, especially where members' own savings are on-lent to those who do not repay.

What role should promotion of these groups therefore play? Should we be arguing that NGOs stop using these approaches because they seem unable to implement them well enough? If we seek to improve these approaches is this a sensible use of further aid funding? Can approaches to improving these systems be undertaken in cost-effective or even financially sustainable ways? Is expecting deeper outreach simply asking too much of NGOs and microfinance organizations?

Community-based savings and credit groups are unlikely to ever provide the quality of services of the formal financial sector or the emerging tier of licensed and commercial MFIs, but they do offer a key means through which those poor people not reached by this sector can smooth their consumption and accumulate funds for small-scale investments in their livelihoods. In this context therefore it is necessary to consider how these services can be improved. As indicated above, one issue is simply to reduce the losses people face in these systems – both in their traditional groups and NGO-facilitated ones.

The argument of this chapter is that improving the performance of these groups to address the repayment problems they so often face requires a deeper understanding of the constraints imposed by the internal dynamics of their power relations and in particular, the constraints to implementing sanctions on defaulters. We describe the approach as one of 'institutionalizing suspicion'.

This chapter draws on research carried out for the Decentralised Financial Services Project in Kenya, which is an action research project working with a number of NGOs operating microfinance initiatives in rural areas. The hypothesis of the project is that in order to reach remoter areas of Kenya with sustainable financial services, it is necessary to develop a complementary strategy to that of the mainstream 'top-down' provision, with a 'bottom-up' strategy that builds on the ability of self-help groups to manage their own services (Johnson et al, 2006). Understanding the weak performance of these approaches, the project worked with NGOs to develop training tools to improve their performance.

The next section outlines the argument for the need to 'institutionalize suspicion', reviewing the ways in which myths about the role of social capital and peer lending in microfinance groups have obscured the complexity of the power relations involved, and the approaches that mainstream MFIs have in fact employed to overcome them. The chapter then presents findings from the research to show how these dynamics operate in practice and how these findings suggested the need for a new emphasis on sanctions in the development of training tools. The conclusion summarizes the findings and addresses the question of whether such an approach is in fact worth implementing.

Reaching remoter areas with microfinance: The challenge of user ownership and management

Reaching remoter areas, and poorer populations in them, with sustainable and secure financial services means being able to cover the higher transactions costs that arise. Poorer people in these areas tend to need services providing smaller deposits and loans in a context where poor physical infrastructure and increased lending risks – due to poorly diversified livelihoods and economies – impose higher costs on providers. Historically, financial sector institutions have struggled to serve these areas and existing mainstream MFIs that have moved to financial sustainability are also finding it a challenge to reach them (Johnson et al, 2006).

Nevertheless, the ubiquity of ROSCAs and ASCAs in rural Africa is well known and these provide a very basic level of financial service provision (Ardener and Burman, 1995). ROSCAs are systems in which a number of people form a group and contribute an agreed amount on a regular basis. At each meeting the fund is usually given to one person who takes all of the money, until everyone in the group has received the money in turn. The order of rotation may be determined by ballot, by age or seniority, or other social systems of preferment. Where these involve an auction system an interest rate is implicit. ASCAs are systems where members' contributions are made into a central fund that is in turn used to make loans to members usually with interest. The fund accumulates as interest and continuing contributions enable it to grow.

Indeed, it is partly the presence of these groups that has encouraged NGOs to consider the use of savings and credit groups as entry point activities in their rural development initiatives. Moreover, the social capital literature of the last decade has also emphasized the solidarity and strength of local social networks in enabling these groups to function well. At the same time, features of these systems and the related design features of peer group lending in microcredit schemes have been analysed from the perspective of transaction cost economics to emphasize the role of local knowledge in lowering the costs of screening, monitoring and enforcement in lending.

While much has been learnt from the analytical contributions of social capital and transaction cost economics, these analyses have also supported the view that strong repayment performance in microcredit schemes arises mainly from these aspects of their design and that SHGs have their own successful means of implementing sanctions. As a result these analyses have introduced some rather unhelpful biases, even myths, in the discourse around microfinance, since the analyses do not capture the full reality of these systems. For example, it was pointed some time ago by one observer that the effectiveness of repayment enforcement in the Grameen Bank system was not the result of the institutional design of peer lending systems alone but also of the strong management structures and follow up and enforcement by credit officers in the field, which was supported by a strong organizational culture (Jain, 1996). The managers of MFIs know well that it is the close and strict monitoring of group activities and implementation of repayment schedules that ensures loans are repaid. Indeed, if this were not the case then the transfer of the methodology to more remote areas would not appear to present a problem, that is, less supervision would not create a repayment problem if it was solely the design of incentives for clients that mattered.

NGOs working with savings and credit in more rural areas have often not set up the rigid supervisory arrangements seen in the weekly meetings and adhered to the insistence of timely repayment of the mainstream MFIs. One view would be that they are simply 'doing microfinance badly' and that they should be prepared to implement these more rigid supervisory arrangements. However this begs the question of cost and how to get a cost-effective balance between the benefits in monitoring and enforcement and the transactions costs these activities impose in remoter areas.

To develop viable user-owned and user-managed models we need to understand the reasons why these models do not work well in more detail and find ways to tackle the issues that arise. Much of the literature on ROSCAs and ASCAs has lauded their ubiquity, flexibility and durability, suggesting that repayment problems and default are minimal. However, a closer look at this literature also offers clues to their pathologies. The lack of records often means that researchers take reports of low default at face value and anthropologists have often seen this as temporary default (Bouman, 1995).

Previous studies have shown that local leaders may abuse their power in the system to obtain wealth, and age can act as a means through which elders dominate these groups (Bouman, 1995). Including close kin or friends in groups can increase the risks of default and make sanctions difficult to pursue (Velez-Ibanez, 1983). Underlying problems of illiteracy and hence difficulties in overseeing the books can either be a source of power, since those keeping them can falsify them and other members will not know, or simply a source of mistakes that can lead to failure . Problems of illiteracy and the potential for fraud become more acute in ASCAs than ROSCAs, since the former necessarily involve more complex systems of bookkeeping and may also involve the custodianship of funds belonging to the group that are not lent out. By contrast, ROSCAs have in-built mechanisms for transparency. For example, the uniformity of the contribution and payout, the fact that all the money is paid out at each meeting, enables members to know immediately whether a member has not paid. Research in Uganda into the losses involved in financial systems suggests that ROSCAs are less risky for poor people than ASCAs. Wright and Mutesasira (2001) found that the percentage lost of the amount saved in ROSCAs over the previous 12 months was 6 per cent compared to 21 per cent in ASCAs.

Given that NGO intervention has so often failed to enable such groups to function better, Bouman pessimistically concludes that 'we must finally accept that indigenous self help societies have their own ways of helping themselves and their own views of what Utopia looks like and at what tempo to get there' (Bouman, 1995) . However, perhaps we should also recognize that NGO training programmes are largely based on western values, although the importance of social and cultural factors is often acknowledged, and 'the strange aspect is that... little attention has been paid to cultural reasons for possible ineffectiveness' (Zegers, 1989).

How then can we better understand the relationship between concerns for transparency and accountability that are embedded in NGO training initiatives and the social and cultural factors that influence their implementation? An earlier analysis of the failure of agricultural cooperatives addresses this point and offers a clearer insight into the central problem that needs to be tackled. Ronald Dore (1971) recognized the potential for cooperatives to work well because of the extent to which people know each other in a local context and have relationships of solidarity and cooperation. However, this traditional solidarity at the same time faces patterns of traditional authority, and while such societies may be cohesive, they are not necessarily egalitarian. It is the tension between this solidarity and authority that lies at the heart of the problem. Attempts to enforce the rules strictly are likely to create discord, while if the rules are overtly flouted then the organization can no longer function. Groups cannot be expected to be able to effortlessly 'institutionalize' the 'modern' notions of accountability and transparency that are embedded in the training that is given. For Dore, 'the trick lies in retaining these elements [the sense of mutual trust between members and the sense of loyalty to the group] while at the same time introducing the rationalized accounting methods... [which allow] a strict apportionment of benefits to contributions and... the devices of institutionalised suspicion which prevent the abuse of leadership powers. The trick is an immensely difficult one'. Although this 'trick' is difficult, the success of strategies to improve the functioning of user-owned group systems require that we pull it off and are able to institutionalize suspicion in appropriate ways.

The idea behind the Decentralised Financial Services action research project is that a bottom-up strand of microfinance delivery is needed to complement centralized provision to more rural and remote areas. It sought to do this by developing toolkits that NGOs or the groups themselves could use that would help them understand how the group should operate, keep records and better organize themselves. In contrast to group training materials available from many NGOs, which are directed at staff, the idea here was to try to produce participatory training materials that could be used by NGO or CBO workers with very little training and could even be picked up and used by group members themselves.

The research component sought to understand the baseline situation of the groups with whom the NGOs were working and to follow up and understand whether the implementation of the tools was in fact having the desired effect. The methodologies of the NGOs varied but usually involved some injection of external funds, except in the case of the managed ASCA organizations (Johnson et al, 2002). The baseline survey involved nine NGOs spread across Western, Rift, Central and Coast Provinces. In-depth follow-up research was carried out with nine groups spread across three of the participating NGOs – SAGA, WEDI and Coastal Rural Support Programme – in three different parts of the country and in three separate research visits over a period of 10 months from March 2004 to December 2004.

Findings: Default, misappropriation and power relations

The baseline survey of 97 groups produced an indicative snapshot of their performance. First, it was notable that average savings per member at Kshs3,722 (approximately US$50) are a significant sum for people in more rural areas. Second, the average loan outstanding per borrowing member was Kshs16,668 (US$222), which appears quite high for rural contexts, however, this data includes some groups that were located in Nyeri, which is a relatively wealthy district. This figure compares with an average outstanding loan balance of Kshs23,000 (US$300) for MFIs in Karatina in Central Province in 2003 (Johnson, 2004a).Third, the survey suggests that on average 50 per cent of the portfolio was overdue. This may not be surprising given the agricultural context of many of these groups, but nevertheless illustrates the nature of the problem that these groups tend to experience. The challenge in financial service delivery terms is to improve the circulation of funds and ensure that this does not represent a situation where outstanding payment becomes bad debt and results in members losing their savings completely.

Since the key problem that faced these groups was poor repayment, the in-depth qualitative research investigated cases of default and misappropriation in order to explore the dynamics around them in greater depth. At the beginning of the research seven cases of default were identified affecting five of the groups involved in the in-depth research. Two further groups – both all women groups – experienced more complex situations: one group was being revived and reformed and hence there were still past debts that had not been repaid; a further group had experienced widespread default whose origins were difficult to establish. In the seven individual cases, six involved men and only one a woman, and three of them involved office holders, of whom two were men, and the only female defaulter was also an office holder.

This evidence suggests a clear gender dimension to default in these individual cases, since overall membership across the nine groups involved a majority of women (73 per cent). However, there was a clear majority of men in only one group, with two further groups having only a majority of one man in a more or less evenly split group. Moreover, it also suggests that office holders are more likely to default. The action taken against the office holders presented a further pattern. Of the three cases, in two the office holder was removed from his/her position to become a general member again. However in one case, the holder had not been removed and the members said they would remove him only after he repaid the loans; none of the office bearers had in fact repaid their loans completely. Moreover, in the four cases that were resolved, the NGO got involved by deducting money from the group fund and hence precipitating action by the groups against their defaulting members, and this was in turn resolved by deducting money from the defaulting member's shares.

It became clear from these cases that the members did not regard someone as being in default but only to be 'delaying' if the member still attended group meetings and paid something of the outstanding debt. It was only if the member stopped attending completely or clearly refused to contribute at all that the group could clearly identify the person as a defaulter since they showed no intention to repay. This pattern is not surprising since the incentives for members to force each other to repay are weak when these relationships are seen in the broader social contexts and livelihood strategies involved. However, it represents a clear difference between local notions of default and the expectations of good microfinance practice.

Five cases of misappropriation were identified affecting four of the groups, but these were usually described by members as cases where 'records were not kept properly', rather than misappropriation. Three of these involved male office holders and two were female. A similar pattern of action could be seen as in the cases of default. The two women office bearers were removed from their positions but remained members of the group. However out of the three male office holders, one was left in position for the reason that they wanted him to pay first. The second resigned from the position and only then was he accused of the misappropriation, and in the third case, the members removed the man through an election before dealing with the misappropriation. This again suggests that the male members exerted more power when holding official positions, and this may also have been because they were more educated than the general members and had strong connections to the NGOs concerned and within the community generally.

It became evident from the research that the sanctions that groups were prepared to use in relation to default or misappropriation were relatively weak. They described the fact that they would first 'insist' that the member pays and then, as one woman put it, ask the person to 'repent' and repay. While members indicated that they could visit homes and remove assets, no actual case of this was reported. A final resort was seen as taking the case to the local chief and this had helped in two of the three cases where such action had been taken but not in the third. Indeed, when asked how they treated members who had delayed or defaulted on loans outside of the group in the context of wider community activities, there was a mixture of responses. It became clear that only in cases where the defaulter had clearly developed some animosity with the group that cooperation in wider social activities was withdrawn. In other cases, this tactic might be used in a modified manner, for example, attending a family funeral but not contributing financially, or making the member the last person to benefit from reciprocal farm labour activities. However, once a member was repaying again there was a view that they should benefit from social support.

Johnson (2004b) has used the term 'negotiability' to refer to these aspects of flexibility in community-based financial systems. She argues that it is the fact that the underlying social relationships allow for renegotiation of debts that is a key reason for the popularity of these mechanisms in central Kenya in the late 1990s. This negotiability means that the risk of entering debt relations through these systems is reduced, compared to borrowing from the formal sector, and hence in the context of uncertain livelihoods it is more compatible. However, it is this element of negotiability and its intrinsic flexibility that contains both the greatest strength of these systems and their greatest weakness since it also enables powerful individuals to manipulate them to their own advantage. Both kinship ties and the need to support others in return for being supported at particular times of need, mean that demanding repayment in cases where someone has not actually refused to repay is seen as potentially damaging. This means that it is preferable to only resort to the use of stronger means when absolutely necessary.

The outcome of the research was therefore to realize that the tools the project had devised were deficient because there were none that overtly dealt with the implementation of effective sanctions. The research therefore engaged participants in discussions of the effectiveness of different sanctions. The sanctions that groups reported were: 'insisting', writing letters, taking members to the NGO, taking the member to the local chief and taking a member's asset. They were asked to rank their social acceptability, effectiveness in achieving repayment, legality and timeliness. This brought out some interesting points regarding social acceptability. Groups preferred to keep the matter within the group as far as possible. While taking a member to the local chief or seeking to take an asset from their house were seen as the most effective means of enforcement, using these approaches raised concerns in the groups about the way the wider community would view this action because the group itself would get a bad reputation. However, it took time for groups to realize that the results of members default affected the welfare of the whole group and once they had done this and agreed that they should implement these more strict sanctions then they felt they could in fact explain this to others outside the group. The following examples help to illustrate this.

At the outset of the research, one group identified a male office bearer as a defaulter and a woman office bearer as having misappropriated funds. The woman was removed from her position and told to repay the money. While at this stage the group did not agree with taking assets from members who did not pay, by the last stage of the research they had in fact adopted a new policy and she was the first to be asked to sign a contract pledging an asset to the group. Since the male defaulter had absconded from the group he was termed a defaulter. Despite this, he was not in fact removed from his office bearer position because they said that they were afraid he would not repay. Since the group wanted to apply for a new loan tranche from the NGO involved, they had to clear his loan themselves using the group's funds and at this point removed him from the membership, but were still debating how to get him to repay. The differential treatment of these two office bearers was very stark, along with their inability to discipline the absconding member. By the last phase of the research, the group's record-keeping system had been strengthened and the financial transactions were more transparent, with all the members now talking more freely about issues related to the group's well-being. The male secretary of the group was one of the most powerful members of the local community and someone who was able to assist members when they needed help. He had been getting loans from the group both on his own behalf and through his three wives who were also members, but in the early stages of the research had not been paying on time. The members had started to talk more openly about this but gave the justification that he ultimately repaid his and his wives' loans, however, he along with others had now started paying the instalments on time.

A second group had started as a women-only merry-go-round (ROSCA) but was reorganized when an NGO arrived in the area. It became a mixed group with a majority of women but led by a few powerful men. In the first stage of the research it was clear the male chairman dominated the meeting (which few attended) and the treasurer had misappropriated group funds. Members reported that they were unhappy with the leaders as there was misunderstanding between them and it was clear that they were not comfortable talking about these issues. By the second visit, a dramatic change had occurred. The chairperson had resigned, the meeting attendance was significantly improved and the members were questioning the office bearers on the accounts of the group. At this stage, they had also identified another case of fraud by the chairperson and made him admit it and agree to pay back the funds. By the final research round, it was clear that one of the training tools had helped the group assess whether their leaders had the right qualities and precipitated their first ever election. They also called in the NGO to assist them with this and as a result removed all but one of the officials. The ex-treasurer, who had denied misappropriating funds previously, was taken to the local chief and made to sign a contract to repay. After this he admitted the offence and started to repay. By this stage, group attendance and participation in discussion had increased dramatically. The group realized the importance of mobilizing their own funds and lending to each other as well as borrowing from the NGO, but at the same time introduced the policy of pledging assets before loans were given. These changes were attributed by both group members and NGO field officers to the training they had received.

These examples illustrate well how power and gender relations were entrenched in the groups and undermined their ongoing viability. The participatory training tools operated to 'institutionalize suspicion' by opening up discussion about group dynamics in ways that enabled members to address the problems they were facing, often in the face of resistance from dominant leaders.

Conclusion

One of the key failures of microfinance has been in its limited outreach to remoter areas and poorer people in them. Emphasis on financial sustainability – especially in the Kenyan context – has meant that mainstream MFIs have focussed on easy-to-serve and relatively better-off populations. The success of mainstream MFIs has not been the reliance on solidarity and peer lending that much of the 'myth' suggests, rather it has been their willingness to implement rigid rules through the management procedures of the MFI itself in its monitoring and enforcement. This is in turn why the model is difficult to immediately transplant into remoter areas because the costs of doing this are unsustainable.

Reaching further out with services therefore requires new methods and we have argued here that one part of this approach is to work on a bottom-up approach to service delivery to complement centralized provision. However, doing this requires that we learn from past failures. Those NGOs that have worked in these areas and not rigidly applied the rules of repayment run the risk of making – and probably have made – people poorer as their savings become the unrepaid debts of others who are usually more powerful. While it is no doubt impossible to make these systems work perfectly, they are an important means through which poor people can access financial services that help them manage their livelihoods. As a result, it is necessary to at least help them to work better and reduce the losses people face. This means institutionalizing suspicion by equipping groups with the means to hold powerful members accountable. This is, of course, not a quick fix solution. It requires engagement through training and discussion of the local constraints involved, while a willingness to facilitate means that local people find acceptable for solving such problems within their cultural contexts. As is evident here, gender relations are a feature of these dynamics that need further consideration as to how greater awareness of them and potential counterbalances can be built into the training tools.

The question remains as to whether such an approach is worth implementing and this is harder to answer. The point made here is that it is not only NGO-promoted groups in which members may experience losses, but also indigenous ROSCAs and ASCAs. Such systems will never be perfect but it may be cost effective in public policy terms to seek to reduce these losses, especially if sufficiently low-cost means can be found to effectively promote better management and governance of the groups. The Decentralised Financial Services project is now working to make these training methods integral to managed ASCA organizations that are already financially sustainable, and seeking to find out whether improving group performance improves the bottom line of the organization. If it does, then their improved sustainability also offers the possibility of extending outreach to remoter and poorer rural people.

At the same time, it will not be possible to prevent NGOs from promoting savings and credit with community groups. While many NGOs often now recognize that they lack skills in microfinance and are prepared to leave this to specialist MFIs, they often do not actually operate in the same geographic areas so this is not an option. The approach of institutionalizing suspicion, proposed here, should however be of interest to many NGOs concerned with empowerment and rights. The shift to rights-based approaches emphasizes demands for transparency and accountability in wider societal and government structures. Ensuring that power is exercised accountably in community-level groups can therefore be seen as an initial building block for the development of effective poor people's organizations. The need to effectively address internal power relations and internal transparency and accountability in community groups in order to enable savings and credit functions to operate better is therefore compatible with their other NGO activities and approaches, and should therefore be of interest to them.

Note

1 The authors are grateful to Markku Malkamaki, the project manager of the Decentralized Financial Services Project, Nairobi, for supporting the research and undertaking some of the fieldwork. We are also very grateful to the staff and members of the collaborating NGOs for their assistance with the research.

References

Ardener, S. and Burman, S. (eds) (1995) *Money-Go-Rounds: The Importance of Rotating Savings and Credit Associations for Women*, Berg, Oxford/Washington DC.
Bouman, F. J. A. (1995) 'Rotating and accumulating savings and credit associations: A development perspective', *World Development* 23(3): 371–84.

Dore, R. F. (1971) 'Modern cooperatives in traditional communities', in Worsley, P. (ed.) *Two Blades of Grass: Rural Cooperatives in Agricultural Modernization*, pp. 43–60, Manchester University Press, Manchester.

Helms, B. (2006) *Access for All: Building Inclusive Financial Systems*, International Bank for Reconstruction and Development/World Bank, Washington DC.

Jain, P. (1996) 'Managing credit for the rural poor: Lessons from the Grameen Bank', *World Development* 24(1): 11–21.

Johnson, S. (2004a) 'The impact of microfinance institutions in local financial markets: A case study from Kenya', *Journal of International Development* 16(3): 501–17.

Johnson, S. (2004b) '"Milking the elephant": Financial markets as real markets in Kenya', *Development and Change* 35(2): 249–75.

Johnson, S., Mule, N., Hickson, R. and Mwangi, W. (2002) 'The managed ASCA model: Innovation in Kenya's microfinance industry', *Small Enterprise Development* 13(2): 56–66.

Johnson, S., Malkamaki, M. and Wanjau, K. (2006) 'Tackling the frontiers of microfinance in Kenya: The role for decentralized services', *Small Enterprise Development* (forthcoming).

Velez-Ibanez, C. G. (1983) *Bonds of Mutual Trust: The Cultural Systems of Rotating Credit Associations Among Urban Mexicans and Chicanos*, Rutgers University Press, New Brunswick, NJ.

Wright, G. A. N. and Mutesasira, L. (2001) 'The relative risks to the savings of poor people', *Small Enterprise Development* 12(3): 33–45.

Zegers, M. (1989) 'The influence of cultural traditions on management training for small-enterprise owners', in von Gelder, P. and Bijlmer, J. (eds), *About Fringes, Margins and Lucky Dips: The Informal Sector in Third World Countries – Recent Developments in Research and Policy*, pp. 163–800, Free University Press, Amsterdam.

CHAPTER SEVEN

SHGs in India: Numbers yes, poverty outreach and empowerment, partially[1]

Frances Sinha

Abstract

India is brimming with SHGs – groups of about 15 women who come together with the guidance of NGOs, or (increasingly) government agencies or staff of regional rural banks, to start small regular savings. Linked not only to banks but also to wider development programmes, SHGs are expected to confer many benefits, both economic and social. SHGs enable ('poor') women to grow their savings and to access the credit that banks are increasingly willing to lend. SHGs can also be community platforms from which women become active in village affairs, stand for local election or take action to address social or community issues (the abuse of women, alcohol, the dowry system, schools, water supply).

Seeking out the reality, this chapter draws on a recent study of over 200 SHGs in two southern states and two northern states to find that, whilst the number of SHGs is growing even faster than targeted, the social and empowerment effects are not as widespread or as long lasting as perhaps hoped for, the poor are included but not exclusively, and, on the financial side, account keeping is weak. SHGs are a good start, with the promise of new opportunities and empowerment for women. But the social context of established traditions and gender disadvantage means that SHGs need more effective mentoring and strategic guidance from promoting agencies, and probably over a longer time period than is usually provided, if they are to realize some of the expectations that lie behind the increasing numbers.

Did you know that more than 400 women join the SHG movement in India every hour and that an NGO joins our microfinance programme every day?

This is the statement that greets visitors to the microfinance home page of the National Bank for Agriculture and Rural Development (NABARD), the apex bank that has since the early 1990s actively promoted the SHG 'bank-linkage' programme. The strategy involves forming 'small, cohesive and participative groups of the poor', guiding them to open a group savings account in a local bank, regularly pool small amounts of savings, use the pooled savings to make small interest bearing loans to members, and in the process learn the nuances of financial discipline. Subsequently, usually after about six months of group formation, bank credit is made available to the SHG to augment its resources for lending to its members.

NABARD (and others) sees this model not only as financial intermediation (a means to provide financial services to the poor in a sustainable manner) but also as an opportunity for women's empowerment. Ninety per cent of SHG members are women. In their groups, women can pick up new skills, gain mobility and visibility, and begin to play a role in village community affairs. Linked not only to banks but also to wider development programmes, SHGs are seen to confer many benefits, both economic and social. SHGs enable women to grow their savings and to access the credit that banks are increasingly willing to lend. SHGs can also be community platforms from which women become active in village affairs, stand for local election or take action to address social or community issues (schools, water supply, roads, issues of social justice, alcohol sale, the dowry system).

NABARD's vision was to provide financial service access to one third of the rural poor through linking (that is, providing bank credit to) 1 million SHGs, or 14–15 million SHG members and their families, by 2007. With an annual growth rate now at around 30 per cent, target numbers have been exceeded, with over 2.2 million SHGs linked to banks by March 2006, and bank credit to SHGs during 2005–06 of nearly US$1 billion. The SHG numbers are the cumulative figures, showing the total since the late 1990s when the bank-linkage started. Even allowing for some level of dropout and groups breaking up, the numbers are very substantial. Indeed, NABARD's statement on their website is, if anything, an understatement: assuming that SHGs do not get linked during the night, the number of women who join every working day is more in the order of 1,200!

If the numbers have been achieved, what are the stories behind the numbers? How effective is the credit? Who are the members? Are they the poor? Who drops out? On the financial side, how effective and transparent are the groups in managing their financial transactions? Are the groups sustainable? Are they equitable? On the social side, to what extent have SHGs been able to mobilize for social or community action? How effective have such actions been?

To explore these questions, a consortium of donors – Catholic Relief Services, USAID, CARE and GTZ/NABARD – all supporting SHG promotion in India, commissioned a study covering 214 SHGs (with nearly 3,000 women members) in four states, two in the south (Andhra Pradesh and Karnataka) and two in the north (Orissa and Rajasthan). The sampling criteria included representation of different agro-climatic and socio-economic regions, SHGs formed before March 2000, usually bank-linked, representing different promoting agencies (NGOs, government, banks), including tribals and preferably with some example of social action or a 'story' to tell. Fieldwork was undertaken during 2004–05, with visits to 108 villages. The study was undertaken by EDA Rural Systems Pvt Ltd, Gurgaon (EDA) and Mahila Abhivruddhi Society, Andhra Pradesh, Hyderabad (APMAS) – and is referred to in this chapter as the EDA/APMAS study.

In each village we were interested in a range of issues and we wanted to 'triangulate', or cross-check for different experiences and perceptions.

Accordingly, we reviewed the available group records and talked not only to field staff of the promoting agencies, to SHG leaders and members in focus group discussions, but also to individual members by themselves, to drop-outs (if we could locate them), and to members of broken groups. We also interviewed village leaders (usually men) to understand their perception of the SHG programme and their role. We were interested in the 'stories', whether 'light' or 'dark' and had detailed discussions on these, most of which were developed into case studies to illustrate the study findings. The complete study, *SHGs in India: The Lights and Shades*, is available at www.edarural.com/SHG-study.html

The findings of the EDA/APMAS study reflect the challenges around SHGs – enabling access for the poor, maintaining sound records of financial transactions, with effective communication and accountability, and, on the social side, beginning to make a difference to women's role in traditional rural communities. In this chapter we focus on the evidence for SHGs enhancing women's social role and engagement – in village politics, community services and activities, and actions on issues of social injustice.

Poverty outreach

We used a number of different indicators, including a poverty estimate from participatory wealth ranking of each of the sample groups, matched with an index of indicators roughly benchmarked to the national poverty line. This was based on the methodology for poverty assessment designed by EDA as part of a national baseline study of 20 MFIs in India, by which wealth rank indicators (of housing quality, assets, food security, income sources, children's schooling) are correlated with estimated per capita income for a sub-sample of households.

A comparison, in Table 7.1, of the sample profile with all-India data shows fairly substantive outreach to the poor, (half the SHG members are below the poverty line) and to those recognized as structurally poor (scheduled castes and scheduled tribes). The proportion of scheduled tribes in the study sample reflects a research design focus to include this community. If around half of SHG members

Table 7.1 SHG members: Poverty profile

	Sample *(women SHG members)*	*Rural India* *(households – secondary data)[a]*
Number	2,968	
< Poverty line	51%	26.8%
Vulnerable non-poor	32%	
Scheduled caste	30%	16.2%
Scheduled tribe	25%	8.2%
Women heads of household	11%	10.2%
No schooling	74%	61.7%

Note: [a]Sources of this data are: Planning Commission, 2002; NSSO, 2002; Government of India, 2001 (literacy data – rural women).

are poor, this is a considerable achievement, but is nevertheless not the same as *all* members being poor, which is what is claimed.

Of course, our sample mainly covers groups that were at least four years old. After a number of years, you might expect to see a reduction in poverty, which would affect the poverty profile. When we analyse the study data by time (and the sample does include some women who joined SHGs in the previous two years, as well as women who have been SHG members for five to seven years and more) we do find some changes in the poverty profile, though only in the first four years and not after that. What the data show is that even after five or seven years, around half of member households are still below the poverty line.

These and similar findings from other initiatives to assess poverty levels (Van Bastelaer and Zeller, 2006) underline two issues in microfinance: first, the fact that microfinance does not only attract the poor; and second, the challenges of poverty reduction.

As shown in the Table 7.1, literacy rates amongst rural women (poor or not) are very low across India. In the study sample, 74 per cent of SHG members had no schooling. This has implications for record keeping and their use for transparency and accountability. There are several types of records for SHG transactions: savings and loan ledgers for the group, savings and loan passbooks for individual members, meeting minutes, receipts and vouchers. For the EDA/APMAS study, we needed information on group transactions and financial sustainability. We accordingly reviewed the records of all the sample SHGs, including a quick audit exercise of all the books for the previous two years, if available, cross-checking entries for completeness, accuracy and consistency across ledgers and passbooks. The audit exercise took up to two hours for each SHG with records available. What we found was that as many as 40 per cent had weak records – most records had not been updated for three months or more (commonly 12 months or more), or if updated were incomplete (many entries blank) or inconsistent (with errors). Only 15 per cent of the SHGs had good quality records (complete and up to date with virtually no errors); another 39 per cent had records of moderate quality (mostly up to date, though with some errors). In 6 per cent of the groups the records were not available, since the person maintaining the records was not in the village at the time of the visit, or (a few cases) the records were at the office for the promoting NGO.

The basis of SHGs is financial intermediation, for which the records of accounts need to be well maintained with systems for verification and transparency in place. The fact that this is largely not the case is partly explained by the relative complexity of the records system. Record keepers – who may be office bearers of the SHGs, or someone (educated) recruited as a bookkeeper

Table 7.2 Poverty profile of SHG members by time of membership

Time as member	< 2 years	3–4 years	5–6 years	7+ years
Number	163	575	1,269	961
Poor	59%	49%	52%	51%

from the village or nearby, or a staff of the promoting agency – find the accounts difficult to manage; group members – many of whom are illiterate as we have seen – do not find them useful, nor are they easy to explain. This is an area that needs more attention to make a sounder basis for women's empowerment as SHG members. Some interesting initiatives for simpler, sounder systems are being tried by NGOs.

Empowerment

But now, we turn to questions around the potential role of SHGs to provide an empowering community platform for their women members. In the EDA/APMAS study we were not looking at empowerment at the individual and household levels (improvements in women's skills, confidence, decision making and status), so much as how these elements of empowerment may be translated – through the medium of SHGs and networks of SHGs – into action and agency by women at the community level.

We used the data from 214 SHGs to address a number of questions: in how many groups has a member been elected to the village *panchayat*? How effective are such elected members in village governance? How many groups have played a role to improve community decisions and action on, for example, delivery and maintenance of services (schools, health care, roads, veterinary care) and on issues of social justice, especially those of concern to women (domestic violence, dowry, bigamy, treatment of widows)? How effective or successful have such actions been? And, when SHGs undertake group-based enterprises, how viable are such enterprises?

The evidence from the EDA/APMAS study is that examples of community empowerment through SHGs are not as frequent as might be hoped for – this even from a sample that was not entirely random (we were looking for examples of social action by SHGs).

In India, local government is decentralized through the *Panchayati Raj* system, which vests local village councils (*panchayats*) with some powers of resource allocation and decision making. Since 1992, one-third of *panchayat* seats have been reserved for women, with elections held usually every five years. Legal fiat for women's reservation led to a spate of 'proxy' women candidates; women were elected but were hardly involved in elections or governance since male relatives (in the form of the *sarpanch pati* or the *sarpanch* husband) continued to manage the *panchayat*'s affairs. Over time, though, there have been examples of women beginning to campaign in elections and, once elected, developing into active ward representatives and leaders, maybe with support from male relatives but no longer acting as mere 'rubber stamps'. NGOs have sometimes played a role in this process, by guiding women's candidature and facilitating interactions between women leaders.

In our study sample, we found that in one out of every four SHGs, a woman member had been a candidate, and in one out of every five SHGs, a woman member had been elected to the *panchayat* as a ward representative, sometimes as the chairperson (*sarpanch*). Those elected included ordinary members as well as leaders of SHGs. Some (43 per cent), nevertheless, were proxies, or largely disengaged in the sense that although she might attend a *panchayat* meeting, her presence is largely ignored by others (men – who continue to be two-thirds of members). Over half the elected women, however, were active in attending meetings and were seen to make some contribution to *panchayat* affairs.

Our interviews and case studies suggest that SHG membership can contribute to women's election to *panchayati raj*, but does not appear to influence what they can achieve if elected. Probably more important than SHG support is the fact that the members (or their families) often had political leanings and activities even before they were members of SHGs – reflecting too the increasing involvement of political parties in *panchayat* elections. We also found the most active women representatives were those (from families) with political connections, and/or with a background of employment in government programmes. And we did not find any link between the women *panchayat* representatives and the community actions that SHGs became involved in.

Thirty percent of our sample SHGs reported a community action, sometimes more than one such action. A smaller number of groups (12 per cent) reported action on issues of social injustice. The actions usually involved more than one SHG, including other SHGs in the village who were not part of the study sample, and non-members too especially in the southern states. Women SHG members took action through rallies and demonstrations. Most of the actions reported were single, one-off events. These were all actions that represented some degree of *agency* by women, in terms of decision making and enhancing women's contribution to the community in a way that goes beyond traditional gender roles. Not included, therefore, are activities such as cleaning the village before village functions, which community leaders increasingly find SHGs useful for. Nor have we included general participation in campaigns or rallies (pulse polio, literacy, anti-dowry, for example), for which SHGs are becoming a means of mobilizing women, especially in the southern states.

Based on SHG members' own assessment of their community role, around half of these actions were successful. Actions to improve access and quality of community services and infrastructure were mostly effective: a water supply was provided, hand pumps were repaired, a school was started, a road was sanctioned, a committee was set up to review hospital services, a local alcohol outlet was closed. Examples of mixed outcomes were: sanction obtained but service not implemented, a veterinary doctor appointed to visit the village but he turned out to be incompetent, a school building built with a cash contribution from the SHG, but the SHG was not reimbursed (by the *panchayat*) for their contribution.

The most common single type of action taken up by SHGs is the attempt to close down local liquor outlets. We found that alcoholism – and the accompanying problems of domestic violence from men, the drain on household finances, impaired health – prompts perhaps the most anger amongst women, but also despair. Dealing with this issue is a major struggle that pits women not only against a behavioural syndrome, but also against institutional and business elements that have a vested interest in continuing to sell alcohol – and make money out of it – including the local *panchayat*, which derives a substantial revenue from leasing out contracts.

As shown in Table 7.3, most of the anti-alcohol cases were assessed as having 'mixed' outcomes, since, although a local alcohol outlet was closed and alcohol consumption was reduced, this improvement was sometimes short-lived when the outlet reopened some time later, or men began going to a neighbouring village where alcohol was on sale.

The examples of social injustice that SHGs tried to address usually involved a SHG member herself or someone from her family. The success in dealing with them depended largely on the type of issue, as shown in Table 7.4. Problems that can be dealt with through a specific action (preventing bigamy, obtaining compensation, marriage of an orphan girl or a separated woman) appear successful since they have an immediate result. Private behavioural problems (domestic violence or sexual abuse) are far more difficult to address successfully. The very fact that they are brought out in public appears to be a significant action, but an effective result – ending such violence – is more difficult to achieve.

Table 7.3 Type of community actions by SHGs and reported success

	Total actions	Outcome		
		Effective	Mixed	Failed
Total community actions	53	28	19	6
	100%	53%	36%	11%
By type of issue:				
Community services – improving access and quality	24	13	9	2
Anti-alcohol	18	7	8	3
Building community infrastructure	7	5	2	
Natural resource access/management	4	3		1

Table 7.4 Issues of social injustice addressed by SHGs and reported success

	Total	Effective	Partially effective	Failure
Total actions	20	10	6	4
Ending domestic violence	6		4	2
Preventing bigamy	5	4		1
Marriage of a girl orphan, remarriage of a separated woman	2	2		
Compensation for dowry death	1		1	
Prevention of child marriage	1	1		
Ending sexual harassment	1			1
Justice for husband/son (compensation for injury, unfair arrest)	4	3	1	

Another group activity, of interest to banks (as a means of enhancing credit absorption) and to SHG members (for employment and income), is collective enterprise. Forty-six groups (21 per cent) of the sample had been involved in a new collective enterprise or an enterprise contract, linked to government programmes. Collective enterprises (by 30 groups) included joint marketing (of milk), or using credit for the group to lease land or ponds for production, to purchase materials for processing (stones, rice) or assets for renting out (a tent house). Half of these group enterprises appeared to be viable, usually with low supplementary earnings for SHG members. Even less successful was group management of government contracts (by 16 groups), such as running ration shops (as part of the Public Distribution System), cooking the midday meal for school children, or managing a subsidized fodder depot. Two-thirds of these were not viable. Lack of viability was linked to unrealistic business planning, issues in managing cash flows combined with women's lack of experience in management and accounting.

Finally, there are some expectations around women members of SHGs beginning to address communal divisions linked to caste. SHG membership is open to all women, irrespective of caste. Nevertheless, the groups tend to be formed on the basis of caste. This reflects the concept of affinity and the practical requirement of neighbourhood proximity (members living nearby can more easily get together) and could be seen as effectively reflecting if not reinforcing caste divisions.

In the study sample, two-thirds of SHGs are single caste, in terms of all members belonging to the same broad caste or social community. One-third of SHGs have some members from different castes. Twenty percent of groups (especially NGO-promoted groups) in fact cross the main hierarchies (between scheduled castes and tribes and the other castes). In fact NGOs that have a village-wide development focus try to emphasize interactions across castes, including scheduled castes and different sub-castes, in training programmes and network meetings. In many of the community actions reported in the study, different SHGs with members from different castes did mobilize together. We found that some prejudices are beginning to reduce, though the evidence is, unsurprisingly, that social attitudes that have been prevalent for years, if not centuries, will take time – and considerable initiative and persistence – to change.

What were the factors that made a difference to the SHGs' collective roles – between action and inaction, between success and less effective outcomes? The situations and dynamics are often quite complex and much can depend on the type of issue. Broadly speaking, we found the following:

- A critical underlying element is mobilization across a number of SHGs; nearly all stories involved a number of SHGs, at least three to four in a village, more than this in larger villages; occasionally, huge numbers of groups across villages, brought together through a federation structure. The numbers provide a 'critical mass', which gives visibility and security.
- How do SHGs get mobilized? This happens most often through opportunities provided by the self-help promotion agency (SHPA) – a village level meeting

of all SHGs in the village, a cluster meeting of SHGs from a number of adjacent villages, and a federation meeting of representatives from over 50 SHGs.

- A high proportion (71 per cent) of the actions necessarily involved women from different castes and social groups mobilizing together.
- The action usually comes as a response to an issue raised in village or cluster meetings, prompted by sharing of experience by SHG members, by suggestions from the SHPA staff or from village leaders.
- The actions involve a new boldness and confidence for women – to approach the authorities (*panchayat*, district officers, police), to take decisions and carry out their functions (to stage rallies and blockades), and varying degrees of skill in negotiation by SHG leaders.
- Guidance from the SHPA seems essential, especially initially – in creating forums for SHGs to come together, identifying issues, helping to formulate strategy, assisting in formal procedures involved in drafting petitions to district authorities.
- Also essential is persistence, not backing down when things don't work out immediately.
- Ensuring men's support (tacit if not overt) and engaging the village leaders, having them on the women's side; going over their heads to a higher authority sometimes works, but not always.

Conclusion

In conclusion, SHGs – and networks of SHGs (the power of numbers) – represent an opportunity for social action and empowerment through women's involvement in considering, addressing and participating in issues that affect their members and their communities, including issues that affect women in particular. They are a platform too that includes the poor and marginalized communities, although it is not exclusive to them. Although the examples of SHG action that we found were not as numerous or as effective as hoped for, the fact that such initiatives happen at all can be seen as a good start in a traditional, patriarchal society that has usually marginalized women's roles and agencies.

Note

1 The author would like to acknowledge the work and contribution of all those who participated in the study, especially Ajay Tankha, Shashi Rajagopalan, the APMAS team led by C. S. Reddy and K. Raja Reddy, my colleagues in EDA, including Amit Brar, Nishant Tirath, Sakshi Varma and A. K. Bijoy; our advisors, Malcolm Harper and Girija Srinivasan; and staff of the sponsoring agencies: Lyn Carter (USAID), Snigdha Chakravorty (CRS), Marie-Luise Haberberger and R. Ramakrishna (GTZ/NABARD).

References

Government of India (2001) *Census of India*, Office of Registrar General, Government of India, Delhi.

Government of India (2002) *Household Indebtedness in India*, National Sample Survey Organisation, Delhi.

Planning Commission (2002) *Human Development Report*, Government of India Planning Commission, Delhi.

Van Bastelaer, T. and Zeller, M. (2006) 'Achieving the Microcredit Summit and Millennium Development Goals of reducing extreme poverty: What is the cutting edge on cost-effectively measuring movement across the $1/day threshold?', in Daley-Harris, S. and Awimbo, A. (eds) *More Pathways out of Poverty*, Kumarian Press, Bloomfield, CT.

CHAPTER EIGHT
Microfinance and farmers: Do they fit?[1]

Malcolm Harper

Abstract

A relatively small proportion of microfinance loans are used to finance crop farming enterprises; most are taken to finance trading and processing activities, for livestock or for consumption. There are many reasons for this, including the usual terms, amounts and repayment schedules, which do not fit the financial requirements of farming, and the predominance of women borrowers. This chapter investigates whether there is also a mismatch between microfinance interest rates and the rates of return that can be earned from typical farming ventures. It concludes that the margin between interest costs and financial returns from farming is much lower than from other common investments, that this is an important problem, and that although microfinance interest rates can be reduced and yields on small crop investments can be increased, the gap is unlikely to be totally bridged.

Introduction

Ali's mobile phone (a Grameen phone of course) buzzed as we sat chatting in his home town of Bogra in Bangladesh. He glanced at the text message. 'It's quite extraordinary', he said, 'the world's biggest loan shark has just got the Nobel prize'. Ali was being unfair, of course, but microfinance interest rates are rather high; does it matter?

'New paradigm' microfinance has largely replaced old style rural finance, which mainly subsidized low-cost farm credit. The 'old paradigm' rural development finance institutions have often disappeared, and others have been converted into what are effectively specialist microfinance MFIs. Does new paradigm microfinance effectively address the needs of farmers?

For the purposes of this chapter, farming is defined as the cultivation of crops, and animal husbandry of any kind is excluded. This is not because animal husbandry, such as raising goats, dairy cattle, pigs, poultry or any other animal, is unimportant, but because such activities already are one of the most popular uses of microfinance, and 'new paradigm' microfinance seems to suit them well. Crop cultivation is different. Most microfinance portfolios include rather few loans for crop cultivation. The smaller community-owned village banks and cooperatives are constrained by their lack of funds (Klein, 1999) and few NGO MFIs are engaged in crop lending (Coffey, 1998).

MFIs that have ventured into crop financing, such as Basix in India, have had relatively poor experiences with this kind of loan (DiLeo, 2003). In the Bangladesh Grameen Bank's 2004 list of activities financed, about 500,000 loans are stated to have been made for 'agriculture and forestry', out of a total of 3.5 million, whereas over a million loans were taken for trading and shopkeeping (Grameen Bank, 2004). Since farming is and will presumably continue to be the main economic activity of many rural people, it is worth asking why microfinance is not more used for farming, whether it matters, and what can be done about it if it does matter.

There are some fundamental differences between farming and other income generating activities, which may affect the match between microfinance and the farmer's needs. These include the following:

- Most farming products are themselves a means of survival. They can be eaten as well as sold.
- Farming tends to be an ancestral activity. Most small-scale farmers are following their parents' footsteps and farming it is not new to them.
- Many (but not all) farmers already own the basic asset required for farming, which is land. They do not have to finance its acquisition.
- Land is traditionally the most acceptable form of collateral, as well as being basic to farming.
- Farming land, unlike most other assets, usually increases in value in the long term, but in the short term it declines in value if it is not used. Its value can also be reduced through overuse or misuse, but if it is not used at all the owner must usually invest heavily in bringing it back in to production. This does not apply to land used in shifting cultivation, but this type of land use is not the dominant method in most regions.
- Most farming families live on the land that they cultivate; it provides space for shelter as well as for cultivation.

On-farm versus off-farm credit use

To compare farm credit with microfinance loans, we should first examine the typical uses that a rural household might make of microcredit. These can then be compared, to see how 'classic' new paradigm microfinance fits or does not fit them.

Five typical examples are proposed:

- So-called consumption credit, for medical care in case of sickness;
- Petty trade, dealing in consumer goods, often from home or as a mobile peddler;
- Livestock, the purchase of a dairy cow;
- Seasonal crop finance, for farm inputs;
- On-farm investment, for minor irrigation.

The following table attempts to compare these, along the following parameters:

- Amount of investment/loan needed. How much does it cost?

- Lumpiness of investment. Is it in one payment, or can it be spread?
- Financial return on investment. What is the percentage return on the investment?
- Lumpiness of return. Is the return in one lump or continuous over a period?
- Delay. Is there a delay between the investment and the first return?
- Predictability of investment. Can the client predict when the payment will be needed?
- Risk of loss. How secure is the return and the asset that earns it?
- Seasonality of investment and of return. Do the investment and the return depend on the season?
- Centrality to household livelihood. How important is the income from the investment to the household's total income?
- Male or female managed. Is the asset generally under the control of men or women?
- Skill needed. Does the return depend on skills that the client may not have?
- Access needed. Does the return depend on access to supplies or markets that the client may not have?

The right-hand column suggests the ideal requirements for each of these parameters to fit the demands of a typical microfinance programme.

Rural people's livelihoods have diversified, in part thanks to microfinance, but farming is still the most important single source of income for most rural people, in kind and in cash. At least at first sight, the match between the features of the investments and the requirements of microfinance in the last column

Table 8.1 Microfinance uses and requirements compared

Feature	Sickness	Petty trade	Dairy Cow	Crop loan	Minor irrigation	Requirements of typical microfinance programme
Amount	Small	Small	Medium	Medium	Large	Small
Lumpiness of investment	High	Medium	High	High	High	High
% return on investment	Nil, but enables wages	High	Medium	Medium	Low	High
Lumpiness of return	Low	Low	Medium	High	High	Low
Delay before return	Low	Low	Medium	High	High	Little or None
Predictability	Low	Medium	Medium	High	High	High
Risk	High	Low	Medium	High	Medium	Medium
Seasonality	Medium	Low	Low	High	High	Low
Centrality to household income	High	Low	Medium	High	High	Low
Gender	Woman	Woman	Woman	Man	Man	Woman
Skills needed	None	None	Medium	Medium	High	None
Need for market linkages	None	None	Some	Some	High	None

appears to get worse as one moves from sickness and petty trade to farm inputs and irrigation. Does this in part explain the following features of MFIs?

- They serve mainly women, and landless people.
- Their loans are used mainly for consumption or off-farm investment.
- Few of their rural clients 'graduate' to mainstream banking as one would expect they might if MFIs addressed their main livelihood needs.
- There is little evidence that microfinance has radically transformed the livelihoods of rural people.
- The main farm-related use of microfinance loans is for small-scale trade and processing, and livestock.
- Few MFIs have ventured into farm credit, and their results have generally not been good.

There are obviously many reasons why rather few on-farm investments are financed with microloans. The topic was discussed at the 2004 Asia/Pacific Microcredit Summit in Dhaka. Dr M. A. Hakim of PKSF suggested that it could be explained by the perceived high risks and seasonality of farming, the history of politically induced defaults and the misplaced notion that farm financing required specialist technical skills. Neither he nor any of the other discussants, however, mentioned the issue of interest rates and rates of return (Asia/Pacific Micro-credit Summit, 2004).

A recent CGAP paper (Christen and Pearce, 2005) lists 10 features that can make microfinance more suitable for farmers, but they do not include lower interest rates. In fact, 'old paradigm' agricultural finance schemes are by implication criticized for attempting to charge interest rates that are 'affordable related to the rate of return on agricultural investments'.

The interest rates charged by MFIs are higher than the usual commercial bank rates, and it is presumably believed that the rates of return that clients will earn by investing the borrowed funds will be higher still, so that their net incomes will be increased. The remainder of this chapter will focus on this particular feature of microfinance, and its possible mismatch with on-farm returns.

Returns on investment

One particularly important difference between activities is of course the rate of return that can be earned from them. Microcredit is generally more expensive than traditional formal institutional credit because of the high transaction costs that have to be incurred to provide the accessibility and other service characteristics that have been shown to be more important to poor people than the rate of interest they have to pay. These interest rates are usually lower than moneylenders' rates, which are most microfinance customers' only alternative, but it is also important to be sure that the returns on their investments are sufficient to cover the interest costs.

The *Mix Market Bulletin* (2006) gives a range of yields on portfolio for microfinance institutions. The average nominal rate for all MFIs is 38.1 per cent, and there is some variation when the figures are disaggregated by types of institution. The average rate for NGOs is 43 per cent, for community-owned institutions it is 29 per cent, and for banks it is 31 per cent. These figures include loan-processing fees and other supplements that many MFIs add for a variety of reasons, and are therefore more indicative of what clients really pay than plain interest rates, particularly when these may be quoted (or misquoted) as 'flat' rates. The Bulletin also includes 'real' yields, which are corrected for inflation, but the orders of magnitude are similar.

It can of course be argued that it is inappropriate to associate any particular loan or source of loans with any particular investment. Money is fungible, and microloans, like any other finance that comes into a household, go into the common pool from which money is withdrawn when it is needed. If one objective is to improve customers' incomes, however, MFIs should surely want to be sure that the returns on the largest and most common type of investment their clients were likely to make were well in excess of the cost of their loans.

Like any service provider, therefore, MFIs should set their prices not only by calculating what their costs are, but by assessing what their customers can afford to pay. The competition is still usually the moneylender, whose rates have often come down in recent years, in part because of competition from MFIs, but moneylender interest rates are still well above most MFI rates. Business investors compare the cost of money with the projected yield on their investments, and they do not invest in projects whose long-term return is lower than their cost of funds. Bankers are well aware of this, and they compete with one another accordingly. Many MFIs are still quasi-monopolists, in that their only competition is moneylenders, but MFI management should surely nevertheless examine the returns earned by their clients on the ventures in which they invest their loans. If the interest rates are higher than their clients' returns, the long-term impact will be to impoverish and not to enrich them.

Rates of return on and off farm

Rates of return generally decrease as the scale of investment increases. A rickshaw puller can earn a higher percentage return on his investment in the rickshaw than a taxi driver can earn on his car, and a tailor can earn a larger proportionate return on the cost of her treadle-powered sewing machine than an investor can make on her investment in a garment factory. Most microfinance institutions, however, are not in the business of financing taxis or garment factories. Their high interest rates, as well as their often quite onerous demands for group membership, regular savings, weekly meetings and so on, effectively discourage larger borrowers from using their services, and thus protect them from 'client drift'. People who can access mainstream bank loans, like the readers of this paper, are generally not interested in microfinance.

The concern here, however, is if it is possible to compare the returns on farm and non-farm investments of similar scale. If investments in farming yield a generally lower return than investments of similar amounts in what has come to be known as 'the non-farm sector', then this may be one explanation for the fact that most microcredit is used for consumption or for non-farm activities.

An attempt was therefore made to compare the percentage rates of return on a range of farm and non-farm investments of similar scale. Data on the returns to non-farm microinvestments was already available. This data has been reported elsewhere (Esipisu et al, 1998; Harper, 1998). The information was acquired by students, microfinance practitioners and government and donor staff who participated in a number of training programmes in Asia and Africa, and who collected the data as part of field exercises.

One purpose of this was to show that MFI clients could afford to pay high rates of interest, and thus to overcome policy makers' and bankers' fixations on the need for subsidized interest rates. Although the field visits were undertaken mainly in rural areas, and the participants were free to select any enterprise they chose, very little data was obtained for on-farm investments. This was partly because teashops and vegetable vendors can be found in any village, whereas farms and their owners are usually scattered in the countryside and are not easy to find during a half-day field training exercise.

The data was collected from 215 microenterprises. The businesses were of all types, apart from farming, and they were selected at random by the students along roadsides and in village market places. About one third were owned by women. The sample is not of course representative of all non-farm micro-enterprises, but the figures are at least indicative of what can be expected. The figures for investment were not whatever sum the owner had invested at the start of the business, but were an estimate of the total value of the investment at the time of the visit, at current prices. All the figures were adjusted for seasonality, and the opportunity cost of labour was generously estimated. There were only 37 cases where this cost was nil, because there were clearly no possible opportunities for the owners to earn any money from employment. In every other case, there was some way in which the owner could have earned something during at least some of the time she or he spent on the business. This was usually casual labour.

Failed businesses were not included, because they were not there to be studied, and the figures make no allowance for the risk of failure and loss of the investment and the earning capacity it had generated. Many of the businesses had been in existence for five years or more, and although many owners spoke of earlier failures, these did not usually seem to have involved total loss of the investment. Equipment had been sold, and the working capital had been extracted for consumption or reinvestment in another venture.

The average annual incremental return on these 215 investments, after subtracting the opportunity cost of their owners' labour, was 847 per cent. The returns ranged from minus 480 per cent to plus 19,200 per cent, and only in 40 cases, mainly the larger businesses with investments of over US$500, was the annual return less than 100 per cent. The return was over 1,000 per cent in 44 cases. There were only 10 businesses where the owner would have made more money by being employed. These extraordinarily high returns do not of course mean that the owners of these microenterprises were wealthy. The amounts invested are very small, and the opportunity costs of the owners' labour are often very low. An 847 per cent annual return on an investment of US$100 is only US$847, which is about US$2.30 a day and may be the sole income for a household of five or more people.

For the purposes of this chapter, an attempt was made to obtain similar data for farmers. Little data of this sort is available from most international financing or microfinance support institutions, such as the World Bank or DFID. The CGAP slide presentation on interest rates states that rates of return on microfinance investments vary between 117 per cent and 847 per cent, although no source is given for this data.

Basix Finance were, however, able to provide some Indian examples, and the participants in the December 2004 Dhan Foundation international training programme on 'The Art of Up-scaling Microfinance" in Madurai in southern India were asked to interview farmers and acquire some comparable data. Table 8.2 summarizes some of the findings for individual farmers that were obtained from Basix and by the students on the Madurai programme:

Table 8.2 Small farm investment returns

Place	Madurai	Madurai	Anantapur, Andhra Pradesh	Mehboobnagar, Andhra Pradesh	Madurai, Tamil Nadu
Activity	Replace cow dung with fertiliser for paddy	Plant paddy on 0.4 acres newly irrigated land	Year round irrigated double crop, groundnut and red gram.	Rainfed cotton irrigated paddy	5 acres
Cash invested	US$100 for fertilizer	US$60 for fertilizer	Seeds and fertilizer, US$300	Seeds, fertilizer and pesticides US$450	Fertilizer/ pesticides, US$54, hired labour US$15
Opportunity cost of family labour	No extra labour needed	30 days labour @US$2 = US$60	US$100	US$100	US$87
Gross return	20 addnl bushels of paddy @ US$9	Value of crop US$130	Value of crop US$600	Value of crop US$900	30 bags @ US$6 = US$180
Period	6 months	3 months	1 year	1 year	3 months
Return net of investment	US$80 per 6 months	US$10 per quarter	US$200	US$350	US$24
Annual % return	160%	31%	50%	64%	61%

In no cases do the investments include the cost of land, nor the capital cost of any irrigation works, which were substantial in two of the cases. The farmers were paying no fees for the irrigation, which had been provided by government. No allowance is made for risk, which is of course particularly high in rainfed crops. It is also assumed that the initial capital was all invested at the start of the season or other period, which is not always the case, but it is rare for any cash return to be realized until all the inputs and labour have been expended.

Some other data are also available. Four small irrigation investments in Nigeria, using two and three inch portable pumps, achieved rates of return of 45, 78, 107 and 119 per cent, and the cultivation of maize and millet was said to earn 25 per cent, and yams and cassava, 53 per cent (Yaro, 2004). In Benin, the return on maize and soya cultivation was assumed in a FAO/IFAD proposal to be 40 per cent (Republique du Benin, 2005). Similarly, a study of the economics of irrigation for potato cultivation in Colombia concluded that the return on the investment was 42 per cent (Holden, 2006).

This is only a small and non-random sample, and the methods of data collection and analysis were not necessarily consistent. Indian cases predominate, but this may not be unreasonable in the light of the fact that some 700 million Indians live and work in rural areas, of whom most are very poor by any standards. All the data were obtained from farmers' own recollection, rather than from diaries or any other more systematic means. People do not usually like to talk of failures, although some farmers may have been tempted to understate their returns because of a mistaken impression that the researchers were dispensing subsidies. Alternatively, of course, they may have exaggerated their success out of pride or to demonstrate their eligibility for loans. There are many reasons why the data may be inaccurate, but the errors are equally likely to have been positive or negative, and there is no reason why the returns from farming data would be any less accurate, or more understated, than the returns from non-farm enterprises. The orders of magnitude are probably reasonably correct, however, and readers should be able to confirm (or contradict) the figures with examples from their own experience.

The highest of the above annual rates of return was 160 per cent, only three were over 100 per cent, five were between 50 and 100 per cent, and five were under 50 per cent. These returns are reasonable or even quite high returns by normal commercial standards, but when MFIs are charging annual interest rates of 36 per cent or higher, as many do, there is only a small margin to cover risk, profit and any imputed return on the often very high value of the land. Two of the return figures were actually lower than the average microfinance interest rates that were quoted earlier in this chapter, so that farmers would be worse off if they invested microfinance loans in these crops. However approximate the data may be, the returns from farming are dramatically lower than the returns from the earlier sample of 215 non-farm businesses.

Does the mismatch matter?

It can be argued that the low margin between the cost of microloans and the returns from on-farm investments is not a serious problem. The following arguments might be adduced to support this view:

- Microfinance is aimed at women, from the poorest households. They tend to own no land, and many of them use their microloans to start or expand non-farm microenterprises from which they will supplement or even replace the minimal wages they earn as labourers on their better-off neighbours' farms. Microfinance is irrelevant to most farmers.
- Farmers may already have sources of funds to finance their crop production. The traditional 'old paradigm' credit providers still survive, in some places at any rate, and there are many other fund sources, apart from their own funds, such as credit from input suppliers and advances from crop traders, not all of which are exploitative. Microfinance aims to complement and not to replace these sources, and enables clients, particularly women, to diversify their livelihoods.
- Population pressure and the resulting smaller family holdings, the growing capital-intensity of farming, water shortages and World Trade Organization-induced global competition in commodities such as edible oils and food grains, mean that small-scale farming is becoming uneconomic. Rural families must move into non-farm activities, and microfinance enables them to do this.

The strength of these arguments will vary from one context to another, but there are strong counter-arguments to support the view that microfinance should be an appropriate source of funds for on-farm investments as well as for non-farm microenterprises and 'consumption' expenditure:

- The neo-liberal market-led view is still in the ascendant, and appears likely to remain so. Some MFI interest rates are higher than they would be if the institution was totally efficient, but the differences between the returns from farm and non-farm ventures are such as to make it quite impossible for the surplus to be earned on the farm to come anywhere near that which is available from non-farm enterprises.
- In many countries, traditional commercial bank branch numbers are being cut drastically, and in some places they are being replaced by MFIs, such as the recently privatized National Microfinance Bank in Tanzania, which runs the rural branches of the old public sector National Bank of Commerce, or the Centenary Rural Development Bank of Uganda, an MFI which has effectively replaced the Uganda Commercial Bank as the country's rural commercial bank, albeit with fewer branches. The 'old paradigm' rural credit system has not always survived.
- Farmers' cooperatives, which used to be many cultivators' main source of seasonal finance, are in disarray in many countries. In India in the year 2000, 142 of the countries' 367 District Central Cooperative Banks were technically insolvent, and 332 of them were capital inadequate (Berkhoff,

2003). The financial position of their 93,000 affiliated primary societies was even worse, and their cooperative status was also deeply compromised by political interference and government control.

- Farmers need more finance than before to be able to buy more expensive inputs and equipment, so that even if their traditional sources are still available, they are not sufficient to allow farmers to invest the sums they need to be able to compete.

Irrespective of these arguments, however, the basic point remains: if the cost of finance exceeds the return that is earned on investment, the investor will lose money.

What is to be done?

This chapter has only dealt with interest rates and rates of return; issues such as cash flows, risk or gender have not been covered. Many recent developments in microfinance can be interpreted as attempts to correct the mismatch on some of these issues. Some MFIs, such as Grameen Bank under its Grameen Two programme, have modified their rigorous fixed weekly or monthly repayment schedules to allow for the timings of cash inputs from farming, and some now offer or even require life and health insurance. A number of microfinance institutions such as Basix Finance are also pioneering new forms of protection against crop failure in order to reduce the risk of non-repayment.

There have been a number of innovations in farming systems and technologies, such as the irrigation treadle pump, pioneered in Bangladesh and India, and lower risk crops, integrated pest management using less inputs, and new technologies that are under the control of women. Some of these increase rates of return while others reduce the amounts needed for investment. IDE of New Delhi, for instance, has pioneered low cost drip irrigation for small farmers, and initial trials showed that an investment of about US$215 on a 1.6 acre plot could increase net income by a total of US$550 over the projected four year life of the equipment. This approximates to an annual return of about 75 per cent, well below what can be earned from petty trading but well over the returns on most on-farm investments (IDE, 2005).

Nevertheless, these changes are far from being universally applied, and, even if they were available everywhere microfinance would not be wholly suitable for farmers. What more needs to be done to bring microfinance and farming closer? Answers to this question will of course vary from one place to another, but there are certain trends which are already evident, and other steps which can be taken, which may in part address the issue:

- MFIs need to be more efficient and reduce their costs. The pressure to date has been for MFIs to achieve 'sustainability'. For a financial services business, this presumably means profitability, including some return on equity. MFIs have only reached 10 per cent or less of the potential microfinance market in most countries, and moneylenders and other informal credit suppliers are still their main competition. The easiest way to cover costs, therefore, is to charge high interest rates; partly as a result of their quasi-monopoly position, many MFIs are already highly profitable. The 209 'financially self-sufficient' MFIs in the *Mix Market Bulletin*'s list for 2004 made an average after tax profit of 4.8 per cent on their total assets. Returns on assets of over 2 per cent are unusual for normal commercial banks; such a high figure is far beyond their reach. Competition is increasing, however, and this will of course be the main driver of efficiency, and of the lower interest costs, greater flexibility or other service improvements that their customers will demand. The mismatch between interest rates and returns that we have identified will presumably be reduced over time.

- The increasing presence of commercial banks in microfinance (Harper and Arora, 2005) may also bring interest rates down. The figures quoted earlier in this chapter showed that banks' microfinance interest rates are about 7 per cent lower than NGOs, and banks are sometimes reluctant to charge their poorest clients higher rates than those paid by the better-off. Their activities are more visible, they may be state-owned or at least substantially beholden to the state, and they have more opportunities to cross-subsidize what is usually only a small part of their business, particularly since it has high public relations value and some microfinance clients may 'graduate' to mainstream status.

- Loans to women dominate most microfinance portfolios. There are very good business and social reasons for this, and it may be heretical to question it, but on-farm activities are still mainly male dominated. Competition may force MFIs to look for neglected niche markets, and male farmers may be one of these. Some institutions have started down this road. The Pandyan rural bank for instance, in Tamil Nadu state of India, is heavily involved in microfinance for women, and has financed over 13,000 women's SHGs, with around 15–20 members each. The bank has more recently also started lending direct to small-scale farmers, usually men, using joint liability groups of about five members each, who guarantee each others' loans. The transaction costs are low, for both the bank and the farmers, with no requirements for regular meetings, and the repayment experience has been as good as that from the women's SHGs (*The Hindu*, 9 May 2005).

In spite of these emerging trends, however, the fact remains that most MFI credit products are unsuitable for financing on-farm investments; they are too expensive and too inflexible. Microfinance staff, however, seem to be unaware that they may not be serving the farming market. The most immediate need is for MFIs, and for those who advise, finance, train and study them, to examine the issue more rigorously than has been possible in this short note, to find out if there is indeed a problem in their area and then to address it.

Note

1   An earlier version of this chapter appeared in *Small Enterprise Development* in September 2005. A number of people made useful comments on this chapter, in particular Nana Opare of Cranfield School of Management, D. S. K. Rao of the Micro-Credit Summit Organisation, Susan Johnson of Bath University and Jennifer Heney, Michael Marx, Maria Pagura and Ake Olofsson of the FAO.

References

Asia/Pacific Micro-credit Summit (2004) *Asia/Pacific Micro-credit Summit*, transcript of remarks, Dhaka.

Berkhoff, A. (2003) *Microfinance in Rural India: Linking Self-Help Groups to Cooperative Banks and Primary Agricultural Credit Societies*, unpublished diploma thesis, IWW Universität Karlsruhe, Karlsruhe.

Christen, R. P. and Pearce, D. (2005) *Managing Risks and Developing Products for Agricultural Microfinance: Features of an Emerging Model*, CGAP, Washington DC.

Coffey, E. (1998) *Agricultural Finance: Getting the Policies Right*, FAO/GTZ, Rome.

DiLeo, P. (2003) *Building a Reliable MFI Funding Base: Donor Flexibility Shows Results*, CGAP, Washington DC.

Esipisu, E., Harper, M. and Rao, D. S. K (1998) *The New Middlewomen*, ITDG Publishing, London and Oxford, and IBH, New Delhi.

Harper, M. (1998) *Profit for the Poor, Cases in Microfinance*, ITDG Publishing, London and Oxford, and IBH, New Delhi.

Harper, M. and Arora, S. (2005) *Small Customers, Big Market – Commercial Banks in Microfinance*, ITDG Publishing, London and TERI Publications, New Delhi.

The Hindu (2005) 'Business line', 9 May.

Holden, D. (2006) *Indicators for Comparing the Performance of Irrigated Agriculture Systems*, IWMI, Colombo.

IDE (2005) *(India)'s Market Creation Approach to Development*, IDE, New Delhi.

Grameen Bank (2004) *Annual Report*, Grameen Bank, Dhaka.

Klein, B. (1999) Better Practices in Agricultural Lending, FAO/GTZ, Rome.

Mix Market Bulletin (2006) *Mix Market Bulletin* 12, CGAP, Washington DC.

Republique du Benin (2005) *Programme d'Appui au Developpement Rurale*, FAO/IFAD, Rome.

Yaro, M. (2004) *Loan Management, National Special Programme for Food Security*, FMARD & FAO, Rome.

PART TWO
Institutions

CHAPTER NINE
The moneylender's dilemma

Kim Wilson

Abstract

In the late 1980s Catholic Relief Services (CRS) joined the microcredit industry and its evolution from economic provider to global moneylender began. Along the way, CRS learned that through microcredit the poor were poor twice, once from initial circumstances and twice from high interest rates. Though best practices argued for high interest as a route to sustainability, best practitioners operated in contexts where few laws protected consumers, where consumers were desperate and where subsidies surged, but not to clients. While these conditions welcomed the profiteer, they repelled CRS. In 2005, CRS decided to fully divest its holdings in microcredit in favour of savings-led microfinance.

> As he went through town that day he was obsessed with thoughts of money. His mind rang with the words he had said to villagers: 'I am only trying to help you get out of your money worries'. He began to believe it himself. He saw himself a saviour of mankind.
>
> The Financial Expert, R. K. Narayan

In 2005 CRS issued to its field offices a paper called *Microfinance 2010*, which mandated divestiture of all microcredit holdings within five years:

> Microfinance exacts a toll on the agency. Due to their special requirements, MFIs chafe at our financial, audit and accounting systems, human resource policies, and annual planning process. Questions of subsidiarity come into play, and our explicit mission to serve the poor and marginalized may not receive the same attention as concerns for financial profit. This confounds us. Do we continue along a path pronounced good by serious international donors or do we follow the wisdom of our principles?
>
> (CRS, 2005)

CRS was getting out of the moneylending business. The agency would no longer invest in new MFIs and would phase out its MFI loan and equity portfolios. It would support MFIs in finding other investors and lenders but would itself disengage as an investor or lender.

The decision to step back from credit was sweeping and controversial. It came at a time when some of CRS' microcredit programmes were quite profitable, when the agency's coffers were flush with private and public money, and when CRS' new fund dedicated to microcredit, 'Lifelines', was doubling in size.

For years CRS had advanced along the frontiers of lending, confident in its benefits. Now within a matter of months the agency was in full retreat. On the surface the question was: how could CRS make such a cavalier about-face? But the evidence had been mounting for years. The deeper question was: what took us so long?

In such a large and decentralized agency, where carrying on is far easier than changing course, I am surprised we made the decision at all. It took an enormous force of will for so many to come together and decide 'enough', that doing-well-by-doing-good had become a conceit and had outlived its usefulness, that it was better to face the sting of peers and the 'best practices' hegemony, and better to reject the promise of more funds than to keep up the charade.

The dilemma for CRS was that we had become a moneylender, a subsidized one. Perversely, the subsidies never travelled to the poor in the form of low interest rates, great service or social impact, but stayed within the confines of our partner microfinance institutions, often off the MFI's books. We had not attained the double bottom-line where financial profit matches social returns. In aggregate, we had attained the benefits of neither bottom line but the purgatory of a double top line, where MFIs benefitted from subsidies along side extraordinary rates of interest.

An abbreviated history

With US$25,000 and a pledge to follow a documented methodology, CRS bought the Village Banking™ package from FINCA International. It was the late 1980s and microcredit seemed unrivalled in its power to change the economic fate of vast numbers of poor people. Inadequate credit was considered the primary barrier to financial opportunity for the self-employed, a category that fitted many of the people the agency aimed to serve. Loans used productively could boost a marginal activity like selling charcoal, tea or shea nuts into a prosperous family business. Village banking not only represented vital resources for the agency's primary clientele, it conferred other benefits as well, social cohesion and empowerment among them. Most important, village banking was something that CRS' thousands of grassroots partners could do. It was systematic, simple and easily mastered by local staff. In those days village banking had a beginning, a middle and an end. After nine or so rounds of external loans from the partner-lender, borrowers within a village bank could pool enough savings to meet local credit needs. The partner could shift its loan capital to a new community. The simplicity of microcredit paved the way for expansion. CRS could capitalize on its thousands of grassroots partners and help them bring financial resources to the most rural locations.

In the 1990s, microcredit broadened its scope to include all forms of finance to the poor, yet most programmes still focused on credit. The prevailing practice was for organizations like CRS to help local partners create sustainable institutions. Borrowers, it seemed, wanted more money than their group funds would supply. By charging higher rates of interest and providing continued credit to an ever-growing base of borrowers, partners could sustain credit operations indefinitely. However, microcredit was no longer something every partner could do. It had become a specialized business that warranted technical expertise. The agency in the mid-1990s began to push for the formation of independent microcredit businesses that would merit the investment of commercial sources of capital.

By 2005, CRS supported microcredit in 21 countries with an agency portfolio of about US$19 million and far more on the books of partners. Some programmes followed a modified village bank methodology. Others were Grameen replicators. Still others adopted the solidarity model. All were similar in that partners used group guarantees as the primary means of security. All included a savings feature of some sort (or were supposed to) and all were to focus on women. The agency had developed a set of standards for reviewing programme performance, engaged a network of microfinance advisors worldwide, and invested substantial public and private funds in microfinance activities. CRS was supporting loans to hundreds of thousands of clients in Europe, Asia, the Middle East, Latin America and Africa. In total CRS managed 17 country programmes that had some form of financial relationship with one or more MFIs and four country programmes directly involved with wholesale microfinance institutions.

The following is a personal reflection on the many small awakenings that led CRS to stop seeing microcredit as a strategy to uphold its mission and start seeing microcredit as an obstacle to achieving it.

A night to remember

I attended a conference of practitioners, many from CRS, in the mid-1990s. Microcredit had unofficially morphed into microfinance. New to the industry, I felt as though I had stepped though a portal to an alternate universe. Steered neither by commerce nor charity yet drawing on both, this universe enjoyed its own language, which brimmed with commercial diminutives. Microentrepreneur substituted for ragpicker or street hawker and microsavings replaced involuntary acts of thrift. Small grants became microequity and moneylenders were now microbankers.

The kick-off dinner of salads, fruits, sautéed sole, cheeses, wines and deserts, was interrupted by a surprise. The kitchen staff – cooks, waiters, dishwashers – walked into the dining hall and encircled the tables, then began a gentle applause. Someone took the microphone and announced the staff had learned that the topic of the dinner was microfinance and that they wanted to wish us well. They had relatives in other countries who could benefit from small loans.

For a magic moment I am absolutely certain that every dinner guest in that room was transfixed, thinking the same thing as I. In 10 years time how would our well-wishers see us? As social pioneers, merchant profiteers,or naked emperors? The gesture took us off guard. It was not the usual form of village gratitude to which many at my table had become inured. Or the mistaken praise of friends who thought microfinance work as self-sacrificing. This applause was utterly unexpected and sobered our shoulder-slapping bonhomie. We accepted the appreciation with smiles and a promise that one day we would deserve this gesture. Were we up to the task? Would we be heroes or frauds?

New curators of the museum of poverty

In the early days of microcredit, a few protocols steadied our work: do not accept late payments or partial payments; do not allow men into loan groups; place all loans into income generating activities. But soon any deviation from the norm provoked frowns from the ranks of practitioners.

By the mid- and late-1990s we had fossilized. Neither commercial nor charitable, we were subject to the new rules of best practice, which had assumed a papal infallibility. Perhaps the most jarring 'best practice' was a commitment to charge market rates of interest. It was never clear what charging market rates meant in the economies where CRS worked, other than to charge as much as possible. One programme priced its loans at 87 per cent per year in a country with limited inflation. The poor had become the new consumers of debt, fisherman who might fish for a lifetime on an endless line of loans.

It bothered us a little that local moneylenders receiving no subsidy would charge these rates but it bothered us a great deal more that all the grants, technical assistance and idealism that accompanied our own investment held the power to generate such unfettered predation. It seemed that the only thing we were likely to sustain was poverty.

The clash of civilizations

'The call for specialized field staff in specialized institutions – a cornerstone of classic microfinance – can collide with agency reality' (CRS, 2005). The circle that practiced microfinance was no longer a rag-tag collection of development workers but an entrenched set of experts. The agency had begun to see sectoral divides that were not necessarily good for a global institution. CRS staff working in microfinance as advisors or project managers, or in some cases as managers of microfinance institutions (in the absence of independent local partners) had become isolated from other activities of the agency. The fault lines deepened.

We were just doing our job, which was to focus on microfinance. But the synergies that might have happened between sectors, for example between agriculture and microfinance – a natural pair in rural economic development – were not taking place. One part of the agency was intent on building sustainable businesses (MFIs) or helping partners to build them, and all other parts were seeking to deliver humanitarian or development services. Barriers between microfinance and other sectors rose, threatening a kind of balkanization that seemed less like healthy rivalry and more like a cold war.

A well-oiled machine

> That all forms of microfinance consume funds over many years challenges its original claim to self-generate sustainable financial benefits. And while microcredit has proved capable of covering operating costs with operating revenue, it has proved incapable of covering the costs of start up (seed capital) or technical assistance, or of critical management positions. (CRS, 2005)

The amount of working capital and technical assistance needed to transform a microlending programme into a self-propelled credit machine proved gargantuan. By the calculation of some, and it was anybody's guess, an emerging MFI required an investment – net of any interest income or loan funds – of between US$150 and US$300 per client.

As one regional director quipped: 'if microcredit is so sustainable, why is my programme so broke?'. Microcredit indeed had become a leaky ship and some of the funds it siphoned off were undesignated, meaning they could have been used for schools, clinics or agriculture. In the minds of a few, microcredit costs had become synonymous with opportunity costs. Did we continue to pump funds into the abyss or did we start to compare microcredit costs and benefits to other development programmes?

We chose the latter but found it next to impossible to actually determine what it cost to start and sustain a viable growing microfinance institution. To disentangle microcredit expenses from shared programme costs required a hair-splitting calculus that few of us could do. Also, many costs were buried in line items for training, advisory staff and other support. Often key management positions in an MFI, particularly expatriate positions, fell onto CRS' books, omitted from the MFI's profit equation. Also omitted were international travel and the cost of consultants. And once loan funds washed in and out of CRS financial machinery a few times, whether we capitalized or expensed them became a matter of donor preference, further complicating cost estimates.

The industry could only provide data that MFIs themselves supplied. Additional costs that international agencies took on were uncalculated or undisclosed. We did not know if other agencies were reluctant to share true costs or if they were like us and just didn't know them. To gauge cost–benefit we were stuck with dead-reckoning. Our guess was that microfinance was a financial sinkhole.

Change agents

During the last interview in a day marked by dreary conversations, a well-schooled job applicant said: 'I like the clear rules of village banking. I will enjoy managing them'. She had boned up. We responded: 'Though we have a solid system to follow, the programme needs a leader to make sure its services please clients, and even inspires them. We are looking for someone who can empower women, provoke change'. She stared at us blankly. We were in search of a firebrand and our best candidate wanted to run a 7-Eleven, her next interview.

It was 1998 and I had accompanied colleagues to Thailand. We had been interviewing candidates throughout the long, hot afternoon in hopes of finding someone to oversee our village banking organization. Discovering a leader who might turn the programme away from investing in the petrol stations of board members – its latest expression of mission drift – and toward helping the poorest farmers was proving difficult. We wanted more than mission realignment; we were seeking a hero who could motivate staff and transform the lives of the poor. It did not occur to us then as it would later that credit management is a take-no-prisoners war against risk. And risk avoidance calibrated perfectly with a paint-by-the-numbers village banking approach. But, could someone who thrived on tamping down risk – the very quality required to run a credit replication – inspire the kind of transformation promised by microfinance?

Dodging the bishop

Although it was covering costs with interest, Father Paul said:

> I want to close this programme. I am doing it now to please CRS. We are not reaching the far-flung hamlets. The need for assistance is greatest there. The roads are dirt and rough, sometimes impassible. The people living in the interior need far more support than those living near a road. And then there is the interest rate. If I am going to take on the expense of operating an MFI, I will have to charge high rates, nearly the rate of the local moneylender. If I do that, I will have to dodge the bishop. He would never tolerate such a thing.

Though CRS has many kinds of partners, two categories are relevant here: MFI partners that are financial institutions and grassroots partners. CRS supports fewer than 50 microfinance partners (including the institutions CRS started) but thousands of grassroots partners scattered throughout the poorest rural areas of the world. Their programming varies widely. Some emphasize education or health, others agriculture or water, child protection, disaster response, and still others HIV/Aids and malaria prevention and care. Many focus on a rich blend of these activities. They served remote locales often prone to calamity, or with very vulnerable populations. For these partners, microcredit did not work.

Serving two masters

Partner staff at one time (pre-best practices) could afford to show genuine care for their clients and spent extra time to find doctors, veterinarians or agricultural extension workers. They helped deliver babies and cows and tended sick children. They lent emergency money from their own pockets. They worked long hours walking or riding on isolated, dangerous roads, with women staff frequently compromising their safety. They helped buy livestock, advised on kitchen gardens and encouraged borrowers to send their children to school.

Perhaps they could have been more efficient and delegated community work to others, but in many place there were no others. Our partner was the only game in town.

One loan officer in Senegal said: 'I really enjoy this work but sometimes it is hard. The community counts on me for so many things. I am its only visitor'. She was in a bind. Her salary was paid by the microfinance programme, and as such she was compelled to withhold information. 'I cannot tell my clients everything, like the lower interest rate they could get by joining another local programme'.

Friend or foe

Staff wanted to be the champion of a community, yet found it against their self-interest. Collecting late loan payments could further rupture relations. In the Balkans, one loan officer was so upset about confronting late borrowers that she confided she wanted another job: 'They do not see me as helping them, but as an enemy'.

Best practices argued for a commercial approach. MFIs invested a great deal in rules and policies to protect themselves from clients, and urged staff to be draconian. Some of us wondered why not leave commercial approaches to commerce? Why incorporate pseudo-business practices and call them 'best' in the name of development? Tracking down delinquents (often referred to as deadbeats), which is the stock-in-trade of a good moneylender, was taking a toll.

'I am tired of visiting this neighborhood to pressure people', said one promoter. 'Yes, Mrs P. is responsible for the loan but she is sick and a widow. She has been harassed by women in her group and by me. I try to be very nice to her, but my job depends on good repayment. My clients do not tell me their troubles anymore. Now I am a moneylender and I never hear their news'.

Pressured loan tactics took other forms as well. Take the example of the priest who called out the names of tardy borrowers at the end of mass. Our stop-at-nothing training in loan collection had gone too far.

The suffocating world of trust

Human beings can only thrive and achieve their full dignity in community with other people. People see their individual dignity and equality expressed and confirmed in social situations and relations – how they are treated by society, by their community, and by each other (CRS, 1998).

The social guarantee was a promising tonic in development's pharmacopea. Built on trust, it eliminated physical collateral and promoted social cohesion, in theory anyway. But reality spoke of a financial claustrophobia that those of us who can get loans in privacy – beyond the close scrutiny of neighbours or their vigilante tactics – will never have to face.

'I spend a lot of time now thinking about my neighbors and who will pay back and who might not', said one client. 'Some I don't trust as much as I did. I worry that their choices may mean they cannot pay back their loan when it is time. We all watch each other'.

And it brought shame. One client in Egypt said group members 'came to the house of my father where I lived after my husband had died suddenly. They pounded the door until the neighbours heard and demanded he pay the loan back. My father was shamed and asked me to leave'.

What people said they wanted – those who had been clients for a while anyway – were individual credit ratings, ones they could port from institution to institution, in search of a good deal. But, developing credit ratings that could migrate with the client was not in an MFI's best interest. MFIs wanted to access information on deadbeats but did not want their good clients' history disclosed. The group guarantee and its ability to obfuscate an individual's repayment performance served to imprison a client in an endless future of dumbed-down services.

Principles, see how they drift

> Credit and savings are both important means to finance the growth of economic activities. We connect the amount lent to the amount saved to help clients build wealth as they borrow (CRS, 2000).

A key principle of CRS microcredit was to include a savings feature, the only sure way for clients to accumulate assets. In most programmes clients made regular contributions to a group fund. They could borrow from the group fund and also the MFI. What they saved in the fund foretold what they could borrow from the MFI. But self-sufficiency, the mantra of best practices, mandated a more competitive approach. Consider an email that came to me in 2000 (paraphrased): 'The internal account (group fund) competes with our own loans. If borrowers tap their own group fund, they won't borrow as much from us. We are dismantling the group fund'.

> Democratic processes are key to empowering the poorest in a community. Clients are directly involved in the design, management and administration of the services they receive, from creating by-laws to voting on loan applications to choosing repayment schedules. In this way, CRS includes those most affected by decisions in the decision-making process (CRS, 2000).

But how involved in decisions did we really want our clients to be? Under the rules of best practice they were 'valued customers' and critical to institutional sustainability. Best practices implied that an organization must mine each customer for enough debt to contribute to the profitability of the MFI. Our MFIs required continued flows of revenue from repeat customers to stay in business. 'I wanted to stop after three loan cycles', said one borrower in Nicaragua, 'but the loan officer told me that I could never get another loan if I stopped'. She clearly was not a key player in making up the rules.

From time to time following best practices meant leapfrogging local cultural norms. Cultural appropriateness related to several Catholic Social Teaching principles, solidarity and subsidiarity to name two. A partner lamented in a very conservative part of Pakistan: 'To charge market interest rates, I must ignore Islamic Law. Shari'a says we should not charge interest on principal. I was told by a microfinance expert to simply package the interest as a fee. That is what the moneylenders do'. Dared we spread this best practice to others?

Moneychangers in the temple

'Two cords of wood, a pair of oxen, a yoke, a plough, a stove, and 20 bales of grain'. These are just some of the necessaries allowed a debtor under Vermont bankruptcy law in the 19th century. The state considered these assets essential to a person's livelihood, to their survival. The state was attempting to protect its citizens from the ravages of debt. Microcredit clients enjoy no such categorical safeguards. Their protection is a country-by-country proposition.

Debt in the USA emerged as part of a complex financial web, replete with social programmes and laws. First, we have diverse support for people in debt. Many commercial, non-profit and government services help people reduce what they owe. There are debt consolidators and debt counsellors, and consumer watchdog agencies that track abuse. Second, we have laws that protect people from unfair lending practices. The US Fair Trade Commission attempts to limit harassment by the Fair Debt Collection Act. Exemptions permitted under US bankruptcy law limit damage to a debtor's livelihood. Usury laws at the state level limit interest rates and federal rules stipulate a consistent method for disclosing these rates. The US lender liability laws offer borrowers recourse if their bankers have advised them poorly. Most states in the USA have long outlawed debtor's prison. None of these protections are uniformly available to microborrowers overseas. We had not exported our legal buffers along with our debt products.

As we shipped loans to the farthest corners of the world, we depended on our partners to self-regulate. But a nagging thought surfaced: self-regulation was something we ourselves would not tolerate from our banking system; we had come to demand other measures of protection. And if the laws were not there to bring interest rates down or protect customers, was there sufficient competition to engender choice, or could profiteering run wild?

If I only had a loan...

The microcredit industry had promised us scale, sustainability and impact. It seemed relevance was part of the promise too, though never stated explicitly. In 2003 I read what was for me a seminal report. Stuart Rutherford published a financial diary of microfinance in Bangladesh, one of the industry's most saturated proving grounds. The study emphasized the multiple and sophisticated ways that households manage their financial lives. Microcredit, even where competition was thickest, accounted for 10 per cent of lump sums gathered by households over the course of the year-long sequence of interviews. How could microcredit transform households in struggling economies when it accounted for such a small fraction of their financial strategies? Our own evidence suggested that our empowering microfinance was but one small and insignificant financial tool in their lives.

One borrower in Pakistan said after she had dropped out, 'I manage now as I did before with the help of neighbours and the moneylender. Your credit comes in the shape of a box with the weight of a trunk'.

Microcredit it seemed was irrelevant to the lives of the poor in the times of our success – when we were profitable – and very relevant in the times of our failure – when we ran a sloppy ship. If we delivered a loan well, we contributed to a small fraction of a client's household financial transactions. We were insignificant. If we delivered a loan poorly, we could destroy a borrower's life. We were significant. Our power to set people back through debt and shame was far greater than our power to bring them forward.

Whatever happened to microfinance?

Some efforts did seem to match our core goals better – CRS savings-first approaches for example. Partners in South Asia had tried these with success, and partners in Africa had begun forming simple, local savings clubs. In India CRS was reaching more than 500,000 women in savings-led microfinance with costs as low as US$0.90 per woman.

The agency was coming full circle. These savings approaches bore a striking resemblance to the group fund of the village bank model, dropped like a rock in the 1990s in favour of credit institution strategies. In South Asia, SHGs multiplied at a fevered pace as part of an indigenous movement. Groups saved, lent savings to members, and then linked to banks for more credit through an ingenious mechanism devised by Indian apex financial institutions and creative NGOs.

Interestingly, many microcredit practitioners repudiated savings-first approaches. They were not 'real microfinance'. But microcredit had become microfinance for the purpose of broadening from credit to include services like savings. While MFIs were the cornerstone of the microfinance industry, few institutions actually offered savings, and stuck to something they knew how to make money on – credit in the absence of usury laws. Hunkering down into the comfortable realm of credit was not *per se* a bad thing. Managing people's savings is a massive responsibility fraught with risk. But, despite regulated banks in India managing savings of more than 31 million micro-clients, CRS and the industry at large could barely acknowledge the model as a bona fide alternative to the credit-first approach. It took the industry and CRS itself years to accept the SHG–bank linkage model as a viable alternative to MFI-only services.

The night to remember again

So how did we do? What kind of social or financial report might we file to our well-wishers from the kitchen? Those of us there with plans for a strictly commercial venture probably fared best, though I am not sure many represented this category. Poor people had proved themselves as a viable market again and again. Since that night, bona fide full service commercial banks had more aggressively migrated services downstream to serve this new market in many countries. One can hope that consumer protection regulations and competition might serve these consumers in the future.

But those of us operating as moneylenders and masquerading as charities fared less well. With our subsidy gleaned in the form of start-up capital and technical assistance grants, we could linger in a community well beyond the time of a profit-oriented bank. And it was in that lingering that we faced so many dilemmas, all already mentioned. We owed the kitchen staff our regrets. We had not been that helpful. We had never been wittingly rapacious. No, our exploitative actions were the result of a slow, unconscious series of non-decisions, bolstered by a world of best practices, good intentions and subsidized advice. And money. It was time to wake up and draw the curtain.

What CRS did

By spring of 2006, all 21 CRS countries with microcredit programmes had submitted plans to headquarters for MFI partners to divest CRS shares and phase down borrowing from CRS. The objectives of divestiture were messy and context-specific. Were we simply turning over our own problems and ethical dilemmas to other entities? In a way, yes. But, we felt we could live with this decision for several reasons. First, the local Catholic Church in some places was ready and willing fully to manage the balance sheet of these institutions. They could expand or divest as they saw fit. Handing CRS' equity over to the Church matched the Catholic Social Teaching principle of subsidiarity, important to the agency. Second, profitable MFIs were ready to attract commercial investors and lenders. These MFIs would no longer need to juggle the CRS-imposed double bottom line. They could work with a new set of board members who held a clear vision for profit (though we would have a hand in board member selection).

CRS would stay involved in microfinance but forfeit its role as an economic actor in the financial supply chain. Our efforts would focus on neglected rural areas, where savings were a priority, and on legal protection and remedy, where we had the capacity to effect change. We would be free to link clients to resources (banks, post offices or MFIs) and champion their rights in relation to these resources. This would align us with the Catholic Social Teaching principle of right relationships. We would shift private funds away from microcredit toward school programmes for girls, maternal health and emergency relief. We could go back to the real work of charity and see poor people as partners in a shared liberation, and not as experiments in quasi-commerce. Our dilemmas as moneylenders could at last become history.

References

CRS (Catholic Relief Services) (1998) *Summary of Catholic Social Teaching*, internal document, CRS, Baltimore.

CRS (2000) *Principled Practices in Microfinance*, Pact Publications and CRS, Baltimore.

CRS (2005) *MF 2010*, internal document, CRS, Baltimore.

CHAPTER TEN

Princes, peasants and pretenders: The past and future of African microfinance

Paul Rippey

Abstract

This chapter uses an analogy to Shakespearean tragedy to argue that institutions based on Asian models, supported by northern donors, have been the focus of attention and assistance to African microfinance. As these Princes have commercialized, their tragic flaw has been the aggressive marketing of loans, beyond the sustainable needs of their customers, the Peasants, who have become a 'commons', open to exploitation by all. The customers are seduced by credit, while bad products, opacity and donor complicity are exhausting this resource. Neither institutions nor consumers have acted in their long-term best interests, and when the interests diverge, donors have shown more interest in the well-being of the institutions.

New approaches ('the Pretenders'), developed in Africa, hold great promise, including Afriland First Bank in Cameroon, village savings and loans associations from Niger, and consumer protection efforts from South Africa. An important role of international donors should be to help innovations from Africa spread across Africa.

This chapter argues that African microfinance over the last two decades has been largely dominated by institutions based on Asian models, imported and supported by Europeans and North Americans. As these institutions have grown and become commercial businesses, they became increasingly ill suited to meeting the needs of the population they intended to serve; to sustain themselves, they have heavily marketed loans to people whose absorptive capacity for those loans was seldom assessed. In some countries, in fact, the MFIs are reaching saturation in the ability of poor people to absorb any more credit, in part because the customers are treated as a 'commons', a property open to be exploited by all institutions. For their part, the customers are seduced by debt, in an atmosphere in which it is a sign of weakness to refuse to take a loan.

The chapter goes on to say that the future of African microfinance can be vastly better than its past. New types of institutions are being developed, and some old institutional types are finding new favour. At the same time, new financial products and the ability of technology to leapfrog over some of the stages in the development of the industry, all hold promise that the future of African microfinance will be radiant. The chapter suggests that some of the best new products will be African creations, and the role of international donors, hopefully, will be to help promising innovations from Africa spread across Africa.

For the promise of African microfinance to be realized, it will be necessary to make some space for innovations, so we will try to do our part to exorcise the continent of donor-driven, credit-oriented MFIs. The author will, I hope, be permitted to take this stance, having participated in the creation and management of credit-only MFIs in West and North Africa over two decades. I consider myself a reformed microcredit specialist, now doing penance for past sins of indiscriminate debt-mongering.

Two episodes stand out as having raised my doubts about the usefulness of the microcredit endeavour. In the 1980s, I was working in the Washington DC office of an American NGO (the now defunct NGO Partnership for Productivity (PfP), a pioneer in African microcredit). Like countless other NGOs, PfP would season its fund-raising presentations in the US with anecdotes about success stories, including the story of the two brothers who sold bicycle parts in the market in Fada N'Gourma, Burkina Faso. Thanks to a small loan, the story went, the two brothers had grown so successful that they had expanded into a second stall at the other side of the market, stringing a wire between the two shops to connect two battery powered phones. 'Hey, Mamadou', one would call to the other over the phone, 'Got a chain for a 36 inch Schwinn?'.

I had heard that story several times when I lived in the US, so when fate took me to the very market in question, I asked to meet the brothers, only to be told a sad story. When the brothers got to be successful, I was told, one of the other bicycle parts dealers in the market got jealous and paid a master of traditional magic to put a curse on one of the brothers. The result was that each time the brother went into the market, he was struck by uncontrollable diarrhoea. Finally, the poor man lost his stock, and eventually his mind. PfP continued to use the story in their fundraising, without the tragic conclusion, presumably because it illustrated the power of microcredit so well.

Ten years later I was running a USAID-supported microcredit project in Guinea in the early 1990s. I would go out frequently with my local director to visit field staff and clients. A loan officer in Mamou, a large town four hours inland from the capital Conakry, said he had been thinking about the programme, and had ideas about improving it. 'Excellent! Tell us', we asked him, hoping he would enrich the programme with his unique field persective. 'I think', he said, 'that we should limit clients to no more than three loans each'. 'Hm', we wondered, 'Why is that?'. 'Because after three loans', he replied in total sincerity, 'the clients are so poor that it's really not fair to lend them more money'. We of course showed him the error of his ways, all the while wondering how such heresy could have slipped through our training. We assured him that contrary to what he thought he had seen with his own eyes, he was wrong. There was no problem with an indefinite series of small loans. Not only were they actually good for poor people, but our business model depended on them. He never voiced any doubts again, perhaps sensing that to do so would not be a good career move. This organization, by the way, the Guinea Rural Enterprise Development Project, had excellent productivity and repayment rates, but never rose much above 50 per cent cost recovery. The salaries had been set by a North American – myself – and even though I was smart enough to pay salaries much lower than those in other projects, we ended up with a payroll that was higher than we could possibly sustain, and, despite that, had a massive strike while I was there, as the staff compared their monthly take with what their friends who were lucky enough to work for other USAID projects received. When I visited the project around its 10th anniversary in 2001, it was beginning to pay its staff out of the loan fund, a sign of impending death for any credit programme, and I assume that it has breathed its last breath by now.

Donor-funded microfinance in Africa has elements that recall Shakespearean tragedy: our attention is focused on the larger-than-life main characters, the MFIs, whose good intentions do not save them from their tragic flaws. Donors (and increasingly governments) pay tribute to these Princes, occasionally cautioning them against their excesses, but powerless to stop their destructive tendencies. While this drama is unfolding, the Peasants and common folk (now called 'clients') lead their lives largely invisibly in the background. If they suffer as a result of the errors of the Princes, it happens off-stage and doesn't particularly concern us. And, lest it all become too depressing, the saga is interrupted from time to time by episodes of comic relief.

This chapter will look first at the Princes, the donor-driven financial institutions, who with the advent of commercialization became the object of our interest, hope and sympathy. Then we will touch on the effects of the drama on the Peasants, the clients. But while I plunge into these murky waters, please remember that we will surface in a clear pool of hope as we look at the Pretenders, innovative ideas that may be the future of African microfinance. Africa needs to rid itself of yesterday's ideas and yesterday's institutions. If it does so, its own creativity will provide solutions.

The institutions I worked with were all credit-only, prohibited by law from collecting deposits. That credit-only institutions still exist in Africa is largely the result of the widespread acceptance of two beliefs, both, unfortunately, dead wrong. The first erroneous belief is that financial institutions know what is best for them, and act in a rational manner consistent with their long-term best interests. The second erroneous belief is that consumers know what is best for them, and that if we rely on market forces, people will buy the financial services that meet their needs and make their lives better.

These two beliefs are like tenets of religious faith, or, the secular equivalent, 'best practices'. Learned women and men teach them in prestigious settings. Although there is very little evidence *for* them, there are countless articles and studies *based on* them. They are so widespread and so rarely challenged that before I endanger my reputation by questioning them, I feel compelled to quote Thomas Sankara, who said, 'You cannot carry out fundamental change without a certain amount of madness. In this case, it comes from nonconformity, the courage to turn your back on the old formulas, the courage to invent the future.

It took the madmen of yesterday for us to be able to act with extreme clarity today. I want to be one of those madmen' (1983). Lest he be forgotten, I take this opportunity to praise the memory of Sankara, the visionary president of Burkina Faso from 1983 to 1987. He campaigned energetically and effectively for self-reliance and against corruption and donor dependence. Because of this, and because he required citizens to call each other 'comrade', foreign assistance began to dry up. His comrades, led by Blaise Compaore, in an echo of Julius Caesar, murdered him, all the while praising him. Compaore became president for life, and reinstalled corruption as a central element of Burkinabe governance.

Or, to cite a western thinker, management guru Gary Hamel said that by the time something is recognized as a 'best practice', it usually no longer is one. Gary Hamel is also famous for having lavishly praised the Enron business model, a reminder to take his sceptical advice sceptically. Those who follow 'best practices' learned in workshops or through imitation are condemned to work with ageing business models in areas of fierce competition. Microfinance in Africa seems increasingly old-fashioned, mired in 'best practices' developed and documented a decade or two ago. No one knows best practices better than the Princes of African microfinance, the donor supported MFIs.

The Princes

In 1968, Garrett Harding, a professor of biology at the University of California, wrote a paper called 'The Tragedy of the Commons', published in *Science* magazine (1968). The paper has remained current for remarkably long, and in fact has generated a small industry of spin-offs in diverse fields, so that we now find on the internet 'The Tragedy of the Advertising Commons' and 'The Tragedy of the Radio Spectrum Commons', among many others. Remarkably for a paper published in an academic journal, Harding's article and the ideas in it have been widely circulated in more popular media. Harding's ideas shed some light on what has happened to microfinance in Africa.

Some definitions are necessary before we can move on to Harding's ideas. Harding uses *tragedy* in the Shakespearean sense. That is, tragedy is not simply something *bad*, it is something bad that happens as an *inevitable result of unchangeable human nature*. I will argue that something bad has indeed happened to microfinance in Africa, and that perhaps it was more or less inevitable.

Harding condemns the 'tendency to assume that decisions reached individually will be the best decisions for an entire society', and argues that in fact the exact reverse is often the case. Applied to microfinance, Harding would say that simple reliance on market forces, donors, the hidden hand, or enlightened self-interest would be an error. I think we have, in fact, largely had faith that microfinance, and particularly microcredit, was such a good thing that we just needed to fuel it with donor start-up money and training in commercial lending techniques, largely imported from Asia, and it would cause a wave of social goodness to spread across the continent. In fact, I think it has produced a pandemic of revenue-maximizing institutions, many of which have forgotten the social mission they may once have had.

Harding introduces the notion of the tragedy of the commons in this often-quoted passage:

> Picture a pasture open to all. It is to be expected that each herdsman will try to keep as many cattle as possible on the commons. Such an arrangement may work reasonably satisfactorily for centuries because tribal wars, poaching, and disease keep the numbers of both man and beast well below the carrying capacity of the land. Finally, however, comes the day of reckoning, that is, the day when the long-desired goal of social stability becomes a reality. At this point, the inherent logic of the commons remorselessly generates tragedy.

> As a rational being, each herdsman seeks to maximize his gain. Explicitly or implicitly, more or less consciously, he asks, 'What is the utility to me of adding one more animal to my herd?'. This utility has one negative and one positive component.

1. The positive component is a function of the increment of one animal. Since the herdsman receives all the proceeds from the sale of the additional animal, the positive utility is nearly +1.
2. The negative component is a function of the additional overgrazing created by one more animal. Since, however, the effects of overgrazing are shared by all herdsmen, the negative utility for any particular decision-making herdsman is only a fraction of –1.

Harding continues that by adding together the positive and negative components, one has a number close to +1, and the only rational decision is to add another animal, or animals, to the herd. But the same conclusion is reached by every herdsman, and hence the tragedy of the destruction of the commons.

There are ample examples of this pattern occurring – oceans are over-fished, the atmosphere is filled with greenhouse gasses, countries have more people than they can feed, and more cars than their roads can hold. Some people, traditionally liberals, think that appeals to reason and humanity's innate goodness can lead people and institutions to reduce their short-term individual gain for the common good. In fact, many people, even a majority, can be motivated to do just that, but as a policy, appeals to goodness are futile, argues Harding, because 'conscience is self-eliminating'. If, for instance, I am concerned about over-population, and make the generous decision to limit my family size for that reason, then other people's children, who do not have my altruistic genes or family values (whichever you believe is the determining factor in the way children turn out) will be more numerous than mine. The next generation will be motivated less by conscience, more by immediate self-interest. Harding argues persuasively that a solution to preventing the exploitation of any commons is some sort of public coercion. He uses *coercion* in a very broad sense, to include all sorts of incentives.

What is the 'commons' in the financial arena? It is, perhaps not exclusively, the good reputation and trust that people have towards the financial system taken as a whole. In Uganda, the microfinance industry continues to suffer from intermittent poisonous press, strangely interspersed among paeans to the role of small loans in 'alleviating poverty'. One dramatic example, but far from the only one, from Uganda's *New Vision*, a leading national paper, opens on this note:

> Microfinance institutions in Busoga have robbed poor women and the youth blind. More than two thousand women who had borrowed heavily in the last six months have either had to sell off their pieces of land, domestic animals to repay the loans, and where some have failed, they've had to flee to nearby islands or face horrifying prison sentences.

At the least, trust reduces transaction costs, specifically in loan appraisal, reduces repayment problems, and increase retention rates. Some examples of the financial commons being inexorably consumed in Harding's sense would be these:

- *Indiscriminate lending with bad products.* An example might be an institution with a strong marketing arm and unpopular products that processes large numbers of clients through a lending cycle with terms and conditions that eventually drive them away. (One wishes this were an imaginary example.) As is the case with Harding's pasture shared by herdsmen, such behaviour might be tolerable were there a big pasture and only a few herdsmen, or a country just opening up to microfinance where the pool of potential customers, all financial services virgins, seemed to be limitless. Perhaps in such a country, one institution could continue to contaminate customers indefinitely, but in a market nearing saturation, this behaviour will damage the industry, diminishing trust, increasing the need and cost of other forms of guarantee, and reducing the total market. Regulated Ugandan MFIs as a group have had essentially flat borrower totals over the last 18 months. Do they suspect that there is some connection between this fact, and the tens of thousands of people they ran through their onerous group-lending mechanisms over the years?

- *Tolerance of and collusion in pricing obscurity.* The financial services industry in most countries discourages comparison shopping by, among other means, widely adopting practices that make it difficult to know and compare the cost of products (while of course arguing that the methods used of publicizing prices is a *best practice*). In East Africa, institutions regularly use a combination of flat or declining interest calculation, a dizzying set of fees (some fixed amounts and others calculated as percentages of the loans), and a particular regional aberration, high required non-remunerated 'savings', sometimes taken off the top of the loan. A recent addition sweeping Uganda is compulsory loan insurance, offered by a third party insurance company, but administered by the MFI. The insurance company typically kicks back some of the fee to the MFI. I find it excruciatingly difficult to calculate and compare the total cost of loans offered by Ugandan MFIs, and I have a computer, something most poor Ugandans lack.

- *Donor support of superfluous or inefficient institutions.* Donors support flagship projects to protect their investment, save face or keep a presence in a country. The result of overpopulation and tolerance of inefficiency can be slow death for many institutions, with the resulting pain that causes to various stakeholders. One leading Ugandan credit-only MFI recently brought in a new, aggressive and competent manager. Among the manager's first steps was to call for a portfolio audit that uncovered massive fraud and inefficiencies, which will lead to writing off more than half of the portfolio of the institution. The result is that the assets of the institution fall far short of the debt to external lenders, which include two commercial banks. This institution should, by any measure, simply die. Amazingly, the international partner, a faith-based NGO, has committed not only to recapitalzing the MFI, but to paying off its debts. One wonders what would happen if the church-going supporters of this folly knew about it?

Appeals to conscience are not a solution, as they have either no effect or penalize those who respond to them, breeding a race of financial institutions with no conscience at all (if the reader finds that expression disturbingly anthropomorphic, he or she is invited to substitute 'financial institutions more concerned with short-term profit than with the long-term stability of the industry's customer base'). Harding argues that the only hope is for a strong entity to take control of the commons and manage it well. The state in Africa is the obvious choice for this role. South Africa has led the continent in insisting on cooperation among financial institutions and rational use of the microfinance commons. Among many pro-consumer reforms put in place by the Micro finance Regulatory Council (MFRC) were prohibitions against 'reckless lending'. The MFRC's careful definition of 'reckless lending' is worth quoting, because it describes many small loans made by many MFIs: 'Loans made in reliance on the borrower's collateral, without proper evaluation of, or reliance on, the borrower's independent ability to repay, with the possible or even intended result of foreclosure or the need to refinance under duress' (2003). In Uganda, auction of the borrower's goods after the loan sometimes replaces loan analysis beforehand.

In the west, there is a creative tension between regulators on the one hand, and businesses on the other. When things work well, we find a happy medium between the profit motive and the interests of consumers. The cost of this constant battle is that there are occasionally unregulated excesses, and huge overhead costs of litigation. It is not obvious that this model can be exported to poor African countries; national regulation and litigation feel like foreign imports and require expensive competencies. It will be a long time before most African governments can provide effective consumer protection to the customers of MFIs, their citizens, the Peasants.

The Peasants

There is consistent demand among poor people for small loans. However, this fact is no more evidence that microcredit is a social good, than is the steady demand for other products like alcohol, cigarettes and commercial sex. A libertarian might argue that we should leave the market alone in all those areas, including microcredit. Fair enough. I would point out that we don't leave the market alone in microcredit. We actively distort it in many countries with large subsidies.

Amazingly, however, politicians, donors and programmes assume that the demand for credit is a *need* or even a *right*. Universal access to debt is treated with the same sort of urgency as universal access to primary education or to health care. It is assumed with very little question that donors, governments and financial institutions should work together on the urgent task of satisfying the market for small loans.

But the task of getting loans to people is not always easy. Africans are naturally, and wisely, afraid of debt. A West African proverb says, 'a debt is a cord around your neck'. In a study (Wilksen Agencies, 2004) carried out in two districts of Uganda, 59 per cent of respondents said that access to secure savings was more important to them than a loan. However, the media campaigns in favour of debt are undoing this natural caution. Being debt-averse is seen as a sort of weakness. So the task is not simply to satisfy a market, but to create one.

When poor people refuse credit, out of timidity or caution, they are hit with the ultimate weapon, advertising: in Uganda, the popular radio stations play jingles for FINCA in the Luganda language, singing about the ease and benefits of '*vee-lage ban-keen*', while billboards line the roads showing happy successful folks whose new sewing machines or the stock in their store is due to loans taken from the plethora of donor-supported MFIs.

The financial institutions get sophisticated assistance in marketing. Even donor-supported MicroSave, which has done more than almost any other institution to encourage MFIs to treat their customers well, offers toolkits and free management consulting on themes such as corporate brand and identity, product marketing and product rollout, strategic marketing, and costing and pricing. This technical assistance is designed to allow African MFIs to profit from the same tools that help CitiBank and its brothers sell their products. Absent from MicroSave's line-up of free services for MFIs are toolkits on transparency, measuring social impact, or helping clients stay free from debt. The emphasis, as always, is on the institution's success, not that of the client.

The expansion of microcredit was based on two generalizations that in retrospect seem less than certain. First, because anecdotes from Grameen Bank and others showed that small loans could sometimes make a positive difference in the lives of *some* poor borrowers, donors and others took that fact and extended it into the belief that therefore small loans would make a fundamental difference in the lives of *all* poor borrowers. Second, because for-profit firms are a good way to distribute *many* products, it was assumed that for-profit firms were a good way to distribute *all* products. These two assumptions were the beginning of commercialization, the creation of for-profit MFIs. Donors pretend that there is no conflict between the interests of institutions and the interests of poor borrowers, that what is good for the MFI is also good for its clients. This is sometimes but not always true. An obvious counter example is that on at least two occasions in Uganda, expensive donor-funded consultants have come to help struggling MFIs, and prominent among their recommendations was simply increasing interest rates and fees (this in institutions where the annualized total cost of borrowing approaches 100 per cent).

There is further evidence that donor loyalties lie with institutions, not borrowers: when donors complain that information asymmetries are a constraint to the efficient delivery of financial services, they are talking about things that the clients know that the institutions do not – things like information about past borrowing performance, reputation, levels of indebtedness and assets. In fact, asymmetries run in the other direction as well; there are things that the institutions know that their clients do not – things like the real cost of credit, the risks of borrowing, and the pressures that will be placed on the borrower to take subsequent loans.

In the Ugandan study mentioned above, 58 per cent of a random sample of MFI borrowers said that they did not understand all the interest and fees they were expected to pay on their current loan, while 'only' 35 per cent admitted that they had withheld information about other debts from the lending agency (Wilksen Agencies, 2004). At least in Uganda, the clients are even less well informed than the institutions.

A final illustration of the donor preference for institutions over people is that, rather than celebrating when poor people free themselves from debt, donors and institutions worry about their drop-out rates. Underlying this concern is the implicit belief that in the ideal world, all poor Africans would stay indebted to MFIs, automatically renewing their loans, preferably for larger amounts each time.

Like antibiotics, microcredit can be a wonderful thing, if given to the right people in the right doses at the right time, and, again like antibiotics, if misused, microcredit can easily do more harm than good.

If Nobel Laureate Mohamed Yunus had helped a poor woman *save* 70 cents, instead of lending her the money, it would have taken longer for her to be free of her suppliers, but the history of microfinance would have been vastly different. I can imagine what a more secure life African poor would have had, if we had had the 'MicroDeposit Summit', and the UN's 'Year of MicroSavings' instead of the MicroCredit Summit and the Year of MicroCredit.

However, I have no desire to criticize the remarkable Dr Yunus, a thoroughly admirable person. I have no doubt that before he made the first small loans in Bangladesh, he carefully got to know the potential borrowers, rejecting those who didn't have the investment opportunity (however miniscule) or the market or the management ability or the character needed to succeed. Rather, I want to cast some question on his followers, the naïve Grameen-replicators, who regularly seem to confuse the meal and the menu, who take imperfect indicators of success like the number of borrowers and the profitability of the institution and confuse them with the social benefits that they espouse. As I have said, we will need to push some institutions out of the way to make space for the new breed of African innovators, the Pretenders.

The Pretenders

I close with a description of two innovations that hold great promise to revolutionize African microfinance. Both of these innovations are largely the invention of Africans – in the first case, sophisticated and comfortably well-off Africans, and in the other, poor peasants from the Sahel.

Afriland First Bank in Cameroon

Cameroon is located where the continent turns the corner from West Africa on the way to Southern Africa, and also has the incredible virtue of being officially bilingual, French and English. Although it is well situated by virtue of language and location to be a crossroads between East, West and Southern Africa, for various reasons the country is less well known, and much less visited, than the Senegals of the West or the Kenyas of the East. Cameroon though is home to one of the truly innovative financial institutions on the continent, the Afriland First Bank, which is first of all a profitable, locally owned and managed, full-service retail bank. Buried within the bank, however, is a research department that continues to come out with innovative ideas, driving outreach to rural areas.

The bank is a full-service universal bank, and shows healthy profits and steady growth. Its lively research and development department continues to pump out new ideas. They opened a liaison office in Beijing years before it became obvious to everyone else the central role that China was going to play in African affairs. They have developed special products for Muslims, who are adverse to most banking products; their Islamic Savings Account, which neither pays interest nor charges fees, brought in so many deposits that the bank was able to give back a part of the profits they make on it by facilitating Cameroonian Muslims on the annual pilgrimage to Mecca. More important are their programmes of outreach to rural areas and to the poor. These include a network of 65 savings and credit cooperatives called MC2s (*Mutuels Communautaires de Croissance* – Community Growth Cooperatives – whose acronym deliberately echoes Einstein's famous equation), which serve around a half million members. The MC2s are linked to the bank by a web of agreements and partnerships; the bank uses co-branding, cross-subsidies and loss leaders to keep the MC2s growing and to make money while keeping the costs of credit shockingly low in the MC2s. Their strategy is deliberately and self-consciously based on a long-term vision of development. They are nurturing an enormous number of eventual customers, and extending banking services out to very remote and rural areas.

A senior official in the Ugandan government met a delegation from the Afriland Bank and complemented them thus: 'You haven't forgotten that you are African'.

Afriland deliberately embraces the informal sector, uses appeals to traditional values as loan guarantees, and unselfconsciously discusses development, economics, philosophy and ethnology, as well as finance, with visitors. They are gradually expanding into other countries and may become a true African bank. They are not unique – other financial institutions are showing that they understand their clients. Credit Rural in Guinea has found a formula in some ways similar to that of Afriland, marrying local member-owned institutions to a central facility that assures oversight and security. Al Amana in Morocco, though credit only and originally driven by donors, has shown extraordinary growth and profitability, which it continues to reinvest into better products, rural outreach and lower interest rates. Equity Bank in Kenya has also shown astounding growth, in part by creating a corporate culture of innovation, hard work and customer service.

VSLAs

At the other end of the spectrum is another home grown African innovation, the village saving and loan association. These informal structures came out of the deserts of Niger, and many of their features are said to have simply been discovered, as groups made their own innovations to models that had been shown to them.

These self-selected groups of 15 to 30 people save and borrow from the funds saved by the group. They have an extreme transparency, as all transactions happen in front of the group (funds are kept in a box with three locks, each key being held by a different member, which is only opened during the weekly group meetings). All funds stay in the group, which the group has learned how to manage itself; it has no need for outside assistance. The group sets the interest rate for borrowers, typically 10 per cent per month, with all interest being returned to the box. The surprising feature of the groups is that at the end of the year, they conduct an 'action audit' and distribute all resources to the members. Because of the high interest rate on loans, the return on savings will typically be 30 per cent or more. After the action audit, the group reforms, perhaps with some changes in membership or in terms and conditions, and begins another cycle. The groups make small loans – twice I have seen loans of US$3, one invested in trade, one in agricultural production. Other loans run up to as much as US$50 or more.

VSLAs are mysterious to people who come to them from microfinance. They seem, somehow, wrong. They don't require expensive consultants, and in fact groups are frequently formed by neighbours and friends of members of existing groups, who simply observe how they work and imitate them. No one makes any money from them – they perplex MFIs. Government and regulators have little value to add, which frustrates them. While new groups form, old groups don't grow. Although the groups work very well, donors and projects often try to fix them – there are reports from the West Nile region of Uganda of 4x4s with colorful NGO logos on their doors jamming on their brakes and stopping in a cloud of dust when they see a VSLA group meeting under a mango tree. The NGOs want to help, want to participate, want to take care of the cash box. There is something unsettling about these groups handling their own finances, and resolving their own problems, without any assistance.

While they have limitations in the amount of money they can handle, VSLAs serve the needs of their members remarkably well. Every time I visit a VSLA, I ask if any of the members have ever been MFI clients, and if so, how they compare the two systems. The former MFI clients are unequivocal in praising the VSLA for its transparency and proximity, and for the fact that none of their money leaves their village.

We don't know yet how many people can be served by VSLAs, but the number is surely in the millions. In Uganda, 38 per cent of the population live on US$1 a day or less. MFIs will never serve these people efficiently, as the transactions they need are simply too small and banks don't know they exist. All of a sudden, we seem to have a new tool that effectively serves a third or a half or more of the population, at low cost, offering high security to savers. VSLAs are indeed a revolution.

Nothing in this article should be taken to minimize the role that donors can play in helping the Afriland's and the VSLAs, and other African innovations to spread across the continent and adapt to local conditions as they do so. If we rely more on African models to bring financial services to Africans, the future can be radiant indeed.

References

Harding, G. (1968) 'The tragedy of the commons', *Science* 162(3859): 1243–48.
MFRC (Micro Finance Regulatory Council) (2003) 'MFRC clarifies the definition of "reckless lending"', *Credinews*, July.
Sankara, T. (1983) Press conference, 21 August, cited in *Wikipedia*.
Wilksen Agencies (2004) *Knowledge, Attitudes and Practices of Consumers of Microfinance Services in the Districts of Masaka & Mbale: Formative Communication Research Report*, Wilsken Agencies Ltd, Kampala.

CHAPTER ELEVEN

Microfinance under crisis conditions: The case of Bolivia

Irina Aliaga and Paul Mosley

Abstract

We investigate the ability of microfinance to operate under crisis conditions, with particular reference to two microfinance organisations, CRECER and Promujer, in Bolivia between 2000 and 2005, during which period a state of chronic political emergency separated many microfinance organisations from their market and made it difficult for them to repay their loans. We examine the coping strategies adopted by both lenders and borrowers during this period of emergency, and find that they are connected, inasmuch as the poorest borrowers were forced to adopt the 'worst' coping strategies with greatest risks of decapitalisation. We also find that the coping strategies of the two microfinance organisations were successful, inasmuch as arrears rates scarcely increased, and then only temporarily, during the emergency period. We find that this success has much to do with clients' loyalty to their 'parent' organisations, deriving in turn from the support services (health, training etc.) provided to them alongside credit by these organisations.

Introduction

Microfinance is celebrated for its ability to deliver financial services on a large scale to low-income but entrepreneurial individuals, in normal conditions, in densely populated areas of developing countries. On that basis, it has been given pride of place in many poverty reduction programmes and manifestos, some of them very dramatic, such as the promise of the Microcredit Summit (Rogaly, 1998; Morduch and Haley, 2002) to extract 100 million families, about half of the world's poor, from poverty between 1997 and 2005. However, although the achievements of microfinance in favourable environments are unquestioned, what is far less clear is whether its performance remains robust in face of conditions that are far from normal. When microfinance services are forced to operate under suboptimal conditions, for example because of sparse populations, poor infrastructure, resource shortages or civil conflict – all of them conditions fairly characteristic of developing countries – how well does it fare, and can it be made more flexible in order to deal with these conditions? In a book devoted to critical perspectives on microfinance, it would seem important to discuss to examine how microfinance performs under stress, and what can be done to increase its resilience.

In this chapter, these questions are considered in relation to Bolivia, one of the jewels in the crown of microenterprise finance, in which, only a few years ago, one of the microfinance banks, BancoSol, was the most profitable bank in the country (Otero and Rhyne, 1995), by virtue of its competitive cost structure and its ability to tap a fast-growing market previously inaccessible to commercial banks. The Bolivian microfinance sector has fallen somewhat from grace since then, initially because of the entry of consumer-credit houses with weak credit screening and monitoring systems and then, as a consequence of political interference, because of amnesties on unpaid arrears (Marconi and Mosley, 2006). It has even been accused, by one of the present authors, of exacerbating the economic slump and political crisis that the country has experienced since the end of the 1990s, by allowing its arrears to grow, its new lending to slacken and, as a consequence, small business investment to diminish, when instead a policy of counter-cyclical expansion could have helped provide a way out of the recession (Marconi and Mosley, 2006).

However, a closer examination of the diversity of MFIs in Bolivia shows that, in face of a deepening crisis that eventually erupted into street riots causing more than 100 deaths, some institutions were much more resilient to crisis than others: some experienced a collapse of customer loyalty and were forced to close almost immediately, whereas others went from strength to strength and grew throughout the crisis, even during the periods (in 2003 and 2005) when MFIs were prevented from reaching their customers by tear gas and bullets and instructed by their partners not to go to work and thereby infringe the general strike then in force. How did the successful institutions achieve this resilience? This is the central question of this chapter.

Our approach to tackling it will be as follows. First we examine, in brief, the performance of Bolivian microfinance institutions during the crisis period between 2000 and the present. We then focus on the violent episodes in El Alto in 2003 and 2005, examining the response to these of MFIs and of their clients. Finally we draw conclusions for institution building and for policy.

Contrasts in institutional performance

As a background to the discussion of institutional performance we first provide some details of the economic and political crisis still being suffered by Bolivia. Bolivia was one of the countries which, along with Argentina, Brazil, Russia, Thailand, South Korea, Malaysia and Indonesia, was most severely affected by the global crisis originally known as the 'East Asian crisis', which began in Thailand in 1997. But whereas all the other countries recovered from the initial shock within a few years, Bolivia did not. It has experienced continual decline in per capita GDP since 1998 (with the possibility, not yet confirmed, of a return to positive growth in 2006 as a consequence of rising oil prices). This self-reinforcing slump has in turn impacted on the political system (Mosley, 2006), with an increase in the underlying level of political violence, which climaxed in two outbreaks of rioting in February and October 2003, causing more than 100 deaths and the resignation and flight from the country of the centre-right president and mining millionaire Gonzalo Sanchez de Losada. There was a further outbreak of rioting in June 2005, this time causing only one civilian death, which led to the resignation of the interim president, Carlos Mesa, in June 2005. Both of these outbreaks were centered on the satellite-city of El Alto above La Paz, which is the country's main market for microfinance.

It is with the response of the MFIs, both to the general climate of economic decline and to the specific problem of disruptive political instability in El Alto, that we are concerned here. This response, as discussed earlier, was very diverse between MFIs in Bolivia, with most institutions experiencing growing rates of default and as a consequence being forced to cut back their lending so that investment rates among small businesses fell (Marconi and Mosley, 2006), but with a significant minority of institutions (FIE, Los Andes, ProMujer and Crecer) experiencing a decline in arrears and an upward trend in lending through the recession. The contrast between the last two of these organizations and the rest of the microfinance sector of Bolivia is illustrated in Table 11.2. Crecer and ProMujer are pro-poor NGOs, lending to women only, with smaller loans, and a higher proportion of poor and uneducated people among their borrowers than the country average. (Within the group of about 2,000 respondents in eight microfinance organizations surveyed by FINRURAL in 2002, using a poverty line of Bs194 (US$23) per adult equivalent/month, Crecer had about 35 per cent of its clients below this poverty line and ProMujer about 26 per cent; no other organizations had any significant number). They both subscribe to the 'village bank' (*banco comunal*) model of organization. In these groups, lending is to solidarity groups of 10–15 women with poetic and sometimes enigmatic names, such as (in the Senkata centre of ProMujer, where a number of the data for this study were taken) Secreto Amor (Secret Love), Girasol (Sunflower), Amor y Paz (Love and Peace), Mariposas (Butterflies) and Que Felicidad (What Happiness). Incentives to repay are provided through the medium of what is known as 'progressive' or 'step-up' lending, with loan size being increased if and only if repayment performance is good. The instruments and scale of progressive lending vary between institutions and branches of ProMujer, Crecer and other MFIs. In the Senkata centre of ProMujer, a system of penalty points was used in which the penalty for lateness at a meeting was one point, for

Table 11.1 Sliding scale for increases in loan size

Penalty points accumulated	Increase in loan size on previous loan %
0	100
1–4	100
5–6	75
7–9	50
10–11	50
12	0
>13	No loan

absence was it three and for default six penalty points. Eligibility for increases in loan size was then calculated on the basis of shown in Table 11.1.

Complementary services such as maternal and child health, education (financial management advice, health and now languages) and legal support are provided alongside financial services. Importantly for the argument to be presented, an insurance premium is paid on each loan transaction, over and above the interest rate, into a communal emergency fund *(cuenta interna* or 'internal account') on which drawings can be made by clients in case of emergency by individual members if members of her solidarity group approve by means of a majority vote. As is apparent from the performance indicators in Table 11.2, growth of assets has been much higher, and default rates much lower, in these institutions than the Bolivian average.

Why was it that institutions with such a low-income catchment managed to register so much better performance on the part of their clients during the

Table 11.2 Bolivian MFI performance indicators and possible explanatory factors (1997–2002)

Indicator	ProMujer and Crecer	Other microfinance organizations
Well-being indicators		
(as of December 2002)		
Poor and destitute	38.3%	10.6%
Without lowest level of education	14.1%	5.1%
Asset value	US$421.60	US$924.40
Average annual enterprise sales	US$757.90	US$2,502.80
Performance indicators		
(annual average 1997–2002)		
Growth of portfolio	24.7%	5.7%
Growth of customer base	26.2%	-5.3%
Default rate	0.6%	9.8%
Return on assets	6.9%	-1.9%
Design characteristics		
% female clients	98%	57%
'Internal account' for emergency loans	Yes	No
Loan modality	Village banks with solidarity groups	Solidarity groups, with the exception of FIE, Caja Los Andes, most of BancoSol, and the consumer-credit private finance funds (fondos financieros privados)
Average loan size	US$134	US$901
Training services offered?	Yes	No (except for FIE)

Source: performance indicators and design characteristics from FINRURAL, *Microfinanzas*, June 2003 edition; well-being indicators from preliminary results of impact evaluation studies of MFIs conducted by FINRURAL for Ford Foundation.

crisis? We argue that, first, this unexpected outcome can be interpreted as the outcome of an interactive process between lenders and clients. On the supply side, embedded in the institutional design of ProMujer and Crecer were a number of features that helped to make their clients particularly loyal to the organizations in hard times and thus helped to make the organizations resilient in face of declining demand and mounting pressures on their clients' cash flow. In the first place, both MFIs were 'credit plus organizations', providing health services (in particular maternal and child health), educational and training support, and legal advice in addition to credit – contrary to the 'minimalist model' of credit only favoured by USAID and other donors. These additional services were deeply valued by clients because they gave clients a sense of being protected against the hazards of life: 'ProMujer has been like a mother to me', commented one of its clients. These services were often the fundamental reason, more important than credit, why clients sought out the MFIs; since they were so valued, clients made extreme efforts to make sure they were current on the loans they owed in order to be sure of retaining their access to these services.

Second, in those cases where repayment was put at risk by an external shock, the 'internal account' made it possible for borrowers to access emergency liquidity, providing that members of their solidarity group were in agreement. These emergency loans, as we shall see, often made the difference between clients being able to sustain loan repayments and going under.

Third, in ProMujer and Crecer, because of the existence of a larger number of group activities and mutual responsibilities, they had stronger mutual support mechanisms support than other organizations, where groups either did not exist or else existed purely as instruments for the enforcement of joint liability. This social capital represented an asset that could be drawn on in case of need. Members of ProMujer and Crecer simply saw more of one another, often as a consequence of participation in the 'credit plus' activities mentioned above, and as a result of this were more likely to be friends with one another. As a result of this mutual friendship were more likely to trust one another, giving each other emergency *financial* support to supplement the loans from the internal account, but even more important, gaving each other support in labour and morale, which frequently helped them to avoid giving up on their business and enabled them to sustain their investment in it. Finally, the members of Crecer and ProMujer were (as illustrated by the top line of Table 11.2) much poorer than other clients – with average earnings of around US$400 a year, compared with US$1,200 in other MFIs. They were thus less able to access alternative sources of credit, and this made them more assiduous in sustaining their repayments to Crecer and ProMujer.

The institutional designs of Crecer and ProMujer thus included more mechanisms to encourage clients, when their own businesses or their lender organization came under pressure, to practise *loyalty* rather than the other two response mechanisms discovered by Hirschman (1970) in organizations under pressure – voice and exit. This loyalty protected Crecer and ProMujer against having to make cutbacks in lending and investment during recession. As we shall now see, when the recession became still worse and led to political instability and violence by the police and army, those incentives, and the way that Crecer and ProMujer improvised on them, also enabled the organizations to protect themselves against those threats.

Institutional responses to crisis

Between the years 2000 and 2003, the atmosphere in Bolivia degenerated from economic recession punctuated by frequent demonstrations of dissent to state collapse. We have examined the factors underlying this escalation of violence elsewhere (Mosley, 2006): the rise of radical Quechua/Aymara political parties, rash advice from aid donors (including the imposition of income tax increases at the bottom of the recession), and the adoption of a confrontational stance by the Sanchez de Losada government all played their part, but at core lay a perception of persisting inequality, weighted against the Quechua/Aymara majority and aggravated by corruption in government that enabled the already rich and privileged to avoid taxes. (The decline of microenterprise and microfinance during the recession, of course, further reduced the growth of opportunities available for heading off this sense of social grievance.)

At the climax of these protests, in October 2003, the 75-year old president, Gonzalo Sanchez de Losada, fled the country to avoid being lynched by the public, and since that time the level of political instability in Bolivia, although still intense, has calmed somewhat, with one further countrywide episode of rioting, in June 2005, which again resulted in the resignation of a president, this time Carlos Mesa. Throughout this period, the radical Aymara/Quechua parties were making political gains, and since December 2005 the country's first Aymara president, Evo Morales, has been seeking to restore the country's political stability.

We now examine in more detail the response of MFIs to acute crisis in the form of the two specific episodes of street violence that struck El Alto in October 2003 and June 2005. The experience of microfinance borrowers in face of these conflicts, which lasted between four and six weeks, was diverse and in many cases agonizing. First, their market, already shrinking as a consequence of overall economic decline, was now further reduced as a direct result of the fall in economic activity during the period of civil conflict. Second, many clients of MFIs were no longer able to access either their inputs or their market because their access to both was cut off by road blocks. Third and most grievous, many microentrepreneurs were put under pressure not to trade, and indeed to contribute their labour to the barricades rather than to their businesses, in order to enforce the general strikes called both in 2003 and in 2005 by the COB (Central Obrera Boliviana – loosely, Trade Union Confederation of Bolivia).

This pressure was exerted by the *juntas vecinales* (neighbourhood groups) that sought to enforce the instructions of the COB in every street of El Alto, and also by the families and partners of the microentrepreneurs; often, and especially in Crecer and ProMujer, which are women-only organizations, a male political activist would try in every way to prevent his partner from opening her shop. A number of interviewees described these strains to us. A Crecer member said, 'Those who sold goods had their merchandise confiscated, those who did building work (and were therefore visible) were rounded up to make sure they didn't work'. They were thus trapped between having stones thrown at them if they failed to appear on the barricades and foreclosure, putting the family's subsistence at risk. One ProMujer client said, 'We [mothers – including many microentrepreneurs] were forced to stay on the blockade and not send children to school. There was a Bs30 (US$4) fine if you didn't turn up on the blockades'. The potential for intrahousehold conflicts scarcely needs to be underlined. The burden of these conflicts within the household was very unequally shared; according to one woman, 'it is those who have small children who suffer worst'. What is important for our present argument is that all these factors also strained the repayment capacity of all microfinance clients, to protect against which the lending organizations somehow needed to devise a strategy. What did they come up with?

An initial listing of institutional coping strategies is provided in table 11.3. We have divided them into three groups: 'flexibilization' of loan repayments and savings deposits; supplementary support services; and amendments to administrative procedures.

We may now examine some of these institutional coping strategies in more detail, the most fascinating being the strategies that we call 'flexibilization':

- *Flexible payment.* Crecer stretched repayment periods from fortnightly to monthly, and in extreme cases up to three months, and also extended the steps within the 'progressive lending' process.
- *Foodshopping and other essential services.* Both Crecer and ProMujer carried out food shopping on behalf of clients known to be suffering; it will be recalled that Crecer and ProMujer between them contained most of the poorest microfinance clients in Bolivia. These were in effect emergency loans in kind, which augmented the social support services already being provided by those MFIs.
- *Doorstep collection.*The greatest liquidity problems associated with the crisis arose not, as earlier argued, as a consequence of clients' unwillingness to pay instalments but because they were afraid to cross the barricades to pay instalments to the offices of Crecer and ProMujer. In response to this problem, the lenders arranged where possible to collect instalments at the house of the client. This typically did not involve a vainglorious attempt to cross the barricade but a discreet arrangement made through a member of the organization living in the same street as the client. As illustrated in Table 11.3 one of the commonest adaptations to the crisis was to transact both trading and banking business in private, away from the gaze of those responsible for organizing the barricades (often in the early morning or at night). The approach has analogies with the procedure of 'home' or 'doorstep' lenders, such as Provident Financial and Cattles in the UK, which reduce the transactions costs and other difficulties associated with repayment by

Table 11.3 Institutional coping strategies

Design feature	Operating rule under normal conditions	Operating rule under emergency conditions
Flexibilization: loan instalments		
Frequency of payment of instalments	Fortnightly or occasionally monthly	**Crecer:** extension of payment interval to 3 months possible
Possibility of postponing	Not allowed	**ProMujer:** not allowed **Crecer:** one payment may be missed and paid back in instalments
Schedule of 'progressive lending'	As given in Table 11.1	**Crecer:** stretched for some individuals
Form of payment of instalments	In cash by group	**Crecer:** individual payments, rather than group payments, accepted from some groups. Partial payments accepted (including movement on to an interest-only basis, with principal repayments postponed) **ProMujer:** some instalments collected by ProMujer staff from clients' doorsteps
Flexibilization: savings deposits	Notice of withdrawal required for amounts in excess of US$300	**ProMujer:** flexibilization (notice periods for interest-bearing deposits in the non-bank financial intermediary FIE relaxed)
Supplementary support services	Health, education, training/empowerment and legal services	**Crecer:** Food parcels assembled for, and meals cooked for, distressed clients
Administrative procedure		
Frequency of group meetings	Weekly	**ProMujer:** decreased to fortnightly in case of need
Establishment of supplementary collecting offices		**ProMujer:** offices established, not on the main street, to enable individuals to make 'clandestine' payments without harassment

collecting repayments, through doorstep collectors trained to be amiable and flexible in their demands (Collard and Kempson, 2005).

The particular advantage of this approach was that it not only reduced transaction costs, but also reduced the exposure to borrowers to abuse from political militants anxious to stop them from trading. As illustrated in Table 11.3, lenders also attempted to reduce the exposure of borrowers by opening informal subsidiary 'offices' in side streets where payments would be less visible; for extra security, the doors and shutters of such 'offices' would always be kept closed. For their part, clients often sought to reduce their exposure by sending their sons and daughters to make payments for them; wherever possible, latent intrahousehold conflict was finessed by borrowers rather than taking the form of an open confrontation.

- *Extensions of the emergency account mechanism.* Where, in spite of all the above expedients, a client continued to be in difficulties, other group members were encouraged to lend to her through the 'internal account'. The internal account, according to a Crecer worker, thus 'operates in many ways like a *pasanaku'* (a traditional Andean rotating savings and credit association). Since profitable interest rates could be charged on such internal loans, this mechanism gave an incentive to better-off members to support vulnerable members through the internal account during the crisis and keep them current on their repayments and included in the group, rather than to take the more selfish expedient, common in other Bolivian MFIs, of excluding them from the group in order to avoid being contaminated with their repayment problems.

We interpret each of these strategies as an extension of the quasi-maternal relationship that the lending organizations occupied in the consciousness of their clients, and as an *implicit contract.* The organizations offered extension and flexibilization of existing support in return for an expectation of loyalty in the sense of seniority of its claims over those of other creditors. This understanding was typically *implicit* and did not have to be articulated outright.

In conjunction with the ongoing efforts towards empowerment, described in the opening section, these measures achieved their impact: only 7 out of 140 groups in Crecer experienced any payment difficulties at all (in the sense of instalments more than 30 days overdue) between 2003 and 2005 and the overall overdue rates of Crecer remained below 2 per cent, and of ProMujer below 3 per cent, right through both episodes of violence (*Microfinanzas*, December 2003 and December 2005). So little were 30-day overdues affected by the crisis that in 2006, the year after the second great social upheaval, Crecer was able to *reduce* its lending interest rate from 3.5 per to 2.5 per cent per month. This was of course not achieved by the actions of the lenders alone, but through an interaction between their behaviour and that of borrowers. We now examine how this interaction worked through the crises of 2003 and 2005.

Client responses to crisis

According to a Crecer manager, 'The Aymaras for 600 years have been providing us with lessons in survival', and the episode described here can be described as another lesson in survival with particular implications for institutions operating under stress.

To investigate the strategies used by clients in response to the crisis, we conducted two sets of interviews with 37 clients who were poor in 2002. The first interview, in January 2004, focussed on whether a transition out of or into poverty had been made, and what were the correlates of that transition. The second interview, in September 2005, was broader: it continued to monitor the respondent's income and asset status, but in addition examined the respondent's social relations and political attitudes.

In Table 11.4 we identify six different ways in which clients of Crecer and ProMujer attempted to deal with the impact of the crisis on them. In more detail they are:

- *Adaptations in output markets:* changes in the product mix (such as one ProMujer client who switched from selling food to selling vaseline to protesters on the barricades as a protection against tear gas) and changes in the style of salesmanship (such as another ProMujer client who ventured out of her shop to sell drinks to protesters on the barricades, and the many clients who did their selling in the early morning or after dark to avoid confrontation with those – often, as we have seen, in their own families – who were manning the barricades).
- *Adaptations in capital markets:* informal and formal borrowing for liquidity in face of the pressures of the crisis, including borrowing from the 'emergency accounts' of the village banks, and the adaptations of loan terms summarized in Table 11.3.
- *Switches in methods of production:* changes to the gender division of labour (such as made by one Crecer client, whose partner took over selling in the shop, enabling her to go out in the town as a travelling saleswoman), or in factor proportions, including the use of wood fires by restaurants when stocks of bottled gas ran out.
- Increased supply of *labour services.*
- *Cuts in consumption,* such as those endured by a Crecer member, who 'split a potato into two or three pieces and gave it toasted to the children'.
- *Depletion of assets* to meet the needs of either consumption or repayment – often heartbreaking, as in the case of a Crecer client who 'sold her sweater to have something to eat'.

A fuller account of the coping strategies of each individual is provided in Table 11.4. Here we want to understand which coping strategies were adopted by which kind of borrower, and how the decision to adopt a particular kind of strategy interrelated with the lender strategies discussed in the previous section. We make a crude distinction between those strategies that by their adoption are likely to involve reductions in well-being or assets (supply of casual labour, cuts in consumption and outright decapitalization), which we call 'inferior' strategies, and those that do not involve any automatic loss of welfare (output market, capital market and factor-proportions adjustments), which we call 'superior' strategies.

As Table 11.4 shows, there is a correlation between the choice of strategy and the asset and income level of the adopter: those adopting 'inferior' strategies in face of crisis have less than half the income levels and less than a tenth of the asset levels, of those adopting 'superior' coping strategies. As in previous work on Bolivia (for example, Mosley, 2001) we infer that this is because the 'superior' coping strategies required a level of capital and associated protection against downside risk, which the poorest clients did not have. Lacking these attributes, the poorest households could only cut their consumption levels, seek casual labour or dispose of their assets; such actions, of course, moved them one further step down the 'vicious spiral of poverty'. However, the flexibilization strategies of the lenders did manage to arrest the descent of some of the poorer borrowers down the hierarchy of coping strategies, such as Crecer and ProMujer cleints who had incomes below the Bolivian poverty line (about US$60 per month), but who nonetheless were able to take loans from the emergency account and avoid asset sales (typically the sale of their equipment or their shop), which would have crippled or even killed their businesses. The same function was fulfilled by the solidarity nurtured within the village banking system by regular social contacts both at borrower group meetings and meetings for the various complementary services (health, education, civil rights) provided by the two financial institutions. These contacts motivated sharing of consumption which, again, protected vulnerable individuals who had access to this social capital from slipping down the ladder. A Crecer client, a textile vendor and knitter who was well below the poverty line, described the process thus: 'We cooked in a common pot and the neighbours shared. If I ran out of bottled gas for cooking, neighbours would often lend me their cylinders. I would in return happily lend them my bicycle. This, I think, encouraged them to help to mend, or find spare parts for, my knitting machine if it broke down'.

As previously discussed, the spirit of mutual collaboration was by no means universal in El Alto, and many who sought to take advantage of it to protect their livelihood found themselves bitterly let down and impoverished as a result. But where it held good, a process that the lender initiatives described above tended to encourage, it had the ability to rescue individuals from the poverty trap.

Thus, within an already serious recession, poor individuals were hit by the additional shock of political emergency, and risked being forced into severe poverty by having to chose an 'inferior' coping strategy. But some individuals were protected from this outcome, either by the formal safety net of the 'internal account', or by the informal social networks. If we compare the choice of coping strategy, in terms of investment during the emergency period, to the level of income, it is clear that richer households could sustain investment through the emergency by the use of 'superior' coping strategies, and poorer households were forced to decapitalize; however, there were also a number of exceptions, whose investment was higher than their income level would lead us to expect.

One Crecer borrower and five ProMujer borrowers were all at or around the poverty line, but they sustained their investment in spite of their low incomes. It is not entirely clear how they avoided being forced into an inferior coping strategy, but all these respondents had taken loans on the Crecer or ProMujer internal account. They said themselves that these loans had helped them to keep up repayments and at the same time maintain their investment, rather

Table 11.4 Borrower crisis coping strategies

Strategies	Frequency	Correlates:			
		Income	Assets	Crecer/ ProMujer support	Solidarity measure
'Same level' responses					
Output markets: Diversification, change in method of salesmanship, shift in product mix)	11	1,936	3,1057	36%	18%
Capital markets: Diversification of loan sources, informal borrowing and lending, formal borrowing and lending	4	2,617	7,730	50%	25%
Input markets: Changes in gender division of labour, switching between inputs	2	2,440	1,450	50%	0
Sub-total	17	1,868	22,085	43%	15%
'Trading down' responses					
Labour market: Casual labour for others	3	1,386	1,290	0	0
Capital market: asset sale	7	1,042	3,162	50	25
Food consumption: Reductions	4	686	2,056	33	0
Sub-total	12	799	1,762	27%	8%

than being forced into the trap of selling assets to maintain their access to credit. According to one:

> I missed two repayments, but (ProMujer) understood, they wanted me in the group. With the help of an emergency loan to tide me over the crisis period, I was able to catch up after the two missed payments and to continue to fulfil orders, with the help of a number of excursions after dark or in the early mornings to deliver finished garments in defiance of the blockades. I thought I was going to have to dispose of my knitting machines, but the ProMujer internal account saved me from that.

The lenders' flexibility, including the internal account and the other flexibilization measures, *made possible a superior coping strategy for undercapitalized clients who would otherwise have been forced into an inferior one.* An effective institutional design, sometimes in association with informal social networks, enabled some very low-income borrowers to adopt a crisis coping strategy that did not push them permanently into poverty.

These institutional measures essentially provided a form of insurance against the shock caused by political emergency. They prevented people located on the very brink of the poverty abyss from falling into it, by moving the risk/return relationship upwards, as depicted in Figure 11.1. The abyss of decapitalization is represented by the shaded 'disaster zone', with high risks and low returns.

In this way, the flexibilization strategies improved the *dynamic incentive* (Tedeschi, 2006) available to clients by tailoring the required repayment to their ability to pay, and thus improved the repayment rate and reduced the injustices inflicted on members of groups who came under pressure because other members were having difficulty with repayments. It is critical that these improved repayment incentives operated not only for individuals but also for the groups, by increasing their incentive to support one another and reducing their incentive to eject members who were at risk of default. At the same time, the majority of clients reciprocated the trust that was shown in them, and took pride in returning to a normal pattern of repayments after the emergency was over. In many cases the knock-on effect was that they needed to take further loans from relatives, but they usually placed their obligations to their mother institution before all others.

Conclusion

The Bolivian crisis, and most particularly the response of the country to the violent clashes of 2003 and 2005, illustrates what is wrong with

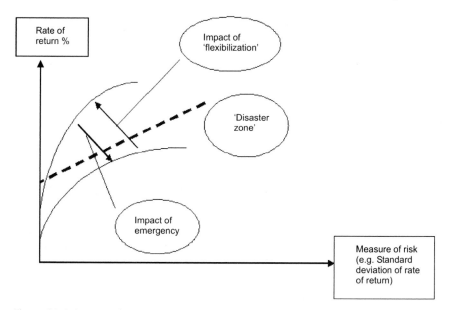

Figure 11.1 Impact of emergency and counteractive measures on risk–return balance

microfinance,what is right with it, and what could be further improved. On the debit side, Bolivian microfinance, having enjoyed enormous success and acclaim during the 1990s boom, fell victim to two traditional bogeys during the subsequent recession: contamination by ill-insured and ill-disciplined consumer-credit lenders, and government-sponsored moratoria encouraging clients to use the 'exit' or default route out of their problems. The consequent collapse of discipline affected small businesses so badly that it had a countercyclical impact on the economy during the slump – damaging, rather than stimulating, the entire economy, exactly when it most needed stimulus.

And yet, on the credit side, the response of many Bolivian institutions to the crisis also illustrates much of what is right and creative about microfinance. First, some institutions did not exhibit countercyclical behaviour, but had in their institutional design the kind of defences against external shock needed to keep borrowers current on their instalments and their levels of investment – even though these were the poorest microfinance borrowers in Bolivia. These defences consisted of supplementary services and, especially, training and collective activities that empowered women.

Their effect was, as we have seen, to encourage loyalty, rather than exit (Hirschman, 1970), on the part of most clients, which caused Crecer and ProMujer to have lower default rates than other institutions in Bolivia. When the economic crisis exploded into political instability and near civil war, this loyalty persisted, underpinned not only by the institutional assets discussed earlier, but also by compassionate creativity on the part of branch managers, manifest in their flexibilization of microfinance services to meet the emergency needs of borrowers. To adopt another of Hirschman's metaphors (1965), the principle of the 'hiding hand' was in evidence: the managers of Crecer and ProMujer may have underestimated how badly the crisis would hit them, but at the same time they also underestimated their ability to respond creatively to it, and thereby protect their clients and their own institutions.

As illustrated by what is now a large literature on civil conflict (for example, Goodhand, 2003), civil conflict is a major cause of underdevelopment and poverty, and the resilience of microfinance in face of that conflict may therefore be an important determinant of poverty trends. We examined the transitions of these clients out of and into poverty, and discovered that they were intimately related with their coping strategy and the interaction of this with the behaviour of the microfinance institutions.

As with people, so it is with institutions that in conditions of crisis one discovers both their weaknesses and their innate creativity. The Bolivian economic and political crises of 1999–2005 certainly exposed a number of the flaws, but also much of the developmental potential of the structure of microfinance as it operates in that country. Both may serve as a source of inspiration for institutions seeking to protect poor people against external shocks.

References

Collard, S. and Kempson, E. (2005) *Affordable Credit for Low-Income Households*, Joseph Rowntree Trust, York.

FINRURAL (2003) *Sistematizacion Metodologica de Evaluacion de Impactos en Microfinanzas*, FINRURAL, La Paz, June.

Goodhand, J. (2003) 'Enduring disorder and persistent poverty: A review of the linkages between war and chronic poverty', *World Development* 31: 629–47.

Hirschman, A. (1965) *Development Projects Observed*, Harvard University Press, Cambridge, MA.

Hirschman, A. (1970) *Exit, Voice and Loyalty*, Harvard University Press, Cambridge, MA.

Morduch, J. and Haley, B, (2002) *Analysis of the Effects of Microfinance on Poverty Reduction*, NYU Wagner Working Paper 1014, New York University, New York.

Marconi, R. and Mosley, P. (2006) 'Bolivia During the Global Crisis 1998–2004: Towards a Macroeconomics of Microfinance, *Journal of International Development* (18)2, p. 237.

Mosley, P. (2001) 'Microfinance and poverty in Bolivia', *Journal of Development Studies* 37: 101–32.

Mosley, P. (2006) 'The "political poverty trap": Bolivia 1999-2006', unpublished paper, University of Sheffield, Sheffield.

Otero, M. and Rhyne, E. (1995) *The New World of Microenterprise Finance*, Kumarian, West Hartford.

Rogaly, B. (1998) 'Destitute women…', *Development in Practice* 6(2): 100–12.

Tedeschi, G. (2006) 'Here today, gone tomorrow: Can dynamic incentives make microfinance more flexible?', *Journal of Development Economics* 80: 84–105.

CHAPTER TWELVE

Methodenstreit and sustainability in microfinance: Generalizations describing institutional frameworks

J. D. Von Pischke

Abstract

Methodenstreit is a clash of methods. It abounds in microfinance, reflecting the values of the 'owners' of MFIs and the organizations they create. A useful way of comparing contesting methods is to examine how they approach subsidy and its role in determining sustainability. Generalizing, the microfinance universe consists of three types of MFIs: for-profit institutions (Type I), NGOs (Type II) and cooperatives (Type III). Their missions are greatly different. Type Is seek profit and want to make the financial sector more efficient. Subsidy is used for start up and network expansion. IIs want to alleviate poverty by expanding services and enlisting more clients. Subsidy is considered essential to this mission. IIIs promote 'affiliation' by recruiting members, offering more services, and forming more and different types of cooperative organizations. Goals include helping people and making markets more equitable and efficient. Subsidy is used whenever useful.

Lots of things are just fine with microfinance. One thing that may be a little misunderstood is the nature of sustainability and the implications of different approaches to sustainability. To get the theme moving, the International Red Cross is not-for-profit. Does this mean that it is not sustainable and should be abandoned? And the Salvation Army? It certainly has a profit motive, but is its existence likely to be threatened because it is dependent on charitable donations?

The great institutional divide

The clash of methods (it sounds better in German – meh-toad'-en-shtrite) has been a central feature of microfinance since the beginning. Possibly the best example is Grameen Bank and the Bank Rakyat Indonesia village unit system (Robinson, 2002). Each was founded at about the same time. Grameen Bank and its founder are widely known for working with poor women in Bangladesh (Bornstein, 1996). BRI's village unit system is not widely known outside the microfinance cosmos but has been a superlative contender in terms of outreach, innovation and above all, savings mobilization. In the mid-1990s each was virtually equal as measured by average loan size divided by GDP per capita (Robinson, 1998). Both Grameen and BRI have massive, nationwide coverage in their respective countries.

Various reasons for this disparity in recognition have been offered. Grameen worked primarily with women; BRI had no gender policy. Grameen management and staff spoke English and could broadcast to the world; fewer did in BRI and Indonesians are often considered less effusive than Bangladeshis. Grameen offered group lending and female solidarity and mutual help, while BRI made individual loans. BRI insisted on a minimalist business model: banking only, on the basis that other things that might improve rural welfare should be the domain of other realms such as government ministries of education, health and agriculture. Grameen offered support formally and also informally among the women who gathered each week at meetings that built solidarity, confidence and spoke to maternal and marital concerns.

Grameen set up a training centre and visitor programme that attracted replicators from around the world; BRI provided similar facilities much later. Grameen stressed the social aspects and the romance of collective action, while BRI was clearly for-profit and diligent in collecting the savings of the poor. At an event I attended, Grameen's founder spoke of a poor woman who owned one sari and one pair of sandals who struggled to educate her two daughters, and after three loan cycles were completed her daughters were attending school wearing shoes. When a leading spokesman devoted to BRI addressed those interested, he enthusiastically described how he constructed a large book of mathematical tables that enabled loan officers to charge interest correctly when loans were being paid off. And BRI was fully transparent, whereas Grameen's accounting and presentation left many professionals more than a little confused (Morduch, 1999; *Wall Street Journal*, 27 November 2001).

What's wrong with microfinance?

The exposition that follows deals with disputes within the microfinance industry. These are happily of less importance now than they were in earlier times: the 1980s and 1990s were to microfinance what the Wright brothers' accomplishments were in the early 1900s. Would this model really fly? Many early concerns focused on whether the poor could pay and whether they would repay given the interest rates required to cover the costs of microlending, and whether commercial practice and objectives were acceptable in what was an otherwise charitable endeavour.

Considerable argument was generated as competing methods and their implications for grant-makers and their recipients were sorted out at the wholesale level. Passage of time and accumulation of confidence led to lower levels of vitriol and *methodenstreit*, grudging acceptance of different models, and later to less concern as MFIs created their own niches and clienteles in a wider range of situations.

For purposes of discussion and to provide generalizations useful for a broad overview, it is useful to begin with the observation that microfinance is a child of subsidy.[1] Microfinance is subsidy driven. Without subsidy, microfinance would be largely unknown, at most a very small corner of the formal financial sector. A case can be made that subsidy, and more precisely views of what subsidy can contribute to any particular MFI, is a reflection and possibly a determinant of how the MFI is structured and how it views its various constituencies. The importance and duration of subsidy varies depending on MFIs' institutional form and purpose. Subsidies are provided by international development assistance organizations, by national and lower levels of government, and by charitable and philanthropic sources. Subsidies are important for providers and also for receivers.

Three stereotypical forms

Three types of microfinance providers may be distinguished, based on their views of sustainability and how it can be assured. These are discussed below as Types I, II and III. Type Is are for-profit, IIs are NGOs or foundations. The boundaries between Is and IIs are strongly determined by their approaches to subsidy, while Type III is defined most strongly by solidarity as expressed over its long history and the unique organizational structure and objectives of cooperation.

Subsidy includes government largess as well as private philanthropy in financial form and as time and effort donated to a good cause. More and more serious MFIs, as opposed to charitable endeavours, charge interest rates that are at some point intended to cover their costs of lending. Subsidy of this sort refers to funds provided at the level of the MFI that are not used directly to reduce the costs of credit for clients. Subsidizing the institution, rather than its transactions with clients, creates capital that provides a framework for institutional development. For example, initial subsidies may cover the costs of training local staff, IT and other systems, vehicles, premises and technical advisors.

If the opposite were the case as MFIs matured – if loans issued to borrowers cost more than interest income received – incentives would be created that would work against the poor. Cheap credit would attract the somewhat better off, and MFIs would have incentives to provide larger loans because the cost of doing so is lower per transaction. This paradigm and these forces were dominant in small farmer credit provided by development assistance agencies in the 1960s through the early 1990s, as amply substantiated in the academic and quasi-academic literature of that time (Von Pischke et al, 1983).

These realizations contributed to establishing cost-covering transactions as best practice in microfinance. An additional value of this approach is that it minimizes the possibility of one MFI grossly undercutting another in a specific market or territory. This behaviour would diminish the effect of the subsidy to the vulnerable institution, partially defeating the objective of the donor providing funds. Donor practice generally discourages this sort of competition.

The distinction between start-up subsidies and continuing subsidies is important in constructing an analytical framework. Start-up subsidies have certainly led the microfinance charge, establishing a very robust basis for expansion and outreach. Continuing subsidies, á là Salvation Army, are an altogether different matter.

A typology of MFIs

Without subsidy there would be little microfinance as we know it today. Different types of MFIs have different views of subsidy and its relation to sustainability. Broad generalizations about MFI types can be drawn from their different views on subsidy, as illustrated in Table 12.1.

Table 12.1 Distinguishing stereotypical features of types of MFIs

Type of MFI	I For-profit	II NGO	III Cooperative
View of subsidy	Dependence on continuing subsidies is dangerous and foolish	Dependence on continuing subsidies is essential and justified	Subsidies may be helpful in meeting objectives
Reason for the view	Subsidy is costly, fickle and habit-forming	Subsidy is required to alleviate poverty	Core objective is affiliation; more members and more services
Character-istics	Commercial, for-profit with a commitment to serving the lower end of the market; minimalist; regulated	Non-profit, political, focus on the poor; maximalist; degree of financial regulation varies	Varies from commercial to non-commercial; regulated under cooperative law
Lending technology	Individual, variety of loan types, plus other financial services	Group lending, some savings, individual lending later; loan disbursement/ repayment cycles same for all members	Usually individual; savings, loans, range varies greatly
Mission priorities	Create more efficient financial markets, build sustainable institutions, serve the poor, expand frontiers	Outreach to the poor, keep poverty high on the public policy agenda, fashion the MFI to attract subsidy	Successful cooperation helps people and makes markets more efficient and equitable
Corporate form	Licensed bank, saving and loan finance company (shareholders)	NGO, foundation (no legal or formal owner)	Cooperative (collective owners)
Ideal board composition	Investors with funds at risk who have a sense of social mission	Management, contributors, 'representative members'	Under cooperative law: elected by and from the membership, one-member-one-vote

Type I MFIs

Type Is take a commercial approach. Costs have to be covered within a reasonable time period. Type Is use subsidy primarily as a contribution to forming an MFI or for expansion. Establishing an MFI requires some initial capital to cover operating costs and funds loaned to clients. Subsidies are helpful in assembling this initial nest egg and even more so in accelerating growth. The start-up subsidy shortens the period in which a new MFI loses money. This period could otherwise be relatively long, such as three years or more. Subsidies may be essential for a small Type I, while for larger institutions or networks subsidy fades in importance as the volumes of funding available dwarf the costs of starting a new institution.

But even in these cases of relatively abundant funding, subsidies are usually forthcoming if the recipient MFI or network is credible according to the criteria of international financial institutions (IFIs) such as IFC, KfW, FMO or BIO that are investors in such MFIs or networks. Funds are likely to be available because microfinance is viewed as a means of stimulating enterprise and reducing poverty. Faster growth promotes better deals for the poor. Well-performing MFIs or networks are attractive to donors and investors, propelling even more subsidy.

Initial subsidy satisfies many agendas in development finance. First, it not only accelerates growth of the new MFI, but also relieves constraints that might be encountered throughout a network of MFIs if no subsidy were available for the new institution. Second, subsidy boosts the return for the investors in the new MFI or in the expansion of the network. By doing so, it expands the activities of these IFIs and other investors generally, which are dedicated to development finance. For example, a grant from USAID to a new MFI in which IFC is a shareholder also increases returns for IFC. (Investors may also provide grants to MFIs or networks in which they are also part owners.) Third, subsidy may accelerate these investors' orderly exit, a disinvestment process that may require a decade or more (Neuschütz, 2004). Somewhat ironically, well-performing MFIs may in fact attract subsidies that they did not solicit because the donor concerned trusts such MFIs' capacity to deliver as instructed.

In a broader context, these IFI investors and by extension those who provide the grants to facilitate the growth of the MFIs in which the IFIs invest, have the objective of improving financial markets generally. This goal arises from the lessons of financial liberalization that got rolling as a development objective in the 1970s. Economies that have more efficient financial markets are better off than others of similar stature that have less efficient financial markets. In addition, the poor benefit disproportionately from more efficient financial markets through employment effects and other indirect factors (Beck et al, 2004).

Subsidies as a temporary remedy

However, Type Is view eventual independence from subsidy as essential to their mission. (They may continue to obtain subsidy, but only for new activities that will become self-sustaining.) Their reason for this view is that subsidy is costly, fickle and habit-forming.

Subsidy is costly in terms of transaction costs, or ATM (aggravation, time and money). Much organizational effort is required to draft proposals and to comply with conditions specified by the donor. Proposals submitted to USAID, for example – a generous and pioneering supporter of microfinance development – consist of a few pages dealing with the proposed grant, and many, many more pages of conditions that have relatively little to do with the project under consideration but rather with boilerplate terms and conditions spanning drug use to discrimination to lobbying and corrupt practices. These requirements are part of procurement procedures developed for defense contracting, space shuttles and other activities, complete with a social agenda attached. And not all grant proposals come through. Some are approved long after they were solicited and for less than the sum requested to get the job done. However, small firms seeking grants or bidding on projects are usually exempted from some of the complexities of procurement.

The fickleness of donors is well illustrated by the World Bank's abandonment of agricultural credit projects around 1990. These projects were generally poor performers in financial terms but of great interest in political terms in the receiving countries, in part because state-owned agricultural credit institutions that channeled the World Bank's hard funds transformed these into soft and very soft loans on the ground. The Bank's disbursements for agricultural credit approximated 10 per cent of its total disbursements for several years in the 1980s, only virtually to disappear soon after. Other donor fads with similar trajectories are not hard to find.

Reliance on donor funding, according to Type Is, is also habit-forming. Can an MFI ever know if it is really efficient if it depends on perpetual subsidy? A remedy is close at hand: at what point and with what effort can an MFI mobilize sufficient deposits from its clients to fund its loan portfolio? In which case – subsidy or a deposit base – does the MFI exercise more control or have more opportunities for expansion? In addition, private equity (venture capital) and capital markets are increasingly interested in microfinance, and these possibilities are more exciting and can provide much more finance than grants ever could.

Type I characteristics

Type Is make individual loans and are usually 'minimalist', concentrating on financial services only, rather than on social services or other endeavours that might assist their clients in areas that are beyond purely financial relationships. The minimalist strategy permits high levels of specialization and relatively uncluttered statements of purpose – to do otherwise would dissipate effort and retard momentum. The minimalist approach includes dialogues with clients concerning information about formal commercial practice and the expectations that accompany it. For its own protection and to exhibit best practice, an MFI should provide instruction regarding contractual terms and expectations regarding the use of funds. Disclosing to the client the amount of interest and fees paid offers a useful start in transparency.

Type Is that begin their operations at the scale of microfinance will usually expand upmarket as they gain experience. Small businesses and even some medium-sized firms may be financed. This flexibility does not mean that microclients are abandoned. One rationale is that successful clients' businesses are likely to grow, and a few microenterprises may become small businesses. If the MFI's target group consists of businesses that have never before obtained credit from a formal source, many candidates are available although the risks and style of interactions with these clients differ from those of the typical microentrepreneur.

The engagement of larger, wealthier clients is sometimes treated as a sell-out, a bait-and-switch tactic that diverts money intended for the poor to those who are a bit better off. However, this objection is misplaced. Three possibilities arise.[2] The first is 'mission stability', which is continued provision of a limited range of services to the poor. 'Mission enhancement', the second possibility, consists of new services offered, new target groups engaged, while the original target group continues to be served, often better. Mission enhancement is consistent with the objective of serving those who have not had prior access to formal finance or to certain financial instruments. These additional opportunities are numerous and include small businesses and professionals as clients, payments and savings facilities as services, and risk management tools such as insurance. This strategy is consistent with the mission of making financial sectors more efficient by continuing to engage those beyond the frontier of formal finance, such as women microentrepreneurs, and by catering to others not well served by mainstream finance, such as small businesses. 'Mission drift' is the third possibility: the institution that once served the poor moves up-market, abandoning the poor. This occurs most dramatically with a change in the ownership of an institution, but it can also happen slowly, creeping out of the small end of the market.

The important point is that mission enhancement should not be confused with mission drift. Enhancement is not drift – it is outreach and development. Mission enhancement makes financial sectors more efficient, as indicated by finer spreads, lower risk premia, new products, lower transaction costs, more participants, and services to an expanded array of clients. Accordingly, this three-part paradigm should be applied in the valuation of service to any specific target group. Mission stability is unlikely to be a viable business strategy except in very small scale operations or in sluggish or stagnant markets.

Governance issues are important for Type Is because of their concern for ownership. Money is at stake, and it is meant to be employed wisely in ways consistent with objectives. This means that the shareholders should be real owners, making decisions and ensuring that plans are well crafted and diligently followed up. Incentives should be aligned with information in productive ways. At the same time, dedication to the target group or groups is important to virtually all microfinance boards. Protecting this aspect may or may not be measured in basis points, depending on the institution.

In my experience, board meetings of large Type Is are highly efficient, consistent with the discipline of the capital markets in which the representatives of these shareholders operate.

Type II MFIs

Type IIs view subsidy as an essential requirement for survival. This view is based on the assumption or observation that subsidies are required to alleviate poverty. Their mission and objective is to alleviate poverty. This is a noble objective and the signature of a caring, liberal society that includes many generous people willing to help.

Some advocates even speak of 'poverty eradication', but can this ever be accomplished? Will there ever be a time when no one is worse off in some way that could be an affront to or blemish on an otherwise relatively just social order? And, would the poverty industry ever want to fold its tents and declare victory, stating that poverty has ceased to exist? 'Ending poverty as we know it' is a moderate version of conquering a social blight, but possibly less powerful in a political sense for those seeking subsidy to fight a good fight.

Subsidy mechanics

Microfinance through this lens as a tool for poverty alleviation is naturally viewed as a non-profit activity executed by an NGO. Advocacy easily moves into the political realm when large efforts for great causes are underway. The realization of results requires an expanding effort that reaches more people with more tools to combat poverty. This strategy keeps poverty on the public policy agenda, and offers microfinance as a partial solution or a palliative that provides comfort where there is otherwise little comfort.

A highly successful Type II practitioner taught an evening microfinance class in one of the universities in the Washington DC area. The project required by each participant for completion of the course was a proposal that would presumably be acceptable to USAID. As a guest lecturer at one of his sessions, I told his class that he could call the Clinton White House and that the call would be returned before the end of the day. The instructor interjected, 'It also works at the new Bush White House!'.

Serious social entrepreneurs will seek more subsidies to serve more poor people in more ways. This strategy is self-reinforcing: the NGO fashions itself to be an attractive and effective institution that helps the poor. At the same time, by providing more services it helps the poor in more ways. Hence, Type IIs tend to be maximalists, offering a wide range of services, from providing meals to maternal health to microenterprise and more, a sort of one-stop shop for social welfare. This diversification increases the client base, drawing in more beneficiaries who in turn will become more loyal or committed clients because of the expanding array of opportunities offered to them. A larger and more diversified client base can attract more government funding and private donations. The maximalist approach is extensive, in contrast to the minimalist or intensive approach of Type Is.

Type IIs are likely to be concerned about impact. Field surveys and studies are often undertaken to demonstrate how and in what way results are being achieved, and for remedial efforts or new strategies in cases in which impact is insufficient given the money and effort expended. Type Is, in contrast are more likely to be interested in market research as an analytical tool. Impact is less interesting because clients are assumed generally to be rational and because the dynamism of the individual lending approach occurs in interactions between loan officers and borrowers. These encounters provide information that is extremely valuable to both parties and that is routinely acted upon.

The Type II lending technology is group based because poor people tend to be willing to work together in groups, at least when there are few other possibilities. Social interaction is also a value in building morale, solidarity and awareness that will help the poor improve their condition. In addition, donors that sponsor Type IIs are quite number conscious – the more clients the better, and fast.

In one African country a large NGO using group lending expanded its operations district-by-district. After the programme was underway in several districts the news about it spread locally through the grapevine. In one district where the programme was being set up, 80 per cent of the groups initially formed appeared spontaneously, showing up on the NGO's doorstep and organized by their members, all of whom traded in nearby markets. This is every NGO's dream and every donor's delight.

Lacking legal owners, NGOs or foundations have boards that are composed of different groups having interests in the particular entity. These usually include the management of the NGO, contributors who provide funds or the agents of such contributors, and 'representative members'. The latter are people who may have little to do with microfinance but who have access to the political institutions that are in a position to provide assistance to the NGO. Another form of representative member may be the illiterate women who have served on Grameen Bank's board.

This board composition is clearly more complex than that of the Type Is. This may mean that decision making is more difficult because of different objectives and perceptions. At the same time, this board composition may provide more information but of a different quality as a result of mixed criteria used in decision-making. More discipline may be required than in Type Is because of complexity.

Transformation

As Type II institutions grow, they may adopt characteristics of Type Is. They may become more concerned about pricing and efficiency. They may want to be regulated as banks or as institutions that can accept deposits and participate in payment systems. This tends to require changes in corporate form, or may involve the formation of separate corporate entities through which the commercial side of their operations can be relatively easily conducted.

A force that makes Type I approaches increasingly attractive is the fact that they can mobilize increasingly large sources of funds from IFIs, capital markets and venture capital. Although many Type IIs are quite well supported by philanthropists, these sources may be less forthcoming in the long run, given the capacity of capital markets.

Type III institutions are cooperatives

Microfinance was quite possibly invented years ago by credit unions, savings banks of different sorts and other financial cooperatives. However, cooperatives did not step forward to claim prior leadership when microfinance got underway, even though cooperatives and their members outnumber microfinance operations in many countries. Type IIIs are different from Is and IIs and subsidies cannot be a focal point that distinguishes cooperative behaviour. Cooperatives take subsidies when it is useful, and cooperative law in many countries often provides different tax treatment than that applied to joint-stock corporations, partnerships and proprietorships. Likewise, their operations extend from the noncommercial to the commercial.

The goal of cooperatives appears to be 'affiliation', which consists of recruiting more members and providing more services. Services expand with a proliferation of apex or second-tier cooperative bodies that perform wholesale or support functions to primary cooperative societies. These second-tier organizations may gain more power as specialization becomes narrower and more demanding. Type III's mission is based on making cooperation successful in ways that help members, and benefiting society at large by making markets more efficient and/or more equitable from a social perspective. Realization of these objectives provides cooperatives and their members greater leverage in the marketplace.

The boards of cooperatives consist of members elected by the membership on a one-member-one-vote basis. This historic form of governance is under pressure in some areas in which the skills required to function well in the competitive modern economy are beyond those of the board members. Failures of two very large agro-industrial cooperatives in the USA over the last 15 years offer examples of these types of governance failures. In Ecuador and some other countries, laws governing financial cooperatives require that managers and others in decision-making positions have certain academic, professional or other specific qualifications. In several countries, credit unions are having to consolidate and merge in order to remain competitive by obtaining economies of scale. This will make management more complex.

Epilogue

Is it odd that I provide no figures? Well, welcome to part of the world of microfinance. Our numbers having to do with subsidies are generally scarce. To varying extents and in the absence of disclosures by subsidy recipients, it may be difficult to determine the real costs of microfinance, the real returns to MFIs and the real stature of our industry and its practitioners.

Subsidy for microfinance is surely not wrong, but it also may not be entirely right. Disclosure has increased tremendously as a result of donor initiative and industry practice. But is it right not to explore our performance even more seriously? How does the quantity of subsidy received compare to the volume of MFI capital? What does it cost to serve different types of clients and of this, how much is subsidy? What other quantitative measures could help to define our frontiers? How can we build on the work of Jacob Yaron, who invented the subsidy dependence index?

What lessons can be drawn from an examination of different modes of microfinance? At the generalized level presented here, different schools contend and there is room in the market for a variety of institutional types. Objectives and outcomes vary in growth, outreach and results. Forms change over time in response to competition and efficiencies.

Notes

1   The typology given here was first developed in J. D. Von Pischke (2002) 'Microfinance in developing countries', in Carr, J. H. and Tong, Z. Y. (eds) *Replicating Microfinance in the United States*, The Johns Hopkins University Press for the Woodrow Wilson Center Press, Baltimore and Washington DC.
2   This argument made its debut in my keynote speech at KfW's financial sector conference in Frankfurt in 2005 and will be available in a proceedings volume in early 2007.

References

Beck, T., Demirgüç-Kunt, A. and Levine, R. (2004) 'Finance, inequality and poverty: Cross country evidence', *World Bank Policy Research Working Paper 3338*, World Bank, Washington DC.
Bornstein, D. (1996) *The Price of a Dream: The Story of the Grameen Bank and the Idea That Is Helping the Poor to Change Their Lives*, Simon and Schuster, New York.
Morduch, J. (1999) 'The role of subsidies in microfinance: Evidence from Grameen Bank', *Journal of Development Economics* 60: 229–48.
Neuschütz, V. (2004) 'Institutional development and commercialization: Optimal exit for equity financiers', in Matthäus-Maier, I. and von Pischke, J. D. (eds), *The Development of the Financial Sector in Southeast Europe: Innovative Approaches in Volatile Environments*, pp. 101–11, Springer, Berlin.

Robinson, M. (1998) 'Microfinance: The paradigm shift from credit delivery to sustainable financial intermediation', in Kimenyi, M. S., Wieland, R. C. and Von Pischke, J. D. (eds), *Strategic Issues in Microfinance*, pp. 55–85, Ashgate, Brookfield VT and Aldershot.

Robinson, M. (2002) *The Microfinance Revolution: Lessons from Indonesia*, The World Bank and The Open Society Institute, Washington DC and New York.

Von Pischke, J. D. (2002) 'Microfinance in developing countries', in Carr, J. H. and Tong, Z. Y. (eds), *Replicating Microfinance in the United States*, pp. 65–96, The Johns Hopkins University Press for the Woodrow Wilson Center Press, Baltimore and Washington DC.

Von Pischke, J. D., Adams, D. and Donald, G. (eds) (1983) *Rural Financial Markets in Developing Countries: Their Use and Abuse*, The Johns Hopkins University Press, Baltimore and London.

Wall Street Journal (2001) 'Small change: Bank that pioneered loans for the poor hits repayment snag', 27 November: 1.

CHAPTER THIRTEEN

Microfinance: Some conceptual and methodological problems

David Ellerman

Abstract

Credit-based microfinance has the characteristics of a development fad; it moves money to get quick heart-warming results on the ground, publicized by selective cases but with little developmental results. Most lending is used for consumption purposes; the few entrepreneurial loans are in easy-entry microbusinesses with little potential. Although defended with a development rhetoric, most support for microfinance seems to be based on simple but superficial poverty relief; it gets some resources to the poor. The methodological heart of the paper analyses the current fad of 'impact evaluations' used to defend microfinance. By comparing programmes to the pseudo-counterfactual of no programme ('doing nothing') – instead of the counterfactual of the best alternative programme using comparable resources – impact evaluations provide the ultimate low-hurdle ('no matter how expensive, it's better than nothing!') for development agencies to give poor but fashionable programmes a few more turns around the hamster wheel.

Introduction

Over the last two decades, microfinance has grown into a major 'development solution'. And now the success story has been crowned with the Nobel Peace Prize for Muhammad Yunus and Grameen Bank. Yet microfinance is not without controversy. Is it really some sort of development solution or is it more of a long-lived development fad?

Development fads 101

Over the last 60 years, development aid and assistance has been increasingly organized as a deliberate, institutionalized and well-financed business. Yet it cannot be reckoned a success. Where development has been most successful (for example, East Asia), international aid and assistance from official or non-profit organizations have had little to do with it (except perhaps as indicating what not to do), and where assistance organizations have had their largest footprint (for example, in Africa), success has been the least.

In most areas of organized human endeavour, learning takes place over the years even if there was much painful stumbling in the beginning. For instance, in the fields of medicine and public health, there are real discoveries as well as mistakes, genuine learning does take place, and it is cumulative. Other fields such as 'management theory' seem to be constantly surfing with the latest fads; the 'classics' are only the latest bestsellers in airport bookstores. Development assistance often seems to be more like management theory than an applied science.

One response to failing organizational effectiveness in business management or in development assistance is chasing ersatz 'solutions' or fads that promise to quickly address long-standing problems or at least their symptoms. Over the course of time, there is indeed some 'learning' but it is a kind of breathless pseudo-learning as one fad after another is taken up and dropped. As each fad proves not to live up its hyped promise, it is quietly abandoned in favour of the latest 'solution' – another cycle in the hamster wheel of fad-driven aid programmes.

How might we identify fads? Any gardener knows that 'successful' weeds are quick to establish themselves on the ground. In a similar manner, a development fad has to show quick results on the ground, results that can then be amplified through public relations activities couched in terms of the latest rhetoric. Nothing seems to be simpler or to get quicker 'results' than offering money to poor people with the cost postponed to the future.

Microfinance might be usefully compared to a more recent development fad, social funds, which also got quick gratifying results. A loan is made to a poor country to establish a social fund at the national level that will then make a gift[1] for local infrastructure to 'qualifying' jurisdictions (for example, localities that support the ruling group). The repayment of the loan by the national government is many years off, probably well beyond the expected political horizon of the sitting government. The qualifying local community is 'empowered' to choose which form its gift will take – a local school, health clinic, road, bridge, water project or the like. Soon after the project is completed, the public relations people from the development agency can descend on the community to do a video of the new school or clinic, and to record the heart-felt gratitude of the local officials and people. Now their children will have a better education, health care, water supply and so forth. Evaluators will also descend on the community to document that they have better school or health facilities than a control group of communities that did not get the gifts. And all this creates the warm glow of moral satisfaction on the part of the supporters of social funds.[2]

Here we see some of the same features that have made microfinance so popular with development agencies anxious to move the money and establish quick heart-warming results on the ground that can then be selectively projected into an image of success. That is sufficient to start a development fad.[3]

But microfinance has even more endearing characteristics than social funds, and thus the appeal of microfinance has certainly been more enduring. For the left, it is a programme that targets the poor and seems to provide a certain measure of poverty alleviation. For the right, it seems to be associated with enabling entrepreneurship and business development so that poor people can then provide for themselves. It has now developed into a world-wide industry (Rhyne and Otero, 2006) with some promise for commercial sustainability. Perhaps it is the mother of all development fads and, thus, it is an appropriate topic for some critical examination.

Development assistance or poverty relief?

Debates about microfinance often involve background assumptions that need to be brought into the foreground and examined. Is the purpose assistance to economic development, or is it more a tool for the relief of poverty?

The international development agencies and organizations were not originally designed to undertake humanitarian relief. Natural and human disasters will always be with us, so there is always the need for some well-defined and short-term disaster relief efforts. But the difficulties in development assistance (Dichter, 2003; Ellerman, 2005a) have prompted many agencies to quietly refocus their work towards poverty relief – all the while describing it in developmental terms.

Much criticism of microfinance has focused on the lack of developmental impact (for example, is Bangladesh on anyone's list of development success stories?). In reply, microfinance proponents hold up a few outlier examples of growing businesses that at some point received assistance from a microfinance programme. Aside from the problem of trying to reason based on the exceptions rather than the bulk of the cases, this response seems to hide a less public discourse. Quiet private discussions in corridors and backrooms have a different tone. The real argument is something like this:

> Look, parts of Africa and some other regions are walking disasters. It is only academic to make these distinctions between development assistance and humanitarian relief. Children are dying, and if we don't address these humanitarian concerns today, then there will certainly be no development tomorrow. Leaving aside all the hyped official rhetoric, the real point is that the microfinance programmes, subsidies and all, are putting resources into the hands of the real poor, and that is more than enough reason to give our support to microfinance.

Such a stance – in public – would be a breath of fresh air in the microfinance debate. Then microfinance would be debated simply as a poverty relief programme.

Getting poor people to take out loans is, for many purposes, a legitimate activity, and it certainly is a way to quickly 'move the money'. In the USA, there is a huge finance industry that is constantly trying to get people to sign up for and use more and more credit cards. And in a handful of cases, microbusinesses might get started by borrowing and shuffling debt around between such credit providers and thus genuine empowerment may be the result (as it might be the result of throwing money out of helicopters or of traditional forms of relief). But few would see 'getting more short-term credit' to poor people as a development solution in the developed world where the business environment is considerably more business-friendly than in most developing countries. While it is a delightful fantasy, there unfortunately seems to be little basis in fact to assume in the developed or underdeveloped world that poor people – who (practically by definition) have trouble getting and/or holding a job – have the necessary entrepreneurial knowledge, skills and opportunities to *start* businesses if only they had access to finance. Outside of a few well-publicized cases, the bulk of borrowing by the poor seems to be consumer-oriented.

This possibility of recasting the microfinance debate as being about relief should not be lightly dismissed.[4] William Easterly, an acute researcher of the official development efforts (for example, of the World Bank), has argued persuasively (2001, 2006) that the major aid agencies have failed and that there is virtually no chance for that to change. Genuine development assistance is much too subtle and indirect an affair for the thundering dinosaurs of the 'dev biz' to have much transformational effect. Since it seems unlikely that the major agencies will be just shut down (they always have powerful inside and outside constituencies), Easterly suggests that perhaps they should retool to focus on poverty relief. Perhaps that is something they could actually do. Hence the retooling of the 'development' institutions away from development assistance towards 'aid' to poverty relief is not only something that is quietly taking place; it is being actively advocated by some critics of the 'dev biz' as something that should be doable.

Is microfinance helping the poor?

Isn't microfinance one of the best ways to 'help the poor'? Microfinance programmes are usually in fact lending-led programmes that can be 'installed' by development organizations using seemingly off-the-shelf models and external finance (see Johnson and Rogaly, 1997; Dichter, 2005b; Rhyne and Otero, 2006). Not only is sustainability an issue, there is an issue as to whether or not that sort of development assistance *should* be sustained. Is that the sort of assistance that builds self-reliance rather than dependency, that builds capacity rather than prolongs incapacity?

In the developing world (and in the depressed parts of the developed world), donor-funded organizations are thick upon the ground to 'help the poor' (Dichter, 2005a). Instead of really helping the poor to become the agents or doers of their own development, the poor are seen as the clients and customers of the multitude of externally funded organizations with the ostensible purpose to deliver services – such as microfinance lending services – to the poor.[5]

Then the question is posed as to whether the microfinance industry should have a more subsidized anti-poverty orientation (with the resulting dependence on continued donor funding) or be oriented more towards a commercial model that might be self-sustaining but that, for all the usual reasons, would tend to leave the poor behind. But I should think the point is that neither of these options promotes the forms of collective self-organization by which poor people have historically improved their lot. There are other forks in the road.

In contrast, a savings-based credit cooperative (or 'credit union' as another type of union) is an organizational form by which large numbers of people, each with small savings, can pool their savings together to finance non-trivial business opportunities (in addition to some consumption-oriented lending). In one sense, cooperatives are commercial (for example, in using corporate forms and accounting standards). But cooperatives are not commercial in the sense of being footloose or free floating so that they could leave the poor behind. A certain identifiable group of poor people are the members of the cooperative and their savings are being put at risk so they have the natural incentive to monitor and control the activities.

There are many ways that donors could subtly help to catalyze and facilitate the development of savings-based credit cooperatives. One way is to foster and partially fund up-stream organizations whose mission is to catalyze and help animators organize savings cooperatives and to help those cooperatives learn on a peer-to-peer basis from each other about propagating the examples and about overcoming the obstacles they face. Another way is to promote partial insurance schemes for small depositors in credit cooperatives so that the fear of losses through organizational or financial collapse will not paralyze individuals from becoming involved in such a collective activity. In any case, the idea is to foster and catalyze the collective agency of poor people to change their own circumstances, not to simply have better services delivered to them as passive customers and clients.

But there are even more ways that donors could provide what might be called 'unhelpful help' – 'help' that tends to crowd out budding attempts at self-organization, 'help' that tends to reward need rather than initiative, and 'help' that tends to create dependence rather than build the capacity for independence (Ellerman, 2005a).

Genuine development assistance, where the helpers do not crowd out and undercut the agency of the doers, is a slow, subtle and painstaking process. Yet various leaders of development assistance agencies, assorted well-meaning celebrities, and a few publicity-seeking academics are constantly badgering the public, the political leaders and the donors to 'do more' to help the poor and to 'do it quickly' because things are getting worse. 'Children are dying!'. Thus donors and the organizations they fund are 'in a rush to do good' – which accounts for much of the 'popularity' and 'success' of installing off-the-shelf loan-led microfinance programmes. But that is rarely how much good is done.

Clear thinking about microfinance also requires getting beyond the carefully selected stylized stories about outlier individuals. The activities of microfinance organizations are described as funding 'entrepreneurship' by the poor when the bulk of loans seem to fall into the category that is better described as consumption smoothing. This includes bulk consumption expenditures on things that cannot otherwise be purchased on credit as well as the various family crises that might otherwise force a family into the embrace of the village moneylender. The point is not that these goals are unworthy but that they bear no relationship to the development-oriented storyline of funding entrepreneurship by the poor.

In the minority of cases where some business activity is being individually funded, it will often be an activity with little or no barriers to entry so many microborrowers may simply end up in cut-throat competition with each other. For instance, one nanobusiness is to buy a spice or staple in some bulk and then to repackage it in small amounts so that other poor people can afford it. Such microbusinesses are easily imitated, have little if any potential for growth and diversification, and do not address the more fundamental obstacle to non-trivial entrepreneurship, namely, people cooperating together to do what they cannot do individually.

It is now commonplace that donations of food surpluses from the north to 'feed the poor' in the south may well end up – in spite of the superficial appeal to 'helping the poor' – undercutting the struggling farmers in the south so that the south becomes even less able to feed itself. In a similar manner, donations of used clothing may undercut local tailors and local cottage industries. It is perhaps less appreciated that another 'entrepreneurial activity' funded by microlending, namely, shuttle trading, has a micro-version of the 'Wal-Mart effect' to crowd-out conventional local merchants, not to mention local producers. Moreover, it is often small- and medium-sized businesses that have the real development potential to engage the market, but their financing needs seem to be crowded out by the quick fix to alleviate the symptoms of poverty by financing individual microbusinesses. In many ways, microfinance programmes may be like fast-growing weeds that will choke the ground before the slower ('development-oriented') crops can grow.

Thus the rush to do good with pre-packaged and easily-installed microfinance programmes may well be another form of unhelpful help that has untoward longer-term effects on the supposed beneficiaries. In this sense, microfinance may be an *anti*-development intervention.

Impact evaluations: The ultimate low hurdle for aid agencies

Microfinance projects, like other development projects, have usually been defended on the basis of evaluations that are, on the whole, positive. But few 'evaluations' can be taken at face value. There is a powerful and by now standard critique of evaluations in the field of development assistance. Basically, the standard critique is that it is well-nigh impossible to get an evaluation that is truly independent. Usually those who fund an evaluation are closely related to the project and will not welcome bad news as it reflects on their judgment and expertise. This lesson is not lost on the evaluators who draw their income from this business. Hence, aside from minor wrist-slapping to show 'independence', evaluators are rarely the bearers of bad news, and project administrators are duly thankful for the 'good job' the evaluators are doing.

But my point is not about this standard critique of evaluation. Recently the undermining of evaluation as a part of the learning process has been taken to whole new level – impact evaluations. Impact evaluations have become a fad in their own right and are now entwined with microfinance as a means to help sustain programmes that have little if any development effectiveness. Hence it seems worthwhile to examine the inherent flaws in the concept of impact evaluations rather than examine the details of impact evaluations of microfinance as if the concept was well-grounded.

The root function of an evaluation is, as the name indicates, to judge the value of something. But the value of something is only determined by considering its costs, which entails comparing it to the alternatives. One of the most basic concepts in economics is the notion of opportunity costs. When certain resources are devoted to Plan A, what is the real cost of the resource commitment? The resources might include time and effort and many other difficult-to-quantify investments so it is not just a matter of adding up the costs. The doctrine of *opportunity* cost says that the true cost of committing those resources to Plan A is the benefit that was foregone by not committing those resources to the best alternative Plan B. Thus the notion of evaluation leads directly to the 'compared-to-what?' question. If the benefit from investing those resources in Plan A was greater than the opportunity cost (that is, the benefit from the best alternative Plan B using those resources), then Plan A has a positive net value and gets a *positive evaluation.*

This basic concept of evaluation is not 'rocket science' – in fact it is just elementary economics. Yet, we now have the fad of 'impact evaluation' in full flower and it is promoted by many economists who should know better. The basic idea of an impact evaluation of a plan or project is not to compare it to alternatives using comparable resources but to compare it to the alternative of doing nothing. In other words, the 'counterfactual' is not the best alternative use of the resources in the current circumstances but what would have happened if no resources had been expended in the current circumstances. If the benefits of the project exceed the benefits from that pseudo-counterfactual of doing nothing, then the project gets a 'positive evaluation'.

When described in such stark terms, one might wonder how impact evaluation could be seriously promoted. One treatise devoted to the subject notes honestly on the first page: 'Notice that in concentrating on impact analysis we will not be concerned in this book with the worthwhileness of a program, as in benefit-cost analysis, for example, but rather, we will limit our concern to certain of its accomplishments' (Mohr, 1988). How can a treatise on 'programme evaluation' not consider the 'worthwhileness' of a programme? Apparently, it is enough to say that it is an 'impact evaluation' or an 'impact analysis'. Inside many aid organizations concerned to justify their programmes, the tell-tale adjective 'impact' is soon dropped so that we have so-called 'evaluations' that do not consider the worthwhileness of the programmes.

There is a classic literature on experimental design in statistics (Fisher, 1951) that is widely used, for example, in agricultural testing or in drug tests. One part of an overall statistical testing programme would be testing a hypothesis about the effect ('impact') of a certain treatment. The design of the experiments involves using groups that are similar in all characteristics except that some groups receive the treatment while the control groups do not. Unfortunately, we now see this 'treatment effects' part of a statistical programme taken out of context and promoted as a means of 'evaluating' social programmes with impact evaluations.

There seems to be some implicit assumption that an evaluation can be reduced to an application of an statistical and econometric scheme that looks just at the current project and the 'counterfactual' of there being no project under otherwise similar circumstances. When the question of alternatives is raised, the statistically-oriented 'evaluator' pleads 'no data' – as if that were another reason to stick to the phony counterfactual rather than a fatal flaw in the whole scheme of evaluation.

> Impact evaluations seemed to get a boost in scientific prestige by being associated with the work of James Heckman who received the Nobel Prize in Economics. In Heckman's nobel lecture, he noted: 'The treatment effect literature approaches the problem of policy evaluation in the same way that biostatisticians approach the problem of evaluating a drug. Outcomes of persons exposed to a policy are compared to outcomes of those who are not' (Heckman, 2001).

> Often a great deal of flashy e-con-ometrics is applied to try to show that the pseudo-counterfactual is otherwise similar to the situation of the 'persons exposed to a policy' – as if that covered all the scientific bases when in fact it ignores the fundamental question of the alternatives (using comparable resources).[6] Towards the end of his lecture, Heckman at least takes a nod in the direction of costs: 'Important challenges to the field include... the development of empirically credible econometric cost benefit schemes for the evaluation of micro policies that link the program evaluation literature more closely to economics' (Heckman, 2001).

Indeed. And via the Economics 101 concept of opportunity costs, the mention of costs will raise the question of alternatives, which will in turn quickly move beyond 'econometric cost benefit schemes' to require some deeper knowledge of the type of social policies and programmes being 'evaluated'.

It might be noted that both Heckman and Mohr assume that the situation would be much improved, if not remedied, by 'cost–benefit schemes' or 'benefit–cost analysis' as if comparison and benchmarking could all be reduced to measuring some one-dimensional quantified cost. They seem to miss the real point of the opportunity cost (also called 'alternative cost') idea, which is to force consideration of all the alternatives available with comparable resources. Why should the comparison of alternatives take the form of measurement along some one-dimensional scale? While it would be a step in the right direction, moving beyond impact evaluation to cost–benefit analysis does not resolve the problem since there is little reason to expect that the whole complex process of comparison, benchmarking, adaptation and learning can be reduced down to computing a net benefit (benefits minus costs) and then selecting the project with the highest net benefit.

A genuine evaluation should be seen as *an integral part of the process of social learning*. Under conditions of uncertainty, local variation and an acknowledged Socratic ignorance of 'The Solution', the best approach to social learning seems to be parallel experimentation and the real-time evaluation of benchmarking and communication of ideas between actual (that is, non-hypothetical) experiments where comparable resources were expended as opposed to no resources (see Ellerman, 2005a).

It is perhaps useful to contemplate what medical research would be like if it limited itself to treatment effects analysis and impact evaluation. Most any sort of home remedy and folk medicine is better than doing nothing. Even blood-letting might have a positive placebo effect (since the practice persisted for centuries). One could imagine a powerful medieval Blood-Letting Guild sponsoring 'scientific tests' where the outcomes of 'persons exposed to [blood-letting] are compared to outcomes of those who are not'. Since the outcomes might generally be positive (due to a placebo effect), the practice would get a 'positive evaluation'. Fortunately, medical and other forms of applied scientific research have only used such a 'treatment effects analysis' as a part of an overall programme that involved comparisons to alternative treatments – not just comparisons to doing nothing.

But it is a different matter for development organizations that are anxious to get a 'positive evaluation' of their programmes and policies. The fad of impact evaluation – with its veneer of scientific respectability – seems custom-made for this purpose. It is the ultimate low-hurdle form of evaluation. A untold amount of resources can be spent on a project and as long as the result is 'better than doing nothing', then the project will get a positive evaluation.

In this, as in so many other aspects of development assistance, the World Bank has been the leading opinion maker and practitioner. For instance, after spending considerable resources on training individual vendors in North Africa in a Grassroots Management and Training programme, the World Bank Institute noted in its 1997 *Annual Report:* 'A 1996 evaluation found that GMT-trained women had systematically better business practices, higher business incomes and felt more empowered than control groups without access to GMT training'. Or to sustain the fad of social funds, the World Bank was careful to apply scientific evaluations to its programmes:

> A good impact evaluation asks the question: What would the status of the beneficiaries have been without the program? 'Counterfactuals' are usually constructed through the use of control/comparison groups... The general evaluation design is a matched comparison between social fund communities or beneficiaries and others with similar characteristics that did not implement a social fund project. (Social Protection Unit, 2000)

It should come as no surprise that the World Bank uses impact evaluations to evaluate not just its social fund projects but also its microfinance programmes.[7]

Indeed it should also come as no surprise that the World Bank Development Economics Department (namely, the Bank's research department) has launched a major initiative to promote impact evaluations themselves as the ultimate low-hurdle way to evaluate development programmes.

> Impact evaluation is an assessment of the extent to which interventions or programs cause changes in the well-being of target populations, such as individuals, households, organizations, communities, or other identifiable units to which interventions are directed in social programs. One way of conceptualizing net effects (or outcome) is the difference between persons or other targets that have participated in a project and comparable individuals, or entities that have not participated in the project.

An impact evaluation must estimate the counterfactual, which attempts to define a hypothetical situation that would occur in the absence of the program, and to measure the welfare levels of individuals or other identifiable units that correspond with this hypothetical situation.[8]

Perhaps there is some irony here. The World Bank often tries to legitimate its leading role by citing its unique standpoint to scan the whole world for alternatives and to ascertain 'best practices'. Yet after decades of failures, it has decided that the best way to evaluate its development programmes is not to compare them to all the actual alternatives that might be undertaken with the same considerable resources but to compare them to 'a hypothetical situation that would occur in the absence of the program'.

Conclusion

I have tried to look at some broader methodological and conceptual issues that arise in the reexamination of microfinance. My main points are as follows:
- Microfinance has the characteristics of a development fad such as moving the money with quick wins on the ground, which can be propagated through selective public relations and by the application of the latest catchphrases (for example, helping the poor, grassroots assistance, market-based, empowering, entrepreneurship and so forth).
- Microfinance is publicly touted as an instrument of development but is privately defended by many practitioners as a form of poverty relief.
- The quick wins of microfinance are quick for a reason: they move the money to 'help the poor' without addressing the financial needs of the small- and medium-sized enterprises with real growth potential (a job for the banking industry) and without making basic changes (for example, in government corruption or in the business climate) needed for broader business development. In fact, the programmes may undercut and crowd out longer-term business development, as when microfinanced shuttle traders crowd

out local producers. Such forms of 'help' are actually unhelpful in creating local business capacity.

- In addition to the well-known difficulties in having independent and objective evaluations of development programmes, the new fad of impact evaluations has carried the corruption of the evaluation process to new levels of sophistication (or rather pseudo-scientific pretense). Any real process of social learning would involve evaluation by benchmarking and peer-to-peer cross-learning between parallel experiments carried out by people in comparable circumstances and with access to comparable resources. But after decades of failure, the major aid agencies such as the World Bank are now promoting impact evaluations to judge development programmes by simply comparing – no matter what resources were expended – the impact of the programme to what would have happened in the 'hypothetical situation that would occur in the absence of the program'. Then microfinance and other development fads (usually) get a 'positive evaluation'.

In view of the above, it is becoming increasingly plausible to argue that the microfinance programmes installed by aid agencies and NGOs are not simply falling short of their hype (most observers agree on that) but are yet another faddish form of unhelpful help, an anti-development intervention that produces a short-run benefit but may misdirect and undermine sustainable development and poverty reduction in the longer run.

Notes

1   There might be something like a 10 per cent 'matching' requirement that can be provided in the form of dragooned local labour.
2   But critics might argue that social funds are in fact indebting future generations in order to put an instrument of political largess in the hands of the government officials and that social funds have zero, if not negative, connection to any capacity building on the part of the national, regional or local governments to provide and maintain their own local infrastructure (for example, Tendler, 2000).
3   See the section below on impact evaluations to understand how these ultimate low-hurdle evaluations are used to sustain development fads.
4   While not the result of official aid programmes, unskilled labour migration is another example of a phenomenon that gets quickly established, is long lasting, and has a positive effect on relieving poverty in the sending country (for example, through remittances) – but nevertheless seems not to be a path to development (see Ellerman, 2005b).
5   For example, one might consider a recent survey and prognosis (Rhyne and Otero, 2006) of the microfinance field commissioned by the Global Microcredit Summit 2006 and written by two leading practitioners based on comprehensive statistics and dozens of interviews with microfinance leaders. The striking thing about this excellent document is that it is entirely framed in terms of the 'microfinance industry' as 'suppliers of financial

services to the poor'. There is no hint that this might have anything to do with the collective agency of poor people's movements; it is all about better serving the poor as the customers and clientele of the microfinance industry. It is as if one surveyed the labour movement and took it for granted that the purpose of labour unions was to provide various services to workers such as access to finance (credit unions and now credit cards), cheaper group rates for health insurance, better retirement plans, and the like – all without any hint that the labour movement might have (at least historically) something to do with the collective agency of employees to 'change the system'.

6   See, for example, Ravallion (2005) for a discussion of 'propensity-score matching, discontinuity designs, double and triple differences' and other impressive-sounding ways of asking the wrong questions.

7   For example, see Dunn (2005) for the World Bank's evaluation of its microfinance programme in Bosnia that was contracted out to a firm called Impact LLC (see Chapter 17 in this volume).

8   On the World Bank's website, www.worldbank.org, click on 'Data & Research', then 'Impact Evaluation', and then 'Overview' to find this description and to find a handbook (Baker, 2000).

References

Baker, J. L. (2000) *Evaluating the Impact of Development Programs on Poverty: A Handbook for Practitioners*, World Bank, Washington DC.

Dichter, T. (2003) *Despite Good Intentions: Why Development Assistance to the Third World has Failed*, University of Massachusetts Press, Amherst, MA.

Dichter, T. (2005a) *Time to Stop Fooling Ourselves about Foreign Aid: A Practitioner's View*, Foreign Policy Briefing Paper #86, Cato Institute, Washington DC.

Dichter, T. (2005b) 'Hype and hope: The worrisome state of the microcredit movement', *eAfrica: South African Institute of International Affairs* 3, 28 August, http://www.saiia.org.za/modules.php?op=modload&name=News&file=article&sid=787

Dunn, E. (2005) *Impact of Microcredit on clients in Bosnia and Herzegovina*, Impact LLC, Washington DC.

Easterly, W. (2001) *The Elusive Quest for Growth: Economists' Adventures and Misadventures in the Tropics*, MIT Press, Cambridge, MA.

Easterly, W. (2006) *The White Man's Burden: Why the West's Efforts to Aid the Rest Have Done So Much Ill and So Little Good*, Penguin Press, New York.

Ellerman, D. (2005a) *Helping People Help Themselves: From the World Bank to an Alternative Philosophy of Development Assistance*, University of Michigan Press, Ann Arbor.

Ellerman, D. (2005b) 'Labour migration: A developmental path or a low-level trap?', *Development in Practice* 15: 617–30.

Fisher, R. A. (1951) *The Design of Experiments* (6th ed.), Oliver and Boyd, Edinburgh.

Heckman, J. J. (2001) 'Micro data, heterogeneity, and the evaluation of public policy: Nobel lecture', *Journal of Political Economy* 109(4): 673–748.

Johnson, S. and Rogaly, B. (1997) *Microfinance and Poverty Reduction*, Oxfam and ActionAid, Oxford and London.

Mohr, L. B. (1988) *Impact Analysis for Program Evaluation*, Dorsey Press, Chicago.

Ravallion, M. (2005) 'Evaluating anti-poverty programs', *World Bank Policy Research Working Papers*, WPS 3625, World Bank, Washington DC.

Rhyne, E. and Otero, M. (2006) *Microfinance through the Next Decade: Visioning the Who, What, Where, When and How*, ACCION International, Boston.

Social Protection Unit (2000) *SPectrum: The End of Charity: How Social Funds Empower Communities*, World Bank, Washington DC.

Tendler, J. (2000) 'Why are social funds so popular?', in Yusef, S. anmd Evenett, S. (eds) *Local Dynamics in the Era of Globalization*, pp. 114–29, Oxford University Press, Oxford.

World Bank Institute (1997) *Annual Report*, World Bank, Washington DC.

CHAPTER FOURTEEN
Learning from the Andhra Pradesh crisis[1]

Prabhu Ghate

Abstract

In March 2006 the state government of Andhra Pradesh (AP) in south India, raided and temporarily closed down nearly all the branches of MFIs functioning in Krishna district. Although the action was an inappropriate use of state power to meet the competition to the state-sponsored self-help group model, it threw up a number of issues relating to the functioning of the MFI model. These stemmed from the rush to grow at all costs to the neglect of more client-centred consumer protection objectives, such as transparency in dealings with borrowers. While the charges against the MFIs were highly exaggerated, the 'quest for numbers' may have led to several questionable practices relating to deceptive interest rates, coercive collection practices and over-lending. This chapter attempts to understand the causes and nature of the crisis, and put it to good use as an important learning experience.

In March 2006 the state government of AP in South India, raided and temporarily closed down nearly all the branches of MFIs functioning in Krishna district. AP is regarded as the 'Mecca' of Indian microfinance, the home of more than half the cumulative number of SHG groups financed by (or 'linked' to) the banks, and the headquarters of India's four largest MFIs. The action came as a rude shock to the sector. It led to widespread negative publicity in the press and did much to reverse the slowly growing awareness and appreciation of the good work being done by MFIs among the educated public. It is instructive to attempt to understand the causes and nature of the crisis, and put it to good use as an important learning experience. Most observers believe that if the MFI sector can successfully do so, it will come out stronger in the long run.

Events and responses

Unfortunately there is still no detailed objective account of what actually happened and why. However, the bare facts are that on the night of 8 March 2006, the collector (district officer) of Krishna district seized the records and closed about 57 branches of Spandana and SHARE in the district, the two largest MFIs in the country, as well those of a few smaller MFIs.[2] Borrowers were given the impression by government staff that they need not repay MFIs loans since the MFIs had violated a number of laws, including criminal laws. About 300 cases are reported to have been filed by the state government revenue authorities during the next few weeks. While many of the branches were soon reopened, MFI field staff were reluctant to continue operations in view of the hostile atmosphere created by a frenzy of negative stories in the press. Repayments went down to about 10 to 20 per cent for some months after the crisis. It is reported that borrowers were told that their loans would be taken over by the government or other banks at a much lower rate of interest.

Although the severity of the state government's reaction came as a surprise, the crisis had clearly been brewing for some time.[3] During a visit of the chief minister to neighbouring Guntur district in April 2005, complaints by MFI borrowers were brought to his notice by local politicians and officials of the District Rural Development Agency (DRDA), the agency at the district level responsible for implementing the programme popularly known as Velugu. Velugu is supported by the World Bank and seeks to 'link' self-help groups of poor village women to local bank branches and organize them into a three-tier federated structure. While Velegu is essentially a credit programme, a number of other services and benefits are also delivered through the groups. In August 2005, after the annual conference of Sa-Dhan, the main network of MFIs in India, which was held in Hyderabad that year, Sa-Dhan board members and prominent MFIs leaders met with the principal secretary of rural development who emphasized the need for preventing 'conflict situations arising out of a lack of understanding', and suggested a broader debate on the activities and operations of MFIs, including 'the need for MFIs to plough back some of their profits for development activities'. Suggestions were made to set up coordination committees at various levels, and it was agreed that a delegation would meet the chief minister to apprise him of the need to exempt MFIs from the purview of a proposed amendment to the state moneylender's act providing for an interest rate ceiling.

In subsequent months there was a series of further news reports in the local papers critical of MFIs. Finally, on 8 March, in response to a demonstration involving stone-throwing by a group of irate borrowers led by a local politician outside a SHARE branch in Krishna district, demanding the return of house title deeds that had been retained as security for housing loans SHARE was making, the collector of Krishna district moved on the branches that night.

There was widespread coverage of the action, especially in the local Telegu papers, mostly expressing support through wildly partisan news reports and editorials. Many of the accounts, even in the national press, were based on basic misunderstanding of MFI procedures, exaggerations and verbatim reproductions of official notes leaked to the press. The press did not speak up for the MFIs – issues like transaction costs do not make exciting copy. A quick factual 'white paper' put out by the sector explaining MFI procedures and costs would have been invaluable. However, on 20 March Sa-Dhan issued an interim, voluntary, code of conduct to be followed by member MFIs, which was publicized through a press conference.

The central bank, the Reserve Bank of India (RBI), expressed its concern to the state government that the action it had taken could have wider repercussions by vitiating the MFI repayment culture in other parts of the state, jeopardizing a reported Rs680 crore (US$150 million) outstanding on loans made by the banks to MFIs in AP. It set up a Coordination Forum to discuss issues of concern to stakeholders and resolve them as soon as possible. At a meeting of the forum held on 20 April it was claimed by the government side that the MFI movement was 'eating into the SHG movement', MFI practices were 'barbaric' and posed a serious law and order problem, and that even the lower interest rates suggested in the 20 March code of conduct of 21–24 per cent were usurious and illegal. Spandana and SHARE announced a reduction in their interest rates, including those on current loans outstanding, to 15 per cent on a declining balance basis. It was left to a respected MFI leader to point out that this rate was unacceptable to other Sa-Dhan members because it was not sustainable, and that the state government had no business to stipulate rates for non-banking finance companies (NBFCs), which are regulated by the Reserve Bank of India and not the state government.

To resolve outstanding issues, discussions continued between Sa-Dhan and a high-level committee of the state government. However the state government maintained its position that interest rates should be reduced further, especially as low interest rates for the poor were a major policy initiative of the state government. A series of highly publicized visits to Krishna district by the state financial commissioner and the state human rights commission took place, and their findings were leaked to the press. There had been no formal outcome of the discussions in the high-level Committee at the time of writing (October 2006), and an air of ambivalence continues to prevail about the state government's final position on interest rates. News reports say that it is reviving the moneylender's act, providing for interest rate ceilings, to be revised by a committee of officials from time to time. In May, RBI came out with guidelines for NBFCs to abide by a fair practices code, including the obligation to specify loan terms to borrowers in writing.

However in late September there were indications that the crisis was finally moving towards an implicit resolution. There were news reports from Krishna district that the major lender, ICICI Bank, had offered to break the stalemate by resuming management of its portfolio in 46 villages that had been identified by the district authorities as being particularly distressed, where it would reschedule loans and collect them though the village organizations (the second tier of the Velugu structure of institutions) at the lower rate of interest already agreed to by the MFIs. The arrangement was widely seen as a compromise, with the MFIs and lenders conceding to the long-standing demand of the government that they should lend through the VOs at a much lower interest, and the government allowing normal operations to resume in the rest of the district. At about the same time the on-time repayment rate had recovered to 40–50 per cent.

The causes of the crisis

Enabling

While it is somewhat arbitrary to divide the causes of the AP crisis into the categories of enabling and underlying, it is a useful analytical device. In the absence of more definitive empirical data, the numbers in the following discussion are taken mostly from two quick small sample surveys carried out by APMAS, and are subject to revision as further studies take place. The first of these surveys was carried out to provide an assessment of the complaints made to the chief minister during his visit to Guntur in April 2005, and sampled 40 Spandana borrowers (APMAS, 2005), and is referred to hereafter as 'the Guntur survey'. After the crisis, a year later, APMAS conducted a second survey in Krishna district of 130 borrowers who had borrowed from either SHGs, MFIs or from both (APMAS, 2006), 'the Krishna survey'. It is important to note that both surveys were borrower perception surveys.

The most important enabling (or contextual) cause was the near-saturation of coastal Andhra with microfinance. AP as a whole has covered a very large proportion of poor families under Velegu and its earlier variants. Ninety-two per cent of poor households in AP had already been covered by March 2005, according to the annual report of the AP rural development department, and the project aimed to cover the rest by the end of 2005 (Government of AP, 2005). For the MFIs, the high proportion of poor landless or near-landless agricultural labour families in the coastal districts and the high population density generally, provided strong demand conditions and important operational cost-saving advantages. Spandana actually started life in Guntur district, next door to Krishna district. Given the high coverage of both Velugu and the MFIs in coastal Andhra, the Guntur survey found that dual membership was as high as 67 per cent, and that multiple membership in Velugu, Spandana and SHARE, was 32 per cent. A year later, the Krishna survey found that multiple membership in all three had increased to as much as 82 per cent. Further, despite the presence in the area of two large MFIs (the two largest in the country) both expanding rapidly, reportedly with considerable rivalry, new local MFIs were still springing up and joining them.

Despite all this competition, the Krishna survey reported the widespread presence of informal lenders, referred to locally as *girigiri* bankers,[4] indicating that demand was still not satiated. 18 per cent of borrowers had taken loans at some time from moneylenders to pay for MFI instalments. However, despite the much publicized 'comeback' of moneylenders, 80 per cent of respondents said dependence on moneylenders had decreased. It is interesting that while increasing loan size is the most prominently reported means of competition in the literature,[5] and both MFIs were increasingly making individual loans above a size of about Rs10,000 (US$220 million), Spandana reports that in view of difficulties being experienced by borrowers, its average loan size had actually come down during the year ending with the crisis. Another interesting consequence of intense competition for clients pointed out by the Krishna study was a 'softening' of practices such as fines for late arrival at weekly meetings.

The second enabling cause was the rapid expansion of bank lending to MFIs that took place after 2003, with the introduction of ICICI Bank's 'partnership' model. The innovation underlying the partnership model was for the bank to take the loans to final borrowers directly on to its own books, as against the earlier practice of the bank 'bulk' lending to the MFI, with the MFI then on-lending at its own risk. Instead, under the partnership model, the MFI provided loan origination, disbursement and collection services for a fee. While in practice this meant no change in procedures, it greatly reduced MFI equity requirements. The arrangement is described in some detail in Nair et al (2005). It greatly enabled stepped up lending to MFIs, especially by ICICI Bank, which accounted for over two-thirds of total lending, with total bank lending to MFIs estimated to have doubled every year in the three years leading up to March 2006. With the financial constraint on expansion lifted, the MFIs were now free to grow as rapidly as they could recruit and lend to new borrowers, who, as it turned out in coastal Andhra, were more often than not existing borrowers of Velugu or other MFIs.

The third enabling or contextual cause was the political investment the current state government had made in cheap credit for the poor as an important part of its election platform, through the *Pavla Vaddi* (literally, 'quarter interest') rate scheme, which derives its name from the fact that the state government stands committed to subsidize any amount above 3 per cent that the SHGs may have to pay the banks for linkage loans (currently about 12 per cent). The subsidy is transparent, since it is financed out of the budget (and is not a cross-subsidy as in many other previous schemes where it was financed by larger bank borrowers) and is 'collective', in the sense that it is deposited into the group's bank account, and that too only after completion of timely repayment, which is made a condition.[6] Politically it must have been jarring to see MFI microfinance not only flourishing, but growing rapidly in the state at much higher interest rates.

Fourth, there was, and still is, widespread lack of public awareness of features of MFI microfinance such as doorstep disbursement and collection in weekly instalments, which lead to the seemingly 'usurious' interest rates they have to charge. This lack of understanding is shared equally by the bureaucracy, politicians and the media and was clearly on display in the exaggerations, misinformation and screaming headlines[7] that followed the crisis. Thus there was a massive external or public relations failure on the part of the sector, and one of the major challenges it faces is a public education programme.

Underlying

One of the longer-term causes was clearly the 'quest for numbers' relating to outreach and profitability that is the main motivation of many MFIs. While extending the depth and breadth of outreach is clearly central to microfinance's mission of making an impact on poverty through financial inclusion, and while sustainability is essential if MFIs are to attract lenders and investors in order to grow, the crisis serves as a useful reminder that there are other just as important client-centered consumer protection objectives such as transparency in dealings with borrowers, and being careful not to saddle them with more debt than they can handle. These are goals that apply equally to minimalist as well as more holistic microfinance. In a sense it is the industry that shares the responsibility for building up a climate of expectations that celebrates the interrelated achievements of rate of growth of outreach, efficiency and field worker productivity without always remembering that these can: first, lead to short-cuts in client selection and training, field worker training and sensitization, and loan size determination; second, be used as the only criteria for incentive payments to field workers; and third, put a degree of pressure on them that leaves no time for issues affecting client satisfaction, other than loan turn-around time, progression in loan size and so on.[8]

MFIs have a social as well as financial mission. Unfortunately social performance is not as easy to measure as financial performance, although a welcome development in India is the new social rating tools being developed by the main MFI rating agency, Microfinance Credit and Ratings International Ltd (M-CRIL), to measure social performance, defined as the 'effective translation of mission into practice, in line with accepted social values'. These tools include surveys to obtain feedback on client protection issues, client satisfaction, reasons for dropping out and similar variables. Interestingly, mission drift in the literature usually refers to moving upmarket to increase breadth of outreach at the cost of depth of outreach. This has not been an issue at all in the present crisis, and it is generally accepted that MFIs following the Grameen Bank methodology generally have a poorer clientele than SHGs. Rather, the mission drift here was to ignore the rest of the social mission at the expense of the financial mission.

A second underlying cause relates to the operational practices of the MFIs concerned, which were the outcome of the rush to grow and become profitable as soon as possible. These practices were probably no different from those of many other MFIs growing rapidly in other areas, but since they have received extensive publicity there is more information on them, allowing us to use them to discuss issues that apply to the sector as a whole. While they were not the real reason for the state government's action, 'usurious interest rates and hidden costs', or what are referred to as 'deceptive' interest rates in the literature (CGAP, 2004) were given prominence in the early days after the closure, before many state government officials realized that NBFCs are free to set their own rates. Indeed they do not seem to have been aware that the state moneylenders act was no longer valid, so that non-NBFCs were likewise legally free to do so.

Spandana's and SHARE's effective interest rates before the crisis are reported to have been 31 and 28 per cent respectively from 2002–03 to 2005–06, when they were reduced to 28 and 24 per cent. These rates are not very different from the modal rate of 2 per cent a month rate charged by SHGs, and below half that of the informal sector (for *girigiri* bankers they are 6.7 per cent a month). They include the loan processing fee, but not a one-time membership fee. The MFIs also required borrowers to make a security deposit as cash collateral. Also, Spandana deducted 1 per cent of the loan amount or Rs50 towards a life insurance premium in which the borrower's spouse received the loan amount, less the outstanding balance, if she died, on which Spandana made a surplus (see Roth, 2005). However this too does not increase the effective interest rate, whether or not one agrees with the view expressed by the press and government that the surplus from the scheme should have been distributed to borrowers. It is true though that borrowers lacked a clear understanding of their entitlements under the scheme, which some studies report is generally the case with insurance products distributed by MFIs in India.

A practice that has raised some eyebrows was charging interest on the entire period remaining on the current loan to borrowers who wanted to prepay their current loan in order to avail of a larger one. This can be a rather high penalty, depending on the period in question. As with many other questionable practices the MFIs were accused of, there is no data on how frequently it was resorted to. The MFIs, like most others in India and Bangladesh, were also using flat rates. Transparency demands MFIs should prominently disclose the effective rate of interest as an APR.[9]

This could place new, start-up MFIs at a disadvantage compared to established large ones, because the higher rate they need to charge to recover higher initial transactions costs will become more 'visible'. The remedy would be to lay down a slab system of suggested interest rates instead of the uniform rate laid down in the code of conduct at present, assuming that it is 'politically' necessary to have suggested rates at all.[10]

The set of accusations that received the most prominence, however, related to coercive collection practices, leading to borrowers having to 'abscond' or migrate out of the village, and even in some cases, allegedly, commit suicide.[11] The respondents in the Krishna survey felt that; first, joint liability (the group paying on behalf of the defaulter); second, compulsory attendance; third, fines; and fourth, keeping all members waiting until repayments are made, are the chief means (in that order of importance) of ensuring a 'cent per cent recovery' rate. Means that would generally be regarded as 'abusive'[12] or at least questionable were mentioned by respondents in the following order of frequency: first, adjusting overdues against the security deposit; second, holding the weekly meeting in front of the defaulter's house; third, MFI staff sitting in front of a defaulter's door; fourth, offensive language used by group leaders or staff; and fifth, putting up a loan overdue notice in front of a defaulter's house.[13]

The point at which peer group pressure becomes coercive is an extremely difficult one. However one clear lesson of the crisis is that the policy of 100 per cent repayment and 'zero tolerance' for default carried a very high cost in terms of client dissatisfaction, and provided ample material to be exploited by interested parties. Clearly there is a need for flexibility to accommodate cases of extreme distress in which a borrower is unable to pay because of critical illness, hospitalization and so on. A second lesson is that there is a great need for action research to provide answers to the question of how flexible MFIs can afford to be, even in cases of lesser distress (such as failure of a business) in rescheduling loans, without affecting repayment discipline generally, and how much operational costs would go up to introduce such flexibility.[14] Third, an additional response should clearly be much wider use of emergency loans and risk funds.

The third set of accusations was that MFIs were 'dumping money on borrowers' who were finding it difficult to repay and having to borrow from moneylenders at a higher cost in order to stay in good standing with the MFI. This is an extremely complicated issue calling for much further field research. While the banks are in a position to lend to salaried borrowers whose total income is relatively easy to assess, MFIs lend almost entirely to the self-employed whose relevant income is that of the household as a whole. Such incomes are very variable and very hard to assess. There was no doubt some over-lending but we need detailed case studies of how some borrowers got into repayment difficulties. This is the kind of research still neglected in India, as elsewhere, and needs economic anthropologists willing to live in villages for prolonged periods and to use participant observation and other methods to get over the limitations of survey-based research and 'quick and dirty' studies.

A third underlying cause of the crisis lay in certain features of the main alternative model of microfinance available to borrowers, the SHG programme. These features made Velugu less attractive to many borrowers as a source of microcredit (although they may have continued to value many of the other services provided through Velugu), and led them to borrow also from the MFIs. Most of these features are inherent disadvantages of the SHG model itself, although the disadvantages may be dominated by the advantages. In the Guntur survey of Spandana borrowers, two-thirds of whom were also SHG members, inadequate loan size was the most frequently cited problem in borrowing from SHGs, followed by the long waiting period for loans. In contrast, timeliness of loans was cited most frequently as an advantage of borrowing from MFIs. In the second Krishna district survey, cumulative borrowing from SHGs was found to be about 40 per cent of that from the two MFIs (standardized for number of loans), although there was less difference in loans outstanding given the longer tenor of SHG loans. MFIs deliver loans of larger average size in a more timely fashion because they borrow in bulk from the banks for relending, whereas SHGs have to wait for the last member in the group to repay her loan to the group before the group can repay its loan to the bank, and secondly, because loan size is tied to group savings and depends on the assessment of the local bank manager on the absorption capacity of the group for a subsequent loan.

Interestingly, the Krishna district survey ranked the availability of individual loans as the most frequent response among reasons for enrolling in MFIs, ahead of timeliness and large loans. Interestingly, again, the most frequent response (90 per cent) for problems with MFI procedures was weekly instalments, just ahead of the high rate of interest, and well ahead of 'rigidity even in genuine cases' (19 per cent). 'More pressure and mental tension' on account of weekly repayment was an important drawback also reported in the first survey.[15]

On balance, given these advantages and disadvantages, only 10 per cent of Guntur district borrowers said they would discontinue MFI membership after repaying their current loan, a proportion that increased to 21 per cent in the Krishna survey. However as the survey report explains, many members who intend to leave, end up 'prolonging' their membership because a member who leaves either has to wait for another drop-out in her original group who she can replace, or organize a new group. In addition she loses her seniority and is on a par with new members in respect of loan size. So the incentives are structured so as to keep membership alive.

Likewise, despite dissatisfaction with SHG membership as a credit institution, very few members actually quit and 'defect'. This is because SHG membership too confers many advantages, with access to a large number of development programmes, services and benefits being contingent on membership.[16] Thus there was no 'poaching' as such, because both models were restricting competition by making it costly for borrowers to switch. The impact of competition is more on regularity of loan repayments and monthly savings in the SHGs. The Krishna survey found overdues amounting to almost half of outstanding in the SHGs that members belonged to. The proximate cause of the state government action was the increasing frustration being experienced by Velugu managers over the effect MFI lending to SHG borrowers was having on Velugu performance, as shown in indicators such as the recovery rate within groups, and of on-time repayments by the groups to the banks and to the Community Investment Fund.[17]

A final underlying cause was the MFIs, in their self-absorption with growth at the cost of other objectives, underestimated the degree to which they were antagonizing several powerful players in the local political economy. Among these were informal lenders such as, reportedly, chit fund organizers, and local *girigiri* bankers, politicians who were embarrassed by the fact that the MFIs were disbursing much more money in their constituencies than they could lay their hands on themselves through their constituency funds, some bureaucrats who felt uncomfortable about anything major happening in their district, even if it was good, without their 'blessings' or at least their knowledge. Even retail traders of consumer durables are said to have felt threatened by the fact that Spandana had earlier set up a consumer store so as to be able to purchase goods in bulk and enable borrowers to benefit from lower prices using vouchers they had the option to accept instead of cash loans.[18] And finally of course there were a number of highly discontented borrowers, as noted above, some of who were championed by local politicians. This powerful combination of interests may explain the lack of public support when the crisis hit.

Lessons and implications for the MFI model

One short-term impact of the crisis was a heightened perception of political risk among banks, who both increased interest rates and reduced new lending to MFIs in AP, especially to SHARE and Spandana, in the first few months of the current financial year that runs till March 2007. It is too early to say what overall lending growth in the country as a whole will be during the year. At least one of the medium-sized lenders has plans to more than double lending this year, but a great deal depends on ICICI, since it accounts for the lion's share of total lending to MFIs. SHARE and Spandana both had to make higher provisions in 2005–06, as well as write-off loans. However they were not the only ones affected. Other AP MFIs had to make higher provisions too.

Another impact has been a sharp reduction in the rate of growth of the MFI model in AP. SHARE's portfolio actually shrunk by about 10 per cent during the first six months of the 2006–07 financial year, while Spandana's had climbed back by September to a level only slightly higher than in March. Although Spandana may have been the larger lender in Krishna district, with Rs74 crore (US$16 million) outstanding in March, it has a larger share of borrowers in the urban and semi-urban areas, and is shifting its rural lending to the Telengana and Rayalseema areas of the state, apart from expanding in Hyderabad and opening branches in Karnataka. SHARE has not opened any new branches in the state since the crisis, but added 15 to its 300 in March, all of them outside the state. It is now has 100 branches in four neighbouring states – Karnataka, Maharashtra, Madhya Pradesh and Chattisgarh, and has plans to open branches also in Rajasthan, Orissa and Utta Pradesh. SKS, another AP MFI is also expanding rapidly outside the state. Thus while the crisis is a short-term loss to the poor families of AP, this will be partly offset by acceleration of growth in other states, many of them badly undeserved.

Hopefully, risk perceptions will improve as things return to normal. The AP crisis was caused essentially by a combination of four factors: first, the fact that the state itself was an active promoter of microfinance through a politically-attractive and highly visible programme, Velegu; second, competition between this programme and MFIs; third, the fact that this competition was damaging Velugu; and fourth, the fact that the state government intervened to protect the model it was promoting or, in other words, let its promotional role dominate the role of neutral umpire between models. Even if the first condition comes to apply elsewhere, the last may not, especially if MFIs ensure that the second and third conditions do not arise, at least in the acute form they did in coastal Andhra. One of the challenges before the sector is to evolve a harmonious relationship with the SHG-bank linkage model, as geographic separation is not possible in the long run, with both models expanding. Nor is it desirable, if the two different segments, the un-banked near-poor and the poor (that is, those below the poverty line) are to be offered a choice of models.

Among positive effects, many of the lessons of the crisis for MFI practices have been recognized and reiterated in the Sa-Dhan's interim code of conduct, and self-regulation mechanisms will hopefully be strengthened to enforce them.

However many difficult questions remain on which much soul searching and hard thinking remains. Lower acceptable interest rates could spur the introduction of technology as a means of lowering transactions costs. With a lower rate of growth, MFIs are likely to be able to devote more attention to good governance, transparency and client perspectives. They are likely to become more sensitive to social performance generally, and the use of social ratings is likely to increase. Other likely impacts are that incentives to transform will get strengthened as NGO MFIs seek to insulate themselves as NBFCs from the uncertainties of interest rate populism. The crisis will hopefully also expedite action on the proposed microfinance bill that recognizes microfinance as a distinct and desirable lending activity.

Another medium-term impact is likely to be downward pressure on interest rates from a desire to conform to public, political and regulatory perceptions of what a 'reasonable' rate is. Several MFIs around the country have already reduced their rates. While large MFIs are in a position to reduce rates with a lower impact on their growth, the growth of the sector as a whole is likely to slow down at least for the next year or two. The high growth rates of some of the larger and some medium MFIs, witnessed in the last few years, are certainly likely to become a thing of the past. The challenge will be to grow steadily even at modest rates, especially for small start-up MFIs.

Notes

1   This chapter is a slightly revised version of Chapter 4 of Ghate (2006) *Microfinance in India: A State of the Sector Report, 2006*, and is included with kind permission of Microfinance India. I am grateful to a number of officials of the AP government for sparing time to meet and discuss with me, C. S. Reddy and Raja Reddy of APMAS for generously sharing the Guntur and Krishna survey reports, and to the MFI leaders concerned. I am particularly grateful to Padmaja Reddy of Spandana for always being so accessible. As she points out, Spandana has never tried to hide its profits (which were much lauded before the crisis, and resulted from Spandana's equally lauded efficiency) and has always opened its doors to researchers, two of whom are cited in this chapter, enabling closer understanding of issues generic to the sector.

2   SHARE had 927,290 members in March 2006, with Rs366 crore (approximately US$81 million) in loans outstanding, while Spandana had 784,323 members and loans outstanding of Rs305. According to a report in the *Economic Times* (30 August 2006), about 10 MFIs had operations in Krishna district, with about 100,000 borrowers, and loans outstanding of Rs130 crore.

3   For prescient observations on the need for Spandana to address political risk, see Sriram (2005).

4   They provide loans of Rs500 repayable in 12 weekly instalments of Rs50 each, after deducting Rs10 for a passbook.

5   As in Bolivia, on the basis of which Rhyne (2002) goes so far as to claim that competition between MFIs is inherently unstable.

6   However SHG group funds ultimately belong to members individually in proportion to their savings.

7   Such as 'Blood Money!'.

8   Ironically, Spandana was widely lauded by the MFI community for being a highly profitable MFI, and for having unusually high efficiency with extremely low operational costs. It was not clear to most observers at the time that it was possible that these were being minimized at the expense of repercussions on client satisfaction. By contrast, Spandana's profitability had attracted adverse political attention well before the crisis, in response to which Spandana had indeed started reducing interest rates.

9   It should be borne in mind that not even MFI field workers know what the effective interest rate (EIR) is, let alone the mathematical formula according to which it is calculated. However, the (EIR) does however serve the essential purpose of enabling comparability.

10   The code of conduct contains a table that explains how the rate of 21–24 per cent is derived. Ten percentage points are accounted for by what is claimed to be the post office money order delivery charge. The charge is actually 5 per cent. Rather than use the money order charge as a proxy, the sector in its public education programme should use the results of well-publicized studies on actual transactions costs as a function of scale.

11   The base suicide rate in AP is 14 per 100,000. There would be cause for concern only if the rate among the borrowers of an MFI were significantly above this. None of the allegations in the press and from government seemed to be aware of this, apart from the fact it is very hard to determine the cause of a suicide. This is not to imply of course, that suicides are not tragic, whatever their causes.

12   This is the term used in the literature (for example, CGAP, 2004). In India, abusive is also commonly used to refer to verbal abuse, another practice field workers were accused of, as noted below, but it should be remembered that what is considered abusive in the latter sense is culturally specific.

13   Only as a 'last resort' were mostly larger, individual, loans, recovered by encashing signed blank cheques, or taking legal action to enforce blank promissory notes. Use of blank documents is of course clearly an abuse, and lay behind the cheating cases registered. Two respondents mentioned physical force, exercised presumably by centre and group leaders, since a lone field worker would risk retaliation (one was in fact murdered soon after the crisis).

14   The Centre for Micro Finance, Chennai, in collaboration with KAS Foundation, an MFI in Orissa, is experimenting with the impact of introducing flexible repayments schedules, such as allowing the client to skip up to two principal instalments through a coupon payment system that simplifies the accounting for both MFI and borrower, or allowing the client

to pay double the principal instalments during the first six months of a milch animal loan when the animal is productive.

15 This is contrary to the widespread advantage claimed for weekly repayment that it makes repayment easier, and to what some women told this author during a visit to a village in Krishna district where repayments stood suspended after the crisis, that they regretted the fact that they were working less because they no longer needed to raise money for the wages to meet the next repayment.

16 The previous government was also acutely conscious of the political importance of Velugu and offered members incentives, especially before election time, such as easier access to gas connections. It could be argued though that competition through 'bribery' is preferable to attacking the other model.

17 The Community Investment Fund is a component of Velugu, under which funds are passed down through the two upper tiers of the three-tier structure, Mandal Samakhya's and VOs, to the SHGs, with the intention to make each tier self-sufficient in the long run through an interest differential added on each stage. The World Bank's original intention was for the fund to finance small collective projects started by common interest groups of the poor, prepared with their participation under micro-plans, but in view of the poor recovery rate (of 45 per cent in 2003–04), it is now used mostly for individual loans by the SHGs, with the recovery rate expected to increase to 60 per cent in 2004–05 (Government of AP, 2005). The fund continues to finance some collective projects implemented by the higher tiers, such as marketing of agricultural commodities and food security interventions.

18 By contrast, except when loans are tied to purchases in particular outlets connected with the MFI, one would expect there to be a strong complementarity of interest between MFIs making large individual loans and the retail trading community generally. Spandana discontinued the business when it transformed to an NBFC (see Sriram, 2005).

References

APMAS (2005) *A Report on Spandana's Microfinance Activity*, mimeo, APMAS, Hyderabad.

APMAS (2006) *Voice of the People on the Lending Practices of Microfinance Institutions in Krishna District of Andhra Pradesh*, mimeo, APMAS, Hyderabad.

CGAP (2004) *Interest Rate Ceilings and Microfinance: The Story So Far*, occasional paper, CGAP, Washington DC.

Ghate, P. (2006) *Microfinance in India: A State of the Sector Report, 2006*, Microfinance India, New Delhi.

Government of AP (2005) *Department of Rural Development, Annual Report 2005*, Government of Andhra Pradesh, Hyderabad.

Nair, T., Sriram, M. S. and Prasad, V. (2005) 'ICICI Bank, India', in Harper M. and Singh Arora, S. (eds) *Small Customers, Big Market: Commercial Banks in Microfinance*, ITDG Publishing, Rugby.

Rhyne, E. (2002) 'Microfinance institutions in competitive conditions', in Drake, D. and Rhyne, E. (eds) *The Commercialization of Microfinance: Balancing Business and Development*, Kumarian Press, Connecticut.

Roth, J. (2005) *Microinsurance and Microfinance Institutions: Evidence from India*, CGAP Working Group on Microinsurance, Good and Bad Practices, Case Study No. 15, CGAP, Washington DC.

Sriram, M. S. (2005) *Expanding Financial Services Access for the Poor: The Transformation of Spandana*, Working Paper No 2005-04-03, IIMA, Ahmedabad.

PART THREE
Expectations

CHAPTER FIFTEEN

The chicken and egg dilemma in microfinance: An historical analysis of the sequence of growth and credit in the economic development of the 'north'

Thomas Dichter

Abstract

The bulk of microfinance practice remains microcredit. There has been a general assumption, promoted to donors and the public, that such credit leads to small business investment or asset creation by the poor and that this therefore is the link between widespread access of the poor to credit and their economic development. The chapter looks at the history of democratized credit and its relationship to growth and poverty reduction in the 'northern' developed countries, and finds little evidence for the connection. In fact the rise of widespread availability of formal credit followed industrial growth and job creation and was linked almost entirely to consumption, while credit for business start-up and small or microbusiness historically came not from formal but informal sources.

Introduction

From the very beginning of the microcredit movement, the presumption has been that the poor lacked access to formal financial services, and particularly to non-usurious credit. (Only more recently, under the larger rubric of microfinance, have we begun to talk about access to financial services in general including savings, insurance and money transfers). In some of the rhetoric of the movement, it has even been presumed that the poor were deliberately 'excluded' from credit access. The response has been to democratize credit, providing access to all, with the expectation that this will enable the poor to work themselves out of poverty by investing in microbusinesses or asset acquisition, which in their turn would feed into economic growth. Pick up almost any article on microfinance in the last 15 years (or more recently any microfinance website) and one finds assertions that reinforce this notion:

> The women I've met in Uganda and Guatemala are so resourceful, and it's just amazing to see how, with their courage and diligence, they create small

businesses with such tiny amounts of money. (Year of Microcredit website, http://www.yearofmicrocredit.org)

the bank gave her a loan of... US$25. Such a small sum to start a business seems laughable, but this was no joke. This was 'microcredit', designed for would-be entrepreneurs in poor areas. (Baum, 2005)

Microcredit programs have successfully contributed to lifting people out of poverty in many countries around the world. (United Nations Department of Economic and Social Affairs, http://www.un.org/esa)

[The Mission of the Microcredit Summit Campaign is] Working to ensure that 175 million of the world's poorest families, especially the women of those families, are receiving credit for self-employment and other financial and business services by the end of 2015. (Microcredit Summit Campaign, http://www.microcreditsummit.org)

We have seen how access to loans and deposit services has empowered millions of people to work their way out of poverty... Microfinance is a powerful tool to fight poverty. Poor households use financial services to raise income, build their assets, and cushion themselves against external shocks. (Helms, 2006)

Moreover, the 2006 Nobel Prize winner and founder of the Grameen Bank, Muhammad Yunus, has famously called credit a 'human right'.

As many practitioners of microcredit (including this author) have learned, however, money is fungible – it can be used for anything. While we knew this in the abstract, it became real as we began to see poor borrowers use their loans for what the industry has come to call 'consumption smoothing', ironing out the highs and lows in cash flow so that crises can be met or large purchases made. But that very term suggests that the microcredit movement is not all that comfortable with the idea of 'consumption' plain and simple, since it is implicitly recognized that poor people using credit for things and services (even if some are necessary such as medicine or education) is not really what microcredit started out to do.

Those of us who work or have worked in microfinance are in fact quite circumspect about a number of things that underpin our work. We tend to skirt around the question of consumption and spin euphemisms around the question of whether the poor invest their loans in business with terms like 'microenterprise', 'entrepreneurial agents', and income-generating activities'.

History – the history in the 'north' of formal and informal credit use for business investment, and the history of formal and informal credit use for consumption – has a lot to teach us about the credit-for-everybody notions of microfinance. My hope is that its lessons might bring our expectations of microfinance more into line with reality. For the economic history of the rich nations suggests strongly that:

- earlier forms of microcredit never played a significant role in business start-up or small business development;

- that the first efforts at democratizing financial services were almost entirely savings and 'thrift' based;
- that economic development in fact came before (or at best alongside) the movements to democratize financial services;
- and that when credit for the poor did come along, it *followed* the savings movement, and developed almost entirely in relation to consumption.

If these lessons are valid, microcredit, still the dominant service in microfinance, seems to have long been on a path that does not lead to the kinds of results that a great many practitioners and advocates have hoped it would.

I will not deal here with the assumption that the poor are entrepreneurial. The distribution of entrepreneurial characters is pretty much the same everywhere in the world. Some people have it, others do not. One of the reasons the assumption of the poor as nascent business people continues to prevail is that in the developing countries, most poor must take to the informal marketplace to generate small amounts of cash and it is this which makes them seem like they are engaged in business – but this is subsistence activity, a *faute-de-mieux* default mode, and not what I call 'real' business. If all other things were equal, one would see quickly and clearly how few people in the world are entrepreneurial.

Instead, this chapter is meant as a *tour d'horizon* of the history of credit access and credit use in the advanced industrial countries during the main period of their development, beginning in the late 18th century and continuing into the early mid-20th. The emphasis will be on North America and Great Britain, with some reference to Germany. But the subject and the literature are extensive and a more thorough review could add much by looking at the rest of Europe and Japan as they became 'developed'.

Do the poor have assets, and if so, how do they husband them?

Since the credit-for-everybody notion is partly based on the belief that the poor need credit so they can build assets, we need first to look at the clients – the poor themselves. Did the poor in the past lack assets, and do they today? Yes and no. The problem is complex. First, many of the assets of the poor, especially the rural poor, have been in the past, and are still today, *hidden* from view, and often deliberately so, to avoid exploitation or expropriation. Read any novel of or description of peasant life from the 19th century onwards and one will read of the peasant's capacity to hide what he has or what he has made, from the tax collector, the landlord or one's neighbour. When houses were taxed on the number of windows, people built houses with no visible windows on the road side. When 16th century farmers in the Alps paid their rent on pastureland with milk, they didn't milk their cows completely during the first milking of the day, and used the excess milk taken during the night time second milking to make *reblochon* cheese. Likewise in rural India, China, Russia or the USA, relatively poor people found (and find) ways to hide or underestimate their assets.

That understandable tradition fits rather well with the altruistic side of the microfinance agenda – it reinforces the belief that the poor are without assets, and much of our research into poverty does little to change that belief. When we do survey the poor prior to setting up a microfinance project, the research (because of time and funding constraints, and perhaps our ideology) is more often than not done too quickly and superficially to unearth anything more profound than the answers the poor want to give to the researchers. Only long-term fieldwork (of the ethnographic sort that would require living in a village for two years or so) would enable us to penetrate the complexity of how the poor make, save and use money and other assets.

Of course just because the poor sometimes hid assets does not mean they were rich. Indeed, they hid (and by extension 'saved') assets *because* of their poverty, their vulnerability to exploitation and often indebtedness. And that poverty shaped some of their behaviour, rendering them often cunning, conservative survivalists, who were forced by circumstance to find myriad ways to deal with crisis, periodic shortages and, of course, death and taxes. Today's microfinance tends to see the poor somewhat patronizingly in one dimension: the poor are needy creatures, with lots of potential to be sure, but with little resilience and few strategies or choices. If anything the rural poor are seen even more simply than the urban poor. But things are not always what they seem.

When the poor in the advanced countries began to have widespread access to formal credit, it was in fact for *consumption*, and indeed the wider accessibility of credit was driven more by the supply of consumables than by the demand for them. As for business development, when formal credit was involved, it was not accessed by the poor (who, if they wanted to start a business used savings or borrowed informally from friends and family) but by established big business. Formal credit for business purposes, whether accessible or not, was not for poor folks, and as we will see, this was often by their own choice.

Credit use by businesses in the past

Historically, the way credit was used by real business people (from merchants and traders in traditional bazaar economies to small businessmen in later 'firm' economies) is more complex than generally thought of in today's microfinance circles. Credit for real business has been in the past, and is often today, intricately entwined with social structure and culture, and with 'rules' that often seem counterintuitive. As some historians, economists and social scientists have shown, the way real entrepreneurs think about credit is different than the way the current microfinance framework sees enterprise credit – in linear, often black and white terms: 'I need capital for my activity, I don't have it, so I have to borrow it, and when my business grows and or when I make my profit I will pay it back'. This is too simple. Consider the kind of local economy found in many developing countries, the bazaar economy. According to anthropologist Clifford Geertz, the traditional bazaar economy is a:

complex and ramified network of credit balances binding larger and smaller traders together. It is this network which provides the primary integrative factor in the [Indonesian] *pasar*, for it leads to a hierarchical ranking of traders in which larger traders give credit to smaller ones and smaller ones have debts to larger ones. These credit balances are only half-understood if they are seen only as ways in which capital is made available, for they set up and stabilize more or less persisting commercial relationships... This is why, for example, traders often prefer expensive private credit to cheap government credit... It gives them more than simple access to capital; it secures a higher position in the flow of trade. (Geertz, 1963)

The great economist John Maynard Keynes once said that if you owe your bank £100, you have a problem, but if you owe a million, it has the problem. The point is that *credit relationships in business can be complicated*, and the power balancing and other optimization or positioning 'games' involved in credit relationships are not easy to understand at first glance. It would seem that the business person and the poor microcredit borrower are two different kinds of people. The vast majority of today's microcredit programme borrowers are more or less straightforward in their behaviour – they want to pay back their loan and get rid of the debt.

In contrast, the smart *business* borrower wants to keep things on as much of a credit basis as possible. We see this occasionally in present day microfinance projects when, for example, a going concern in India with a large turnover of say Rs500,000 per month will take a 12-month loan of Rs20,000 from an MFI. He does not *need* this microcredit in any strict sense, and could repay it instantly. Instead he is using it as an addition to a set of interwoven relationships with others, investing in what he believes (often wrongly) is a potential new relationship that will lead to a loan of a million rupees or more.

Formal credit for business: A result of economic development, not a cause

Which came first, formal credit arrangements or growth in commerce and trade (that is, economic development)? There is ample evidence that growth came first. In medieval Venice, for example, the commercial activity of traders who needed to expand their activity was financed by early forms of private banks, and in 16th and 17th century Mughal Empire India the evolution of a class of people who functioned as early 'bankers' was likewise driven by the expansion of commercial activity. These *sarrafs* supplied credit and undertook money transfers using bills of exchange called *hundi* (Alam, 2006). Both the British and the Dutch East India Companies (early forms of multinationals) raised cash through these *sarrafs*. Clearly once at a certain scale, the two – formal credit and economic development – became somewhat intertwined; but as will be explained later regarding start-up activity, the common source of capital was then (as it is still today) one's own resources and those of friends or family.

Indeed the role of banks in the early years of the industrial revolution in Europe, beginning in Britain in the last quarter of the 18th century, evolved in response to the demand on the part of expanding manufacturing and heavy industries like mining, metallurgy and machine making, for short-term working capital, and many financial instruments were developed including standing overdrafts (Landes, 1969). The historical sequence seems to have been, first the building up of an activity or sector, and then a demand for formal business credit.

Small business start-ups did not want formal credit

In 1825, French writer Honoré de Balzac decided that the only way to control the publication of his books and ensure he received the profits on their sale was to get involved in printing and selling them himself. He began an early version of a 'vertically integrated' business, controlling everything from the writing, to the sourcing of the paper, to printing, advertising and marketing. He needed funds, of which he was perpetually short. He borrowed first from his family and then from his mistress. The business worked for a while but ultimately had to be liquidated. When it was, he was in debt Ffr60,000, 50,000 of which was owed to his family.

In 1923, soon after Walt Disney arrived in Hollywood, he and his brother Roy needed funds to launch Disney Brothers (which later became Disney Studios). They borrowed US$25 from Roy's girlfriend and US$500 from their uncle.

Self-financing (savings) or borrowing from a close social network has generally always been the case for business start-ups, at least from the early days of the Industrial Revolution. As French economic historian Paul Bairoch points out 'self-finance was the dominant and almost exclusive form of business financing at the beginning of the Industrial Revolution' (Bairoch, 1992). Non-bank, non-formal sources of capital for business start-up continue to dominate today, in both the advanced economy countries and the developing countries alike. According to the Global Entrepreneurship Monitor, in a survey of 12 developed and high growth countries in 2000 (including the USA, the UK, Norway, Singapore and Korea), an average of 78 per cent of funding for business start-ups came from informal sources (Reynolds et al, 2000).

Why is this so, or better yet, why is it logical that this be so? Because start-ups are basically experiments undertaken *in situ* – they are not undertaken in a laboratory under 'controlled' conditions, but in the real world. Thus the results cannot be predicted in advance. Most people everywhere seem to recognize this reality, beginning with the entrepreneur. Therefore even when formal financing is available, the preference seems to be for self-financing or informal financing, or more likely both together. Because a loan from a friend or a relative is based partly on a social connection, the entrepreneur gains a hedge since he knows the arrangement is 'softer', more 'patient', more risk-tolerant, and less return-driven than a formal loan. In short, such loans are prevalent not because of a lack of access to formal financing (even when such lack of access may be the case), but because they are *preferable to the borrower from a financial risk standpoint*, a risk that a friend or relative is also more likely than a formal institution to take on.

Indeed there is evidence both from today's microfinance and from past efforts that arose out of altruistic or philanthropic instinct that credit access for business start-up on relatively easy terms *added* risk to the already built-in risk of starting up – a risk inherent in the fact that the money was perceived as 'easy', and thus less care was taken with how it is spent.

A striking example comes from mid-19th century London and the journalism of Henry Mayhew, whose *Morning Chronicle* articles led to the idea of setting up a 'Loan Office for the Poor', a century and a half before the 2005 UN Year of Microcredit, which in effect advocated a world-wide 'loan office for the poor'. Through Mayhew's Loan Office:

> deserving subjects might obtain either small outright grants or loans on easy terms of repayment in order to obtain the necessary stock or equipment to carry on their trades. The sums advanced were petty and the number receiving them amounted to only a few score.

> The largest sum advanced on loan was to C. Alloway, the crippled seller of nutmeg-graters, whose portrait and harrowing story [in the *Morning Chronicle*] brought sympathy and recognition in the streets: 'I am gazed at in the street,' he wrote, 'and observations made within my hearing with respect to the Exact likeness of the portrait.' More than 9 pounds was advanced to him, to be repaid at 1 shilling a week, but he was beset at once with new disasters; he invested in a donkey, ordered a cart, and brought some hardware stock, but the donkey became ill, and the carpenter absconded with his money. The most ambitious effort of the 'Loan Office' appears to have ended in failure. (Thompson and Yeo, 1971)

As for formal bank credit to businesses, historically this was for established businesses where a degree of cruising speed had been reached, or businesses that were at any rate past the start-up stage, and thus something that a banker could have some trust in. Again there is considerable financial common sense to this, and not just a bias for the 'exclusion' of lower income or poor people. It should be noted also that, certainly in the USA, the drivers of economic growth were not poor people getting access to enterprise credit, but the expansion of big business and industry.

The practical dividing line between the standard microfinance client of today (the vast majority of whom are *not* entrepreneurs) and the real business person is the line between consumption and investment capital for business. Credit for the masses has been in the past (and is today) largely for and about consumption. Credit for real business is not for or about consumption *nor does it need to be accessible to everybody*.

As economic historians have suggested, many traders and merchants (and not just in Calvinist Scotland or Switzerland) are known for thrift and asceticism.

They do not approve of excessive consumption (though once they become truly rich they might). Cash, when accumulated, is a business tool, enabling businesspeople to get into a new game; to be in on many different deals. And while the first attempts at expanding formal financial services to the poor were based on strong notions of thrift, the resulting savings were unrelated to business use.

Early formal finance to the poor was based on savings and thrift

From the English 'friendly societies' of the late 18th century to the early German credit union movement associated with Herman Scholze-Delitzsch in 1850 and Friedrich Raiffeisen in 1864, to the postal savings systems, experiments in formal systems aimed at the poor were based on savings. Some of the promoters of these formal financial services, like Henry Duncan who pioneered the Scottish savings bank movement in 1808, were what we would today call 'social entrepreneurs', do-gooders who had a vision on behalf of the poor. Duncan and his followers in Scotland revealed their concern by using terms like 'the debauchery of the alehouse... imprudent expenditures... working class improvidence' and the need for 'moral restraint' (Alborn, n. d.).

There were also insurance schemes, friendly societies (which largely paid out sick benefits) and the penny savings bank movement, begun in Scotland in 1810, and some of these also had a moral reform basis. A study of Scotland in the 19th century noted 'the trend in Scotland towards penny savings banks and friendly societies as a means of training the population in the habits of provident care and self-denial' (Haythornthwaite, 1993).

The very term 'thrift' in these early financial systems of course captures the moral basis of savings. In the USA, the popularity of Ben Franklin's *Poor Richard's Almanac* ('A penny saved is a penny earned') and the coining of the large copper penny in 1793 produced the rage for metal (and later mechanical) penny banks (aka 'piggy' banks).

Henry Mayhew's 82 letters in the London *Morning Chronicle* from October 1849 to December 1850 are considered to be the most penetrating survey of poverty in England in the 19th century. They show clearly that the working poor used various savings mechanisms, despite the fact that they could not always hold on to the money. A tailor: 'When I came to work for the cheap show-shop I had 5 pounds 10s. in the savings bank; now I have not a halfpenny in it. All I had saved went little by little to keep me and my family...'. A boot-maker: 'I had my L100 in the Four per Cents for a long time (I lent it to friend afterwards), and from L40 to L50 in the savings bank'.

In the 19th century, withdrawals from the wide array of financial systems for the poor – burial societies, building societies, cooperatives, penny savings banks, postal savings and so forth – were for medical crises, burials, plots of land, retirement, wedding expenses and so on, similar to what poor people in today's developing counties need cash for. There is, however, no suggestion in the literature that these loans were used entrepreneurially (Gosden, 1974).

There were also, of course, pawnbrokers, as evidenced by another of Mayhew's reports. The wife of a painter: "'I was obliged to sell a dish this morning, sir," said the woman, "to get the only meal of bread we have had to-day, and how we are to get another loaf I do not know"'.

Whether or not the poor were improvident is not the issue of this paper. Of issue is the fact that savings banks and other formal thrift-based financial service institutions often felt the need to teach the value of savings to the poor. More important, the poor who were the objects of these lessons were 'working poor', they had income, but they needed ways (or others thought they needed ways) to put some of that income away for a 'rainy day'. It is significant that these early systems also instituted insurance programmes, both for health and for life. Again, sequence is instructive here, since in the current microfinance movement, *everything seems to have been done the other way around.* The movement began almost exclusively with credit, then much later (and not always with enthusiasm) began to talk about savings, and only now are we beginning to hear talk about other services such as insurance.

Access by the poor to formal credit follows savings and is for consumption

It is not really until the early 20th century that we begin to see a mixing of savings and credit. For example, in 1901 Alphonse Desjardins imported the German credit union model to Quebec and created the Caisse Populaire de Levis. In part through ties with French–Canadians in New England, Desjardins imported the model to New Hampshire in 1909 – this was the first credit union in the USA. By 1925, 26 states had passed credit union legislation.[1]

When mass access to formal credit comes on the scene, it is for *consumption*. In 1910 the first 'Morris Plan Thrift' was established in the USA. These Morris Plan banks were perhaps the first true microcredit precursors since they were aimed at low- and middle-income households and were specifically designed to reduce the power of the moneylender or 'loan shark'. Moreover, they used the concept of joint liability. A loan applicant did not have to put up collateral, but had to have two co-signers who knew the applicant and these two people had to have similar earning power (that is, be of the same economic class). But they were not guarantors of the applicant's loan – rather they were guarantors of his character. This solved the 'asymmetrical information problem' and reduced transaction costs. It is significant that almost all borrowers were employed, that is they were wage earners, and that by 1910, the USA was already heavily industrialized. By 1931 there were Morris Plan lending institutions in 142 cities with an annual loan volume of US$220 million (Phillips and Mushinsky, 2001). Again, the sequence seems to have been, first economic development, then access by the poor to formal savings institutions, and then wider access to credit for consumption.

Morris Plan institutions were largely tied to consumption 'needs', and they need to be seen in the economic development context of the time. Until the end of the 19th century most people in the USA made their living on the land, with a growing number working in industry. There was no appreciable 'middle class' – there were farmers, merchants and traders, working people, and the rich (who were increasingly big-business related.)

Farmers, who were poor in cash terms, often accessed their inputs through supplier credit, and wage-income workers also managed their cash flow through forms of supplier credit (by running up 'tabs' at a local grocery, for example). A great deal of exchange was still in the form of barter. What propelled the formal credit institutions was a combination of growing industrial productivity and technological invention, as well as the progressive movement associated with Theodore Roosevelt, which gave rise to a consciousness of the 'little man'. It was under the first three US presidents of the 20th century (Roosevelt, Taft and Wilson) that all the *formal* innovations in democratizing credit access for the 'little man' took place – credit unions, Morris Plan banks and instalment plan purchasing.

But the 'little man' was not expected to start a little business. If he was not a farmer, he was expected to, and did, work for wages, and to borrow money to buy the things that he didn't absolutely 'need' – consumer goods. In short, the 'little man', for whom mass credit was designed, was already a product of the rise of wage labour, a product of the first fruits of industrialization, which was in effect the west's form of economic development. His role was not as a direct producer of economic growth, but as a consumer of its fruits.

In the late 1920s, President Hoover set up a 'committee on recent economic changes', whose report (with the same title) came out in 1929. It noted that: 'We have long since lost all fear concerning our food supply and so we no longer look on food as a luxury… Our wants have ranged more widely and we now demand a broad list of goods and service which come under the category of "optional purchases"' (quoted in Sklar, 1992).

As economic historian Martin Sklar points out (Sklar, 1992): 'Insatiable as the appetite for goods and services may have become, however, effective consumer purchasing power proved persistently insufficient to satisfy it, and at any rate, production capacity continuously out ran effective market demand'. Sklar is among those who believe that instalment and other forms of consumer credit took off in the 1920s to enable working and lower income Americans to buy new things, and his belief is substantiated today in the fascinating marriage of banking and retailing exemplified by Elektra stores in Mexico. Elektra has already opened branches of Banco Azteca inside its stores to enable the poor to buy bigger ticket items. The system is based on encouraging savings accounts and a cadre of inspectors who visit a client's home to see whether their standard of living matches what was stated on their application. Wal-Mart Mexico is planning a similar system.

Informal credit systems were complex and about consumption smoothing

As opposed to formal credit systems that developed in relation to the growth of consumption (and are relatively recent historically), *informal* credit systems probably go back to the beginnings of the use of money and to wherever there were shortages or crises. Such systems were about 'making ends meet' when there were few state-supplied safety nets or risk mitigation mechanisms. Poor people were on their own, and with few means to meet medical or other crises. There was also the hidden, yet apparently chronic, problem of meagre earnings being diverted by men into alcohol or gambling – a pervasive problem in today's developing countries and one of the reasons behind the emphasis on targeting women borrowers in many microcredit projects. Thus, as is the case in today's poor countries, a 'cash-flow crisis' could occur weekly, or whenever a pay packet arrived home depleted or empty.

Mutual aid clubs of various kinds existed early on the UK, and people moved into and out of them as a need arose, usually for a (relatively large) lump sum, or sometimes for cash-flow purposes. Here, again from Mayhew's interviews with London's working poor in the mid-19th century, is a boot-maker, whose earnings have been hit by growing imports of French leather goods: 'Why, sir, if it goes on this way, the workhouse stares us in the face. But the intention we have is to into a club this winter [*a form of rotating savings and credit association, or in today's microfinance parlance, a ROSCA*], and raise funds to emigrate to America' (Thompson and Yeo, 1971).

In working class Britain in the first decades of the 20th century there was a great variety of informal credit options, as there was in the USA. A recent oral history project involving Belfast workers whose recollections go back to the 1930s is striking: 'Historically most working-class families were familiar with one or more of a list of credit suppliers which included the corner-shop 'tick' [in US parlance 'tab'], credit drapers, pawnbrokers, tallymen, check traders, mail order agents, neighborhood money lenders, and hire–purchase [instalment plan] traders' (O'Connell, 2004).

Moreover, credit strategies were equally diverse and multiple. No source of credit was a preferred source. In post-war Belfast, people still resorted to moneylenders when they reached their credit limits with the credit union. And strategies among networks of friends, acquaintances and relatives were not only innovative but complex in their motivation. Altruism and social ties, and at the same time, profit maximizing and self-interest were all involved. O'Connell talks about a co-op store in Belfast that many community members belonged to because they could buy on credit and get a dividend each quarter as long as their credit was paid in full before the dividend date (called the 'Co-Quarter'). There was a practice of lending out co-op membership books to friends, neighbours and relatives that allowed them to buy goods on credit from the Co-op and repay the 'book's' owner when the co-quarter was due. In this way the owner of the 'book' received a larger dividend because of the increased purchase volume, which was also effectively a form of interest on the loan of the 'book'.

Informal credit systems could also be gender-specific. There were systems for women (based on neighbourhoods and streets within them) and informal credit systems for men based on their particular workplace. These were in effect common bond arrangements with both an economic and (in today's terminology) 'social capital' function.

But again, as with formal credit, all these 'little people' who had access to consumer credit were either savers first and/or wage earners. They were not microentrepreneurs nor did they use their credit to start businesses or as working capital. Consumption and its variants were what credit accessibility was about.

The USA today: Democratized credit is still about consumption

The US Federal Reserve has kept data on outstanding US consumer credit since February 1943, at which time it totalled US$6.577 billion. This was entirely non-revolving credit (auto loans, instalment plans and so on) and did not include mortgages. Credit cards (it is almost hard to recall this) were not in widespread use until the 1960s and this is reflected in the fact that the Federal Reserve did not record credit card debt until January 1968, when the figure (under the heading of revolving credit) was US$1,316 billions. By June 2006, this figure had increased more than six hundred fold, to US$820,650 billion, while total consumer credit had reached US$2,186 trillion, having crossed the US$1 trillion threshold in January 1995.

By mid-2006 there were approximately 1.2 billion credit cards in the hands of the American consumer, a number equal to four cards for every single person (woman, man and child) in the USA. It is hard to imagine a greater democratization of credit, but it is critical to acknowledge that this is largely consumption credit, and as a result of this easy 'credit for everybody', approximately half of all credit card holders in the USA do not pay off their balance every month, and are thus in perpetual debt (we will leave aside how such a situation would look if the banker's risk assessment tool of 'PAR-30' – portfolio-at-risk over 30 days in arrears – were applied).

Finally, the savings rate of the USA reached 0 per cent in mid-2005, the lowest rate since 1933 in the depths of the Great Depression. While the longer term consequences of this phenomenon are still unknown (the USA is at best barely two generations into the phenomenon), it is fairly easy to imagine the ramifications of easy consumer credit and low savings, not just in economic, but in social and cultural terms (for example, the effect of instant gratification through credit cards on everything from community values to personal character to class consciousness). Surely this state of affairs is not what Muhammad Yunus envisions when he says that credit is a human right.

Conclusion

History seems to be telling us that credit and savings services and their role in development have not really changed. The average poor person in the past (and today) is not an entrepreneur and when he or she has access to credit it is largely for consumption or cash-flow smoothing. The average entrepreneur prefers to start with informal credit or savings rather than formal credit. The best financial services for poor or low-income people are savings-based, which in their pure form do not need outside financial help, or for that matter the large microfinance industry that has evolved.

Indeed, in the microfinance world of today, it is increasingly understood that savings are the basis also for the microfinance institution's ultimate health. 'The MFIs that favour savings argue that the self-sustaining threshold is more surely, and in the end more rapidly, reached when the investment cycle is fully financed from the savings of its members' (Gélinas, 1998).

The case of Bank Rakyat Indonesia's Unit Desa system is a good example of a major microfinance success that used hardly any outside resources as a basis for the financial corpus. There are other, less well known, MFIs such as India's Community Development Foundation based on member 'thrift societies' that receive no help from the microfinance industry.

Most important, history seems to be telling us clearly that economic development and its consequent massive poverty reduction did not depend on microcredit being made more accessible for income production or asset acquisition by the poor. Instead, it was the process of development that created jobs, which in turn made the working poor an attractive target for financial services, beginning with savings, and then moving towards consumption so that the goods produced would have a wider market.

While the same exact sequence does not necessarily apply in today's different world, and some key parameters have changed dramatically – for example, technology and automation will inevitably reduce the labour intensiveness of industry even in the poorest countries – there is no compelling reason to think that the underlying dynamic of development does not still apply. As the late British development economist, Peter Bauer, has said: 'To have capital is the result of economic achievement, not its precondition' (Bauer, 1991).

Capital, especially the lending of it, is after all what most of microfinance is about. And we in the microfinance movement have indeed assumed that it *is* a precondition of development. If it is not, and history seems strongly to suggest as much, we need radically to reduce our expectations about microcredit, and thus better align ourselves with reality.

Note

1   Today there are 8853 Credit Unions in the USA with over 87 million members and US$700 billion on deposit, according to the New York State Credit Union League and Affiliates website: www.nyscul.org/News/factsheet.htm

References

Alam, I. (2006) 'Sarrafs (Bankers) in the Mughal Empire', paper given at Session 106, XIV International Economic History Congress, Helsinki.

Alborn, T. (n.d.) 'The Thrift Wars: Savings Banks and Life Assurance in Victorian Britain', unpublished paper, Lehman College, City University of New York, New York.

Bairoch, P. (1992) *Le Tiers-Monde dans l'impasse, Le Demarrage économique de 18ème au 20ème siècle*, Gallimard, Paris.

Bauer, P. (1991) *The Development Frontier: Essays in Applied Economics*, Harvard University Press, Cambridge, MA.

Baum, L. (2005) 'The year of microcredit', *Human News*, 29, September, http://ideaexplore.net/news/050929.html

Geertz, C. (1963) *Peddlers and Princes*, University of Chicago Press, Chicago.

Gélinas, J. B. (1998) *Freedom from Debt: The Reappropriation of Development Through Financial Self-reliance*, Zed Books, London.

Gosden, P. H. J. H. (1974) *Self-Help: Voluntary Associations in 19th Century Britain*, Barnes and Noble, New York.

Haythornthwaite, J. A. (1993) *Scotland in the nineteenth century, an analytical bibliography of material relation to Scotland in parliamentary papers, 1800–1900*, Scolar Press, Aldershot.

Helms, B. (2006) *Access for All, Building Inclusive Financial Systems*, CGAP, World Bank, Washington DC.

Landes, D. S. (1969) *The Unbound Prometheus: Technological Change and Industrial Development in Western Europe from 1750 to the Present*, Cambridge University Press, Cambridge.

O'Connell, S. (2004) 'Credit, Class and Community: Working Class Belfast 1930–2000', research paper, School of History and International Affairs, University of Ulster, Belfast.

Phillips, R. J. and Mushinsky, D. (2001) 'The Role of Morris Plan Lending Institutions in Expanding Consumer Micro credit in the United States', research paper, Colorado State University, Fort Collins.

Reynolds, P. D., Hay, M., Bygrave, W. D, Camp, S. M. and Autio, E. (2000) *Global Entrepreneurship Monitor – 2000 Executive Report*, Kauffman Center for Entrepreneurial Leadership, Babson College, London Business School and Ernst & Young, London.

Sklar, M. J. (1992) *The United States as a Developing Country*, Cambridge University Press, Cambridge.

Thompson, E. P. and Yeo, E. (1971) *The Unknown Mayhew*, Pantheon Books, New York.

CHAPTER SIXTEEN

A practitioner's view of the challenges facing NGO-based microfinance in Bangladesh[1]

S. M. Rahman

Abstract

In Bangladesh, NGO MFIs dominate microfinance. The chapter notes a number of problems and challenges in the sector that suggest microfinance in Bangladesh has yet to emerge as a solid financial discipline. Among the problems noted are: increasing numbers of non-poor people as microfinance clients; high interest rates; a lack of a scientific basis for loan pricing; non-productive loan use (those who borrow do not necessarily use the money for the purposes stated on the papers); NGO MFIs generally not interested in giving medium- or long-term loans to clients; client satisfaction largely ignored; continued dominance of moneylenders in rural financial markets; and weak governance and management, all of which continue to characterize most microfinance NGOs in Bangladesh.

Introduction

In Bangladesh NGOs emerged at a fast rate after 1972, with microcredit becoming an offshoot of their social development activities. In 1985 only 13 NGOs were doing microcredit. The figure rose to 59 in 1990. The number of NGO MFIs climbed to 301 by 1995 (CDF, 2001) and began to accelerate – about 2,000 NGOs are now operating in Bangladesh (World Bank, 2006), and it is likely that all are involved in microfinance in one way or another.

The robust growth of NGO-based MFIs has occurred due to a number of factors. First, a proven methodology, the Grameen Bank's 'classic' approach, was ready to hand. With modifications, many NGOs began to follow this approach. Second, in 1990 the Palli Karma-Sahayak Foundation was set up by the government as an apex organization to provide funds to microcredit programmes. It is the largest wholesaler of loan funds in the country, supplying credit to more than 200 NGOs. The formation of PKSF spurred the sector and kindled hopes in many NGOs. Third, other donor funding was easily available.

Most NGO MFI practitioners generally tend to view microfinance as a social development activity, overlooking its commercial aspect. The term commercialization to many people carries a negative connotation equated with exploiting the poor. This is in contrast with the notion around the globe where many microfinance practitioners are increasingly using the term commercialization to mean the application of market-based principles to microfinance. Yet donor money in the sector is waning rapidly and NGO MFIs will need to access the banking sector.

This is just one thing that will need to change. Again, the NGO MFIs may need to follow the lead of the Grameen Bank. For example, in the past, Grameen Bank used to deduct 5 per cent of the client's loan as a tax to be kept in the group fund, enforcing the group guarantee for securing loans and repayments. The clients appeared to dislike the Grameen classic system (GCS). This is manifest in the words of Prof. Yunus:

> In Grameen Bank II, gone are the general loans, seasonal loans, family loans; gone is the group fund; gone is the branch-wise loan ceiling; gone is the fixed size weekly installment; gone is the rule to borrow every time for one whole year, when the borrower needed the loan only for three months; gone is the high-level tension among the field staff and the borrowers trying to steer away from the dreadful event of a borrower turning into a defaulter, even when she is still repaying; and gone are many other familiar features of Grameen Classic System. (Yunus, 2002).

Since 2000, with the introduction of the Grameen generalized system (GGS), things have changed.

Some problematic issues

Poor and non-poor clients

Women make up 95 per cent of the total microfinance clientele population (CDF, 2004). While the NGO MFIs originally intended to focus on the poor, nowadays they have gone beyond the poor. About 40 per cent of total microfinance clients in the NGO-led industry are non-poor (Zohir, 2001). BRAC is known to have 30 per cent moderate non-poor among its total clientele (BRAC, 2005). Also a significant number of women hand their loans over to their husbands. Accordingly many savings and loan instalment payments are also made by husbands. It appears that microfinance has a two-tier clientele system, where women are the strategic clients to deal with. Basically the loan is intended for the household and the woman is the conduit for channeling the loan. In many cases, group leaders or centre chiefs are the most privileged clients and are provided with much bigger loans and other facilities. They tend to dominate the rank and file clients, acting almost as an unofficial police force of the MFIs. Such group leaders constitute about 13.5 per cent of the clientele population (Zohir, 2001).

Loan use

Loans from the MFI sector carry a relatively high rate of interest (at least 25 per cent) compared with the rates in the banking sector. The effective rate will be higher if other costs are figured in. Unless this money is used in a productive and profitable way, there will be few tangible benefits for the borrowers; instead indebtedness will occur faster. But borrowers do not necessarily use the money for the purposes stated on the loan application papers. About a quarter of the money is spent on meeting household consumption needs, while a significant proportion finds its way into the land rental/mortgage market. Also part of the money is used for repaying past debt. The pace of poverty reduction with microfinance is arguably slow. This is because poverty reduction does not hinge only on microfinance. It depends on macro economic interventions, global trade liberalization and so on. Between 1991–92 and 2000, the incidence of national poverty declined from 58.8 per cent to 49.8 per cent, indicating a modest reduction of 1 per cent per year (Ministry of Finance, 2003). The earlier belief was that the microcredit would meet the requirements of the working capital of the poor for production purposes. This appears not to have been the case.

Recent research commissioned by CARE Bangladesh is revealing (CARE, 2006). Discussions with a wide spectrum of clients suggest that not more than 50 per cent of loans are being productively used in an activity that will produce earnings. Initially loans are used for consumption, and for meeting education and medical costs. Some loans are used for asset creation in terms of buying land, house construction and repairing. In some cases, loans are fully used in consumption. There is no doubt that the loan money is perceived as useful but clearly a fair chunk of it has no earning power and is thus an increased liability to the borrower. The clients like using the loans as per their convenience and choice. They have a hierarchy of needs and they fulfill these needs step by step. As time passes, the clients need more money than an NGO MFI can provide. The clients are found flocking furtively to many NGO MFIs to optimize their credit needs. Surprisingly, some clients are also doing a syndicate loan business whereby they borrow from one or more NGO MFIs and then lend it to others at a high rate of interest.

Unclear laws on deposit taking for NGO MFIs

As per the central bank directive, NGO MFIs cannot take deposits from the general public. They can take deposits from their poor clients, however, and many MFIs are still taking deposits from better-off people. The newly passed Microfinance Act 2006 contains basically the same distinction between the general public and poor clients. But the question arises: are not poor clients part of the general public? Can less poor clients be differentiated from poor clients, and from the general public? Is this kind of separation possible in a population like that of Bangladesh?

NGO MFIs remain reluctant to give long-term loans

NGO MFIs in general are not interested in giving medium- or long-term loans to their clients. The reasons are delayed returns and inadequate resources. Short-term loans can be recycled and earn more profit for the MFI. Long-term loans do not guarantee this prospect. Housing loans are good examples of long-term loans where there is no significant MFI financing in Bangladesh, except the Grameen Bank who have financed more than 600,000 clients for this purpose. A few, however, are doing it with their own resources charging at least 30 per cent interest.

Differentiated products for microenterprise clients and special staff skills are lacking

Those loans that can be said to be genuinely enterprise-related do not go to poor households but to those who are instead classed as 'vulnerable non-poor'. These clients tend to take loans 5 to 40 times larger than a normal microcredit borrower. The loan period for microcredit is generally 12 months (actually 45–46 weeks for financial transactions). This loan period is the same for both enterprise and non-enterprise clients. There are very few NGO MFIs where the loan period for a microenterprise is more than a year. Except for loan size, most NGO MFIs do not have different treatment for different types of clients in terms of loan period, repayment mode, repayment interval, rate of interest or technical support. This is also the case for loans to graduates, which are not differentiated from loans to the poorest or loans to enterprises (McKennie and Rahman, 2003).

Borrowers not treated as customers

There is no customer orientation in much of Bangladeshi microfinance. Many NGO MFIs are now more engrossed in buying fixed assets to safeguard their future than lending money to the clients. The clients' perspective is mainly ignored. Many field workers think they are giving privileges to the clients rather than selling services to them. There is no culture of customer service. In Bangladesh, many NGO MFI staff members still see the clients as 'beneficiaries'. They were 'beneficiaries' a long time ago when they used to get grants from community development organizations – many of which transformed into NGO MFIs. They are now the customers of these same NGO MFIs and are buying services at a price. They should be treated as customers and be duly respected. The field workers often do not explain the products and rules to them clearly and instead keep them confused.

Joint liability (group guarantee) is still widely used

The concept of joint liability sprang from the GCS. But based on their practical experience, the GGS has abandoned the joint liability requirement. Most NGO MFIs, however, continue to follow joint liability.

Loan rescheduling is generally not allowed

Except for the Grameen Bank, there is no provision in Bangladeshi microfinance for rescheduling loans in the case of clients who have repayment difficulties. Yet given Bangladesh's calamity prone location, it is not reasonable to expect all clients to keep to agreed repayment schedules. Tidal surges, cyclones and floods haunt the country every year. When these occur NGO MFIs allow instalments to be kept pending for two or three months at best. But this does not help the clients much. Under the circumstances, they need a longer period during which they can get on their feet and resume normal work after such devastation.

Savings rules often make withdrawal difficult

Despite most NGO MFIs' claim that clients can withdraw savings whenever necessary, in most cases, savings from mandatory savings accounts cannot be withdrawn until the client ceases membership or the client dies. Clients are not generally aware of the often complex rules. The credit staff do not apprise and update them. One client I met remarked, 'We keep savings for meeting our needs and crises. Savings is not a showpiece just to see and not to use'. Another client said, 'My son is down with serious fever for a month. I cannot take him to the hospital. I badly need money now but I cannot use my own savings kept with the MFI. They do not allow savings withdrawal. What is the use of staying in this organization then?'.

Agreed loan amounts are often reduced by complicated deductions and fees

In most NGO MFIs, the clients do not get the exact amount of the loan they applied for. Some NGO MFIs, including the large ones, set aside 5 per cent of the loan amount in the client's savings account. Clients cannot normally withdraw this amount. The MFIs give the money as a loan, charge 30 per cent interest and give the clients 6 per cent on savings. Note that Grameen Bank now does not impose any group tax (which was 5 per cent earlier and non-refundable). Under the GGS, a loan is still being cut at the rate of 5 per cent but the clients will eventually get this amount. What is the difference then? Now a 2.5 per cent cut from the loan goes to the client's personal savings. The savings can be withdrawn. Another 2.5 per cent cut goes to her special savings account (this can be partially withdrawn after three years). This policy helps the bank to earn 20 per cent using the savings, while it will be paying 8.5 per cent to the clients. BRAC has a similar practice, where it slashes 5 per cent from the loans and transfers it into the client's savings account, which the client cannot fall back upon when necessary.

NGO MFIs, including some large ones, sometimes give loans in kind, for example, fish fingerlings, chicks, seeds, saplings and so on. The clients are forced to take these, which they otherwise could have bought from the open market at competitive prices at their own choosing. This economic freedom has been compromised by the MFIs.

There is no interest reduction for loan prepayment

In the NGO-based microfinance industry in Bangladesh, loan prepayment is discouraged. When loans are prepaid ahead of the due date, no interest relief is provided to the clients. The clients say they have to take loans on high interest from the MFIs in view of hard realities. Sometimes they have good cash flow and are willing to make advance payment but the NGO MFIs will not allow this and the debt burden cannot be reduced as it can with banks. If one client takes a loan today and offers to repay the entire loan the next day, the client has to repay the total loan along with the whole year's interest, reckoned on a flat rate system.

Lending rate calculation methods are sometimes misleading

Many NGO MFIs use the flat rate system, which is not easily understandable by the clients. A 15 per cent flat rate interest is equivalent to about a 30 per cent rate on a declining balance system used by banks. Not only the clients but even educated people sometimes have trouble understanding this system. The problem is that the flat rate gives an impression of a lower rate than it actually is. This is misleading and non-transparent.

Loan pricing is not carefully thought out

Both for savings and for credit products, some NGO MFIs do not seem to have any scientific basis for pricing. They do it mostly on the basis of rule of thumb and/or follow what others are doing. This is encouraged by the fact that the spread between savings and loans can be substantial. On average, the NGO MFIs provide 6 per cent interest on savings (at times less or even nothing) and charge 25–30 per cent interest on loans (sometimes more). They know that they have a hefty margin of safety. The cost of operations, cost of funds, loan loss provision, inflation and so on, are hardly taken into account. Since they are not worried, they tend to merrily follow the going prices.

The PKSF-funded NGO MFIs, for example, charge interest at 25 per cent for the moderate poor and 20 per cent for the hard-core or ultra poor clients. These rates are fixed by PKSF for its partner MFIs, and funds are denied if they step out of line. There being a monopoly in the wholesaling of lending funds, the partner NGO MFIs of PKSF have no choice. The grassroots clients regard the rate of interest as too high. They say it is difficult for them to make profits with such high interest rates. Many say it gobbles all of their income, creating difficulties for loan repayment. The chairman of PKSF told a seminar, entitled 'International Seminar on Attacking Poverty With Microcredit' organized by PKSF in 2003, that the interest rate of microcredit is very high (Uddin, 2003). The political leadership both in the government and opposition are always vociferous and critical of the prevailing lending rate. The Asian Development Bank defends high microcredit interest rates on the grounds of high costs (Fernando, 2006).

Microinsurance products are grossly unpopular

Microinsurance appears under various names and premiums are collected in different modes. There are two kinds of insurance: loan insurance and health insurance. The premium is generally related to the loan amount and the loan period. Some NGO MFIs charge an equal fee, say Tk30 (US$0.50) for all clients. There are some who charge two or three types of one-time insurance fees with varying benefits. The benefits generally cover the waiver of the outstanding loans. The insured client's savings are also returned to the nominee. Health insurance is also offered by some NGO MFIs. Those providing this facility charge a percentage against the loan or a specified fee. Those who take higher loans have to pay a larger premium compared to others.

To many clients these insurance practices are exploitive, if not outright shady; in the guise of insurance, MFIs are seen as exacting money from their clients for keeps. Clients argue that insurance should be for a long term, ranging from 8–10 years instead of one year, for which they will pay an agreed affordable premium. After the stipulated period, they should get back all the money with interest they had deposited. They are of the view that in case the client dies, the nominee will get the claims as per insurance policy, and that the premium should have nothing to do with loan amount. Most clients are resentful of current insurance practices. Some clients, however, like the practice of a few NGO MFIs that requires them to pay a small insurance fee (not related to the loan) each time they take a loan, which they promise to return with interest after a certain number of years. One client I met in a group discussion sprang to her feet and said, 'I will not die this year and hopefully even not in the next year; I do not need any insurance. I am not a captive client of the MFI. I must have freedom to exercise my choice and judgement. Insurance should be optional and not enforced – I may take or may not take it. I am not stupid. If I think it will benefit me, I will buy insurance'.

Multiple borrowing by clients

Client overlap is quite well known in the microfinance industry worldwide. In Bangladesh the average overlap rate is 33 per cent (PKSF, 2004). Many NGO MFIs feel that as long as the clients can pay off their loans, they have no reason to worry about this. The clients' view is that a single NGO MFI cannot usually meet their financial requirements, failing which, they approach many lenders to meet their credit needs.

Unauthorized use of savings to pay loan instalments

In the microfinance industry, the practice of taking clients' savings to pay loan instalments is very rare, even when the clients are in dire straits. But some NGO MFIs do just this without the knowledge and consent of the clients. ASA, a leading MFI, is alleged to be indulging in such practices to ensure a high loan recovery rate. When this happens the client is plunged into an awful plight. They are compelled to borrow from other sources exacerbating the indebtedness further. In a bank, savings are safeguarded: under no circumstances will the savings of a client be used to adjust a loan repayment without the client's concurrence.

Use of moneylenders by poor borrowers continues

Even after the great rise of NGO MFIs, moneylenders still reign, especially in rural financial markets. No significant evidence has been found that moneylenders' businesses have been affected by the emergence of NGO MFIs (Choudhury, 2000). A BIDS study reveals that 40 per cent of MFI borrowers borrow from informal sources. The study argues that one plausible explanation may be that eligible borrowers tend to supplement their loans from the MFIs since those amounts are small (BIDS, 1999). In spite of increased outreach, NGO MFIs have not been able to substitute for the informal sector (Sinha and Matin, 1998). The informal sector continues to be one of the most important sources of credit for the rural poor and is widely perceived to function effectively with low defaults and low transaction costs, while catering to the large number of the poor who remain outside the poor-based lending programmes of different organizations (World Bank, 1996). Moreover, moneylenders are no longer a particular professional group – they comprise a cross section of rural and urban society and include shopkeepers, traders, big farmers and local businessmen.

Microfinance personnel are poorly paid

The partner organizations of PKSF have been found to spend 50–60 per cent of interest income for administrative purpose (salary and others), which amounts to 70–80 per cent of total expenditure (PKSF, 2003). The expenditure on administrative cost is high while the salary of field workers is not only low but also the composition of salary is unsatisfactory. The job satisfaction of the credit staff is low compared to their workload and compensation package. The difference in salary between the CEO and the field workers is high. The credit staff, who are the foot soldiers of microfinance's effort to fight poverty, are not well paid. One result of this is occasional fraud.

Most NGO MFIs, except BRAC, take a form of bond security from those staff whose jobs involve financial transactions, in the range of Tk5,000–10,000 (US$77–154). This money is kept in the banks either as a long-term fixed deposit or used in the revolving microfinance loan fund. The staff members get the money along with simple interest of around 5 per cent when they leave the organization. This conveys the message that the staff are not trusted. Moreover, there is a practice of some NGO MFIs placing eye-catching advertisements in the national newspapers asking for job applicants to include a bank draft of Tk100–200 (US$1.50 – 3.00). They are deluged with applications and thus millions of taka are siphoned off from job seekers unfairly.

NGO MFIs are quasi-banking institutions

Operationally, NGO MFIs are quasi-banks in that they deal with deposits and loans. Ultimately many small and mid-level NGO MFIs will leave the scene, due to aggressive competition and a growing inability to match clients' demands. Ingrained with a social mission, it is difficult for the NGO MFIs to think of themselves as banks and look at this issue. These institutions need immediate transformation (Fernando, 2004).

Governance in NGO MFIs is abysmally weak

Weak governance and management characterize most microfinance NGOs in Bangladesh. NGO MFI boards are often nothing more than rubber stamps (Rahman, 1999). It is usual to find friends, close relatives and others on the boards. Many are mere onlookers and remain reticent on important issues, while others support the CEO's every move. The chief executives are said to overpower the boards. Activities of the organizations are conducted mostly on their own whims and decisions. If the chairman of a bank is dismissed, the bank's work continues. The NGO MFIs have a fragile institutional structure, highly dependent on persons rather than systems. In the past, the donors (including PKSF) had pumped huge funds into NGO MFIs in terms of seed capital, capacity development and operational costs. But they have overlooked the issue of governance. They have invested a lot in the larger NGO MFIs, making the whole industry lopsided. Proshika (one large NGO) has meanwhile turned into a risky client of PKSF following its management problems. The savings of its clients are already at risk.

Ownership structure is lacking

There is no clear ownership in the NGO-led microfinance sector. Profits, if any, made out of operations do not go to anybody's pocket. These MFIs are not liable for any loss. The Grameen Bank is a for-profit organization, but it has not been able to pay any dividend to its clients for more than 20 years. What is the meaning of such ownership then? Effectively, both the NGO MFI clients and the Grameen Bank clients are the same. The grants and low cost money acquired by the NGO MFIs have become the sole capital of the MFIs making them the masters of these resources. The benefits to the poor are temporary while those to the MFIs are permanent. The NGO MFI leaders have become quasi-proprietors turning their organizations almost into proprietary concerns.

Taxation is not welcome in the sector

Bangladesh's NGO MFI microfinance programmes are exempted from taxation. But the issue of tax payment is being discussed at the government level. The finance minister of Bangladesh said recently that NGO MFIs should pay income taxes, but the matter remains stalled. Of late, banks are coming progressively into microfinance. Their operations are taxed. The Grameen Bank is supposed to pay income tax but they have managed to avoid paying any taxes. Yet tax payment is an indicator of the strength of an institution. Grameen's non-payment indicates that the bank has not yet come to be at a par with commercial banks, though more than two decades have elapsed since its birth. But most NGO MFIs have an antipathy to paying taxes. PKSF, a government supported microfinance wholesaler, has got an exemption from the National Board of Revenue of the government. PKSF is sitting on huge idle funds (PKSF, 2005). Payment of taxes would have reduced its idle money and enhanced its efficiency.

Conclusion

Overall the pace of poverty reduction in Bangladesh is slow (about 1 per cent of people are being lifted out of poverty each year). Yet most NGO MFIs continue to believe that millions of microfinance clients run productive enterprises. This is a far-fetched idea. The rural poor remain largely disconnected from the dynamic sectors of the market, particularly those where there is scope for benefiting from the opportunities provided by globalization (Sobhan, 2001). The fast growing sectors of economic activity tend to be located within the urban economy where the principal agents of production control the corporate assets. In the rural economy, the major part of the profits also accrues to those classes. The poor are left with very little opportunity for sharing in the opportunities provided by the market economy for value addition to their labours (Sobhan, 2001).

Money cannot always beget money unless the borrowers have sufficient skill and knowledge to leverage that money. A fair chunk of the total loan portfolio in the Bangladesh microfinance industry does not generate any income, but rather increases clients' liability. Microfinance exacerbates the poverty of those who do not have other income and cannot productively use the loans. The number of such people is many but we hear little about them. Even though microfinance may meet many varied and immediate needs of many people, meeting those needs does not mean that microfinance is lifting them out of poverty. The poverty fighting power of microfinance is limited.

Microfinance is unnecessarily being made complex, while it is possible to keep it simple. The products and services should be simple and understandable with no extra fees and no hidden exploitation. Repayment must depend on more than NGO MFI credit workers sitting at the clients' homes for hours, day in, day out, not budging until they collect. Interest rates and their mode of calculation should be clear. Insurance should not be used by NGO MFIs as an alternative tool for getting more money from clients. The MFIs say they charge lower interest than moneylenders. But they rarely compare themselves with the formal banking system. The NGO MFIs should not take advantage of their clients' innocence and illiteracy.

A poor client goes to an MFI branch with a big hope to take a loan. But she returns home with less money than what was agreed. If it is the Grameen Bank, she gets 5 per cent less (this goes to two of the savings accounts of the clients), if it is BRAC, 5 per cent is chopped off (it goes to a savings account where it normally cannot be withdrawn), if it is other MFIs, 1–3.5 per cent is docked as insurance payments. The client should get the sum that has been sanctioned.

Microfinance is not a grocery business and should not be mushrooming everywhere. Its expansion should be controlled. Three mega institutions (Grameen Bank, BRAC and ASA) dominate the microfinance industry, each with more than six million clients – more than the total population of many small countries in the world. To stay in the market, NGO-based MFIs will have to be transformed into some bank-like form, authorized to take deposits from the public. Hundreds of NGO MFIs cannot be effectively regulated in Bangladesh. At best, 250 NGO MFIs would be more than enough for the country.

Creating more wholesale organizations, in addition to PKSF, may pave the way for meeting the increased demand of the clients and fostering sane competition in the market. The governments in the past are liable to a great extent for the oversight of the sector as well as the interest of the clients. A microfinance wholesaler such as PKSF, or a large retailer like Palli Daridro Bimochon Foundation (a self-governed non-bank financial institution created in 1999 by parliament for retailing microfinance) should be brought under the central bank's regulatory regime without delay. Both are currently viewed somewhat negatively by many in the field, and such a move would fortify such institutions and enable them to function efficiently within broader financial systems. Despite the huge proliferation of NGO MFIs, their clients continue to access informal sources at usurious rate. The MFIs' growth could not restrict the moneylenders. Their work goes on unabated.

Many things must change. Grameen Bank itself brought about sweeping changes in its system to get rid of the past wrongs. Until the NGO MFIs also change they will not be solid institutions with financial discipline and adequate systems and policies.

Note

1   The editors have included this somewhat informal personal view of the Bangladesh microfinance scene by a local insider in order to convey a sense of how microfinance is coming to be regarded in some quarters.

References

BIDS (1999) *BIDS Newsletter*, Bangladesh Institute of Development Studies, Dhaka.

BRAC (2005) *Microfinance Program: Expanding Opportunities, Securing Livelihoods*, BRAC, Dhaka.

CARE (2006) 'What the microfinance clients do with the loan money', INCOME III Project, *Microfina Newsletter*, Issue No. 18, August, CARE Bangladesh, Dhaka.

CDF (Credit and Development Forum) (2001), *Microfinance Statistics* 13, CDF, Dhaka.

CDF (2004) *Microfinance Statistics* 17, CDF, Dhaka.

Choudhury, T. A. (2000) *Growth and Implications of Money Lending by Monerylenders and Microfinance Program*, CDF, Dhaka.

Fernando, N. A. (2004) *Micro Success Story? Transformation of Non-government Organizations into Regulated Financial Institutions*, Asian Development Bank (ADB), Manila.

Fernando, N. A. (2006) *Understanding and Dealing with High Interest Rates on Microcredit, A Note to Policy Makers in the Asia and Pacific Region*, Asian Development Bank (ADB), Manila.

McKennie, F. T. and Rahman, S. M. (2003) *Financing Graduates and Micro-enterprises*, a review of microenterprises commissioned by the Joint Donor Group in Microfinance in Bangladesh, Dhaka.

Ministry of Finance (2003) *A National Strategy for Economic Growth, Poverty Reduction and Social Development*, Economic Relations Division (ERD), Ministry of Finance, Government of Bangladesh, Dhaka.

PKSF (2003) *Current Interest Rate and Financial Sustainability of PKSF's Partner Organizations*, Palli Karma-Sahayak Foundation, Dhaka.

PKSF (2004) *Maps on Microcredit in Upazilas*, Palli Karma-Sahayak Foundation, Dhaka.

PKSF (2005) *The Annual Report*, Palli Karma-Sahayak Foundation, Dhaka.

Rahman, S. M. (1999) *Microfinance Status and the Forthcoming Challenges: Microfinance in Bangladesh*, INISIA, Colombo.

Sinha, S. and Matin, I. (1998) 'Informal credit transactions of microcredit borrowers in rural Bangladesh', *IDS Bulletin* 29(4), University of Sussex, Brighton.

Sobhan, R. (2001) *Eradicating Rural Poverty: Moving from a Micro to Macro Policy Agenda*, IFAD/FAO/WFP Public Lecture Series on Rural Poverty Eradication, Centre For Policy Dialogue, Dhaka.

Uddin, J. (2003) *Current Interest Rate and Financial Sustainability of PKSF's Partner Organizations*, Palli Karma-Sahayak Foundation, Dhaka.

World Bank (1996) *Bangladesh Rural Finance: A Study Report of Agriculture and Natural Resources Division*, World Bank, Washington DC.

World Bank (2006) *Economics and Governance of Non-governmental Organizations in Bangladesh*, World Bank, Dhaka.

Yunus, M. (2002) *Grameen Bank II: Designed to Open New Possibilities*, Grameen Bank, Dhaka.

Zohir, S. (2001) *PKSF's Monitoring and Evaluation of MFIs*, Bangladesh Institute of Development Studies, Dhaka.

CHAPTER SEVENTEEN
De-industrialization and social disintegration in Bosnia

Milford Bateman

Abstract

The commercial microfinance model is increasingly seen by the international development community to be the most important poverty reduction and local development strategy in both developing and transition countries. While accepting that the model probably generates some short-term poverty reduction outcomes, this chapter argues that the short-run positive outcomes in Bosnia – a previously quite highly industrialized and technically sophisticated economy – are possibly swamped by negative longer-run impacts and trajectories, particularly in terms of material support for de-industrialization and the destruction of social capital. Overall, the commercial microfinance model seems to have worked against most of the core triggers that lie behind sustainable local economic and social development, and thus it is unlikely to be a factor in achieving sustainable poverty reduction. In Bosnia, as in other countries, the growing popularity of microfinance has therefore probably far more to do with its political and ideological serviceability in terms of underpinning key neoliberal imperatives, principally the desire to discredit state and collective intervention strategies and to increasingly recast community development and survival solely in terms of individual entrepreneurship.

Introduction

The commercial or 'new wave' microfinance model now constitutes the most important local strand of the neo-liberal political project that has uniformly shaped economic policy throughout developing countries since the early 1980s, and in the transition economies since 1990. With upwards of US$100 million of international funds channelled into establishing MFIs in Bosnia and Herzegovina (B&H) since 1996, the commercial microfinance model has been very deliberately positioned as the central policy component of its post-war poverty reduction and community-level reconstruction and development. Leading the way in B&H was the World Bank with its US$40 million Local Initiatives Project (LIP). Alongside LIP came a large number of other microfinance programmes involving other international agencies (EBRD, IFC, UNDP), bilateral bodies (KFW) and international NGOs (CARE). Importantly, almost all of the MFIs entering B&H chose to follow the market-driven operating rules now defined by the World Bank to be 'best practice' – this is to say that MFIs must above all else prioritize eventually becoming financially self-sustainable through 'earning their keep on the market'.

The international community almost immediately began to classify the microfinance model in B&H as one of the most impressive international examples of microfinance 'best practice'. The World Bank rapidly registered its LIP programme as its best development programme in the country, and possibly its best microfinance programme worldwide. Microfinance lobbying bodies, financially supported by the World Bank and (therefore) fully in agreement with its neoliberal policy perspective, such as the Warsaw-based Microfinance Centre (MFC), also began to pick up on and publicize the B&H experience right across the transition economies. And specifically with regard to the post-conflict reconstruction and development context, the very widespread feeling was that, as Nancy Barry of Women's World Banking put it: 'Any worn-torn country should look to Bosnia as a role model' (quoted in Dolan, 2005).

The aim of this chapter is to briefly examine the microfinance model in the case of post-conflict B&H. Critically examining the available evidence and trends in the supposedly 'best practice' case of B&H should help to begin to separate the reality from the hype and rapidly proliferating myths surrounding the supposedly awesome power of microfinance in both transition and developing countries alike.

Some background to the B&H economy

Following the end of the Second World War, the newly designated Socialist Federal Republic of Yugoslavia (SFRY), including the constituent Republic of B&H, immediately adopted a Soviet-style central planning model. For a number of reasons, the central planning model was abandoned in 1948. In its place came the system of 'worker self-management', a form of industrial democracy whereby each enterprise was turned over to its employees to be operated and managed in a broadly democratic fashion. Over the next two decades the Yugoslav economy boomed, becoming known as the Balkan 'Tiger' economy of its day. At the same time, the previously under-developed economy in the Republic of B&H also finally began to make significant progress.

By the 1980s the Republic of B&H economy comprised a mixture of many medium-sized and a small number of large socially-owned industrial units using modern technologies and able to export on a genuinely competitive basis to many countries, particularly to the Middle East. The share of export earnings from the four largest conglomerates based in B&H (Energoinvest, UNIS, Sipad and Hidrogradnja) accounted for up to 40 per cent of the Yugoslav total. At the industrial core of B&H was a very substantial military-industrial complex producing for the Yugoslav army and for export. B&H also had an agricultural sector composed of mainly small-scale family and semi-professional farming units that provided a high level of food self-sufficiency and important additional local income generating possibilities, since farmers could often combine their work on the land with paid work in the new modern factories springing up. B&H also possessed a growing privately-owned SME sector that was also in the process of beginning to react positively to new opportunities opening up in the 1980s.

The economy of B&H thus stood in a reasonably good position in the late 1980s to take advantage of the upcoming changes and likely advent of new technologies, innovations, investments and market opportunities. However, any sort of advance was very quickly brought to a halt by the break-up of the former Yugoslavia and the subsequent outbreak of conflict in 1992. A vicious civil war ensued for nearly four years, Europe's worst conflict since the Second World War. When a peace agreement was concluded in late 1995 with the signing of the Dayton Peace Agreement (hereafter 'Dayton'), the now independent B&H was in a pretty desperate state. Much of the infrastructure was destroyed, many factories abandoned, unemployment was endemic, poverty was at very high levels and inequality had risen dramatically. Immediately following Dayton, the international community set into motion a major reconstruction and development package. On a per capita basis the financial package offered to B&H was to prove to be in excess of the Marshall Plan that helped Western Europe successfully reconstruct after 1945. Along with this generous financial package came technical assistance from the World Bank, IMF and various other foreign economic advisory teams that helped the new B&H government unroll the standard neoliberal package of policy reforms.

In spite of some initial progress, however, it was becoming readily apparent by as early as 2000 that the B&H economy was actually failing to recover. Looking behind the statistical anomaly of ultra-rapid GDP growth in the first few years after 1996, it was found that very little *sustainable* economic development had actually taken place since Dayton. The international development community in B&H finally began to sit up and take notice. In 1999 the EU/Bosnia-Herzegovina Consultative Task Force, a policy coordinating body established in June 1998 by the Council of the European Union, convened a working group to develop an urgent industrial policy response to the worsening situation. It was particularly worried about the rapid decline of the existing industrial sector and the collapse of the associated institutional fabric. Serious concern was expressed about the almost complete lack of new private industrial SMEs since Dayton. Local industrial policies had actually been emphasized by local experts for a long time before and after 1995, the Consultative Task Force noted, and also repeatedly emphasized by many international analysts at the time. But by and large the international financial institutions[1] considered such interventionist ideas to be anathema, and so blocked their adoption (and even their discussion). Overall no real substantive changes were therefore made to the neoliberal policy framework within which B&H was expected to recover and grow into the longer term.

After the new millennium, the output of bad news increased exponentially. UNDP was bleakly reporting in its *Annual Report 2002* that the chances of sustainable economic and social development in B&H were now very minimal indeed, given that the population had effectively been, 'condemned to reliance on a grey, trade-based, unsustainable economy rather than a production-based one' (UNDP, 2002).

As international donor financial support was beginning to wind down, the head of the World Bank in B&H was forced to argue that the country actually now needed major new cash infusions (of around US$250–300 million a year) otherwise it was heading for an 'economic abyss' (*International Herald Tribune*, 18 February 2003). An in-depth analysis by the independent European Stability Initiative went into considerably more detail on the alarmingly negative economic and social indicators (European Stability Initiative, 2004). The US-based and US government financed Centre for International Private Enterprise (CIPE) was forced to concur with the direction and urgency of the European Stability Initiatives analysis, going on to note in its own words that economic policy in B&H had effectively led to:

> Bosnia going through a process of de-industrialisation on a devastating scale. The new private sector is dominated by microenterprises in trade and basic services, generating very little employment. Bosnia seems to be developing backwards: where once it manufactured jet aircraft, it now exports aluminium; where once it exported furniture and finished wood products, it now sells only raw timber. Outside of the larger cities, many Bosnians are abandoning the towns and returning to the land their families left a generation ago. Forced out of the formal economy, they scrape together a living through some combination of casual labour, informal trade and subsistence agriculture. (CIPE, 2004)

Initial IFI predictions that by simply unleashing brute market forces in post-conflict B&H a sustainable recovery would quickly and automatically be vectored into place, thus proved to be as naïve and as wildly inaccurate as in the rest of post-Communist Eastern Europe.[2] At the same time as most developing countries have been desperately trying to move up the value-added, technology and industrial ladders, after Dayton the still quite highly industrialized and technically sophisticated B&H economic structure was effectively allowed to collapse. What has been the contribution of the microfinance model (positive, neutral or negative) to this increasingly depressing picture?

The microfinance model comes to B&H

Very quickly after Dayton and with much fanfare, the international community launched the microfinance model in B&H. The microfinance model was very much seen as a 'quick-impact' poverty reduction policy that would provide a modest cash income to the 'entrepreneurial poor'. But it was also expected that it would play a crucial role in establishing both the growing enterprise population and institutional support foundations necessary for the longer-run 'bottom-up' sustainable growth and expansion of the local economy. In other words, an expanding microenterprise and SME sector was expected to gradually constitute the dynamic core of a revitalizing B&H economy.

Incorporating the microfinance model into the economic policy framework adopted by the first post-conflict government in B&H was not undertaken without some initial resistance, however. The microfinance model's intimate association with a range of developing countries that were all finding it difficult to point to obvious nodes of sustainable local economic development in the wake of significant quantities of microfinance, such as in Bangladesh and Bolivia, raised some real suspicion in B&H government and policy elite circles as to the likely outcome of the microfinance model in their country. The uneasy feeling was that perhaps the main international sponsors behind the microfinance model specifically had in mind for the B&H economy a similar non-industrial, largely informal economy-based future.[3]

However, the international community's belief in the microfinance model seemed to be justified very quickly. Almost immediately after Dayton very many new microenterprises began to kick into operation right across B&H, a large number of them established with microloans from the first MFIs established with the support of the international community. The statistics began to corroborate what was becoming increasingly visible on the ground. In the immediate aftermath of the conflict, the number of enterprises rapidly expanded. Even in the latest time period – 2001 to 2004 – growth in the number of microenterprises and SMEs has continued apace, with a nearly 350 per cent increase in the number of microenterprises employing between one and five employees, while the number of SMEs (11–50 employees) increased by around 250 per cent (Ministry of Trade and Foreign Economic Relations, 2005).

The expansion of the microenterprise and SME sector in B&H has had a number of fairly distinct and inter-related characteristics. First, the overwhelming majority of new entrants were found to be operating in the informal sector. Nearly all of the new MFIs established from 1996 onwards began with a firm commitment to support only formal sector ventures, based on their understanding that an officially sanctioned expansion of a southern Italy-style informal sector would constitute a negative development for B&H. When it became clear to the MFIs that they would simply not be able to achieve financial self-sustainability without extensively dealing with the informal sector, however, this requirement was quietly dropped (Goronja, 1999).

Moreover, confounding the early optimism that informalization was merely a temporary status and would disappear with increasing internal success and external regulation, it turned out that most informal sector ventures once started did not seek to become formal sector operations. For one thing, intense competition from other informal sector ventures could only be met by attempting to 'beat them at their own game', not by moving into formality and accepting added expenses and responsibilities (taxes, social contributions, adhering to health and safety regulations and so on). In recent years, the informal sector has strengthened its hold upon the B&H economy, with informal sector employment rising from 37 per cent of total employment in 2001 to 42 per cent in 2004,

(World Bank, 2004) pointedly now bringing B&H more into line with the majority of developing countries.

Second, the overwhelming majority of new entrepreneurial initiatives established in B&H after 1995 have turned out to be very simple, easy-entry, no technology business ventures, particularly simple 'buy cheap and sell dear' type operations. In its first period of operation, for example, the World Bank's LIP client portfolio was dominated by small-scale trading ventures, making up 44 per cent of the total number of clients supported, amounting to 15,652 individual businesses supported (World Bank, 1999), while even higher proportions of petty traders were involved in most other MFIs operating in B&H.

Third, while the rate of microenterprise entry has been impressive, so too has been the rate of exit. Displacement effects were very high on account of the very simple and very similar business areas entered by most microfinance recipients, leading to intense competition, declining margins and exit for those least able to cope. The World Bank's 2005 evaluation of its LIP programme pointed out that 30 per cent of the microenterprises surveyed in 2002 had failed after just two years (Dunn, 2005). The World Bank-EBRD administered BEEPS Survey in 2005 found that after two years, 23 per cent of its original panel of SMEs could not be recontacted because they had closed down (EBRD, 2005).

In short, thanks to the significant infusions of international donor financial and technical support, the microenterprise sector in B&H was given a significant boost after 1996, and it subsequently expanded quite dramatically. The typical household in B&H now survives through a combination of subsistence agriculture alongside a variety of very small-scale informal sector activities requiring very little capital, technology, scale, skills or knowledge. The overall infantilizing trends in the B&H economy noted above are thus almost perfectly reflected in the programmed output of the microfinance model. In the next section we look at the all-important issue of causation. But what is for sure is that, howsoever it came about, the increasingly primitive economic structure in B&H is now very unlikely to lead to future sustainable growth and development. As noted above, this very fundamental point has been conceded by an increasing number of local and international organizations working in B&H.

The microfinance model and its impact in B&H

The basic claim made for the microfinance model in B&H, as elsewhere, is that the additional income and employment quickly generated through microfinance-induced business activity has been an important factor in immediate poverty reduction and household reconstruction (Matul and Tsilikounas 2004; Dunn, 2005). Individuals and families that received a microloan were able to engage in some sort of business activity that generated an income sufficient to repay the microloan and leave something left over for other uses, including immediate consumption, utilities, health and education. As a result, poverty was reduced, households were able to use their earnings to invest in a variety of assets, and perhaps in some cases a few employees were taken on to create a modest local employment multiplier.

However, while these short-run gains of the microfinance model have been extensively aired by the MFIs themselves and by their international donor sponsors, the longer-run impact – be it positive, neutral or negative – has not been revealed to anywhere near the same extent, if at all. The key question for economic development specialists, as perhaps opposed to the narrow concerns of the sub-set of microfinance 'technicians' (repayment rate, financial sustainability, client retention rate and so on) is: to what extent is the emerging microfinance-induced microenterprise structure and social impact consonant with establishing a sustainable local economic and social development trajectory? The question must be urgently posed because there is mounting evidence that we may be witnessing in B&H an example of what Ellerman (2005) calls an 'anti-development' intervention – an intervention that, like bad medicine, produces some immediate relief (poverty reduction) but at a price of substantially increased longer-run pain, and eventually 'death' (to the chances of sustainable economic and social development). It is to this crucial issue in B&H that I now turn through an examination of five key sustainable economic and social development variables.

Material support for the de-industrialization and infantilization of the B&H economy

A good many economists predicted at the beginning of the transition process in Eastern Europe that neoliberal transition policy would inevitably, and quite unnecessarily, destroy a very large part of the industrial sector and technological base (Amsden 1994; Taylor 1994). As Amsden et al (1994) stressed, the imperative in Eastern Europe was for state mediation and an industrial policy that could help the best-placed enterprises (irrespective of ownership, sector or size) to restructure and survive in the new market economy.

This line of argument also implied the need for a specifically *local* industrial policy approach to deal with the crucial microenterprise and SME sectors. A well-designed local industrial policy would need to involve the establishment of a stock of pro-active long-term focused local development and financial institutions that could support new ventures and marshal the best of the existing stock of microenterprises and SMEs towards higher levels of productivity, innovation and technology intensity, encourage vertical and horizontal interaction and information exchange, and provide direct encouragement for new microenterprises and SMEs to 'organically' emerge from the very many declining large industrial enterprises. As Brunner (1996) warned with regard to the East European post-communist situation,

> Successful East Asian economies have shown that industrial and regional policy programmes are a necessary part of a strategy that does not rely on a belief in a spontaneous rise of the entrepreneurial phoenix. From past

experience it is clear that functioning markets and capable market agents have to be created and sponsored by conscious institutional design and public policies.

However, there was never any attempt to establish a local industrial policy for B&H. Nor was there any significant response to the very public demands from remaining industry/production-based company owners and managers in B&H for special investment financing institutions to urgently help them restructure, reinvest and retool in order to compete in the new marketized economy.[4] Instead, the B&H economy was endowed with the 'market-driven' microfinance-led reconstruction programme. The publicly expressed hope was that the 'entrepreneurial phoenix' would be spontaneously (re)born through a rapidly expanding and increasingly sophisticated microenterprise and SME sector.

The crux problem here, however, is that the microfinance model contains an 'adverse selection' anti-industrial bias. This bias works by filtering out those potential entrepreneurs wishing to work in the industrial sector but who cannot hope to service the onerous terms and conditions offered by the commercial microfinance institutions, and filtering in those ventures incorporating only the very simplest of non-industrial business ideas that just about can. We might call this framework created by the commercial microfinance model a 'disabling environment'. Accordingly, as noted above, most microfinance in B&H has overwhelmingly gone into establishing tiny, informal, non-industrial ventures, with almost nothing directed towards financing potentially sustainable small-scale industry-based ventures. The rub is that the resulting 'shallow' structure of microenterprises is not associated anywhere with the construction or reconstruction of a sustainable local, regional or national economy.[5]

In B&H, however, very much as in the rest of Eastern Europe, the comparatively high level of industrial development, skills and technology in 1995 represented a once only opportunity to establish a core of small-scale, innovative, relatively technology-intensive, industry-related ventures. B&H's substantial military-industrial complex was one particular area where such conditions resided, suggesting this sector as the obvious entry point.[6] As Ellerman (2005) has argued, such an industrial inheritance constitutes a hugely valuable resource of entrepreneurial, industrial and technological 'genetic material' that could and should be catalyzed by outside stimulation and assistance and recombined into rafts of new smaller enterprises.[7]

But working through the microfinance model which, as intended, was pretty much the *only* major local financial support structure in B&H geared up to new start enterprises,[8] such crucially important potentially sustainable local economic development trajectories were repeatedly ignored. Instead, as we have noted, funding was channelled into a raft of largely unsustainable trade- and household-based economic activities. This represents a huge opportunity cost in B&H directly attributable to the commercial microfinance model.

The practical significance of the 'adverse selection' losses brought about in B&H through the commercial microfinance model can be simply illustrated by the experience of the Energoinvest company network, once one of the most technically advanced, innovative and R&D-driven companies in Eastern Europe. After 1996, Energoinvest was forced to seek ways to drastically reduce its workforce. At the same time, Energoinvest provided an almost ideal practical 'breeding ground' for its highly skilled employees to start new and spin-off entrepreneurial ventures based, not on simple arbitrage, but upon reasonably sophisticated and innovative product and process ideas. However, the overwhelming majority of those who responded to the call to set up their own such innovative business quickly found that realistically they could not meet the strict conditions required – namely, high interest rates and short repayment periods – in order to access funds from the network of MFIs. The result was that virtually all of the potential new small business ideas arising from employees within EnergoInvest were aborted or else substantially 'downgraded' into something that the MFI sector would be willing to finance, such as a shop or a simple trading venture.[9]

In sum, the microfinance model has given rise to an 'adverse selection' bias that has materially contributed to the hugely damaging de-industrialization and infantilization trend evidenced in B&H since 1996. Given that B&H possessed a comparatively high level of industrial development, technology, innovation and technical skills prior to the war – an inheritance that most developing countries today are, and should be, desperately striving to attain – the wilful abandonment of this industrial inheritance as a source of enterprise development is an enormous setback to its hopes of establishing at any time in the future a sustainable growth and development trajectory.

The creation of an atomized 'unconnectable' local enterprise sector

It is increasingly accepted that the tissue of interconnections within the local enterprise sector is one of the crucial determinants of a local economy's ultimate sustainability, and not simply, if at all, the *numbers* of enterprises therein. With a variety of enterprises engaged in more demanding areas with regard to technology, innovation, skills, coordination and planning, managerial competences and so on, it is possible for a local economy to gradually advance and prosper in a sustainable manner. This insight is pretty conclusively underpinned by a number of research traditions, such as the new economic geography, industrial districts, social capital theory, cluster and network theory, value chain analysis, the role of technology and innovation, and so on. As Weiss (1988) sums up, reflecting on the great successes of both the Italian and Japanese microenterprise sectors since 1945, 'the core of modern micro-capitalism is not competitive individualism but collective endeavour'.

In B&H, however, generally no strong positive spill-over effects arising from 'connectedness' are possible precisely because the agglomerations of microenterprises and SMEs arising from the microfinance model to date are overwhelmingly unsuited to the task. The microfinance model in B&H has verifiably succeeded in producing significant *numbers* of new microenterprises. However, the overwhelming majority of these individual microenterprises are completely unsuited to forging the efficiency-enhancing horizontal ('proto-industrial districts') and vertical (sub-contracting) connections seen everywhere else as crucial in establishing and firmly embedding a sustainable growth and development trajectory in place.

Programmed failure to reach minimum efficient scale of operations

In all enterprise sectors there exists a minimum efficient scale of production, which is the level of production below which, for a variety of reasons (required technology, economies of scale and so on), it is very difficult indeed to become competitive. The structure of microfinance generally ensures that the microenterprises it supports, in virtually whatever sector, are all well below the minimum efficient scale for that sector. The end result is the entry of large numbers of microenterprises all with very little chance of becoming competitive in the sector within which they operate.

That the microfinance model is patently unsuitable for anything but the very smallest ventures within any particular sector is widely accepted, including in B&H. A major survey by Matul and Tsilikounas (2004) revealed that many people in B&H unwilling to access microloans felt this way because, 'loan terms are too short for business start-ups and loan sizes too small… loans are too small and do not allow to start a "true business"… loans are too small for business expansion'.

Given that many potential entrepreneurs in B&H considered microfinance insufficient to capitalize a 'real' business to the required level for their particular sector, we must then enquire as to what was the end result for those who *did* anyway choose to utilize microfinance. Consider the first wave of microfinance-supported activities in B&H after 1996 – shops and kiosks. This sector began to run into the sand around 1999–2000. Market development and saturation effects (namely, increased competition from other new small ventures, new supermarkets) were combining to undermine their ability to compete. Already wafer-thin margins and turnover began to decline even further, in turn reducing the already minimal level of earnings and wages in the sector. The rate of exit began to rise. At this point, some MFIs in B&H could see the writing on the wall and thenceforth a number began to bar their microloans from being used for such increasingly risky activities. But as many such microenterprises began to grind to a halt right across B&H, plunging those just able to survive into a particularly dispiriting form of 'entrepreneurial poverty', the MFIs were able or willing to do very little to help them. Some MFIs were anyway focusing on which sectors to move into next in order to keep themselves in business.

The next identifiable move made by the MFI sector in B&H was into very small-scale agricultural ventures. From around 2000 onwards, microloans were increasingly being offered to those individuals wishing to undertake some very basic agricultural activity – purchase an additional cow, buy some seeds, repair a barn or store room, or buy the year's required amount of fertilizer. But in the agricultural sector too, once the local market developed, and particularly as local agricultural processors in B&H were privatized and profit considerations forced them to rationalize their local supplier base, this latest wave of very small microfinance-supported subsistence farming operations also ran into a wall. In the dairy industry, for example, the microfinance-induced proliferation of two-to-three cow farms provided a short-term income boost to the farming family. However, these short-term gains were quickly lost for very many farmers when, as predicted, their new patently inefficient farming unit was a little later winnowed out of the local dairy supply chain.

Of course, in B&H some small-scale microfinance-assisted farmers have survived, and a tiny few have even prospered (thus becoming role models for the MFIs and their international donor sponsors). But it is widely recognized in B&H that the emerging overall structure of very tiny farming units is a quite inappropriate foundation for future sustainable growth and development in the agricultural sector. Material support for its perpetuation and extension, as opposed to its conversion, therefore not only added to the huge structural problems already present in the agricultural sector but was a significant waste of scarce international and local financial resources to boot.

In sum, the widespread assisted entry of microenterprises all operating well below minimum efficient scale for their particular sector carries grave risks and serious costs into the longer term. Typically, the structural distortions created require later attention from policy makers, and at a not insignificant cost. At the same time, attempts to survive through hyper self-exploitation ripple negatively across the entire microenterprise sector, leading to falling margins, reduced reinvestment and 'entrepreneurial poverty'. The inevitable decline and eventual exit process for the majority of such unfortunate individuals is then painful, both in financial terms (loss of savings and physical assets, incurring of additional debts) and in personal terms (loss of confidence, loss of reputation, severed social connections). It is clear that there are many negative social side-effects arising in B&H in this regard, such as depression, increased incidence of household violence, reduction in neighbourliness, and so on (see for example, World Bank, 2002). The routine creation of unsustainable rafts of microenterprises in B&H, and then their very predictable collapse – 'houses of cards' – thus involves many long-run negative financial impacts and social costs that can, and probably do, outweigh any initial poverty reduction gains.

Facilitating trade deficits and import dependency

One of the most damaging features of the neoliberal programmes that developing countries were forced to endure during the 1970s and 1980s was the collapse in local manufacturing and agricultural production brought about by instant trade liberalization and an ensuing flood of (often subsidized) imports. Thanks to the basic operations of small importing and shuttle trading ventures, import dependence was quickly embedded into the system. Crucially, the debilitating longer-run impact of import dependency meant that it ultimately destroyed any short-term poverty reduction gains made during the initial phase of trading sector microenterprise expansion. SAPRIN's (2001) conclusion was that the initial uncontrolled surge of imports needlessly contributes to:

> The failure of many local manufacturing firms, particularly innovative small and medium sized ones that generate a great deal of employment. The decline in domestic manufacturing has followed the flooding of local markets with cheap imports that have displaced local production and goods and has been exacerbated by the absence of an industrial policy to support domestic firms in dealing with new conditions or with shocks in international markets'.

Given that simple trading ventures are cheap and easy to enter and require little in the way of special skills, they are very understandably the first destination of many individuals seeking a route out of poverty. And if MFIs are willing to underwrite such business propositions, because the initial profitability is more than enough to deal with their high interest rates and short repayment periods, then a major boost to their numbers is an obvious outcome.

As could have been predicted, therefore, the newly established MFIs in B&H began their life by whole-heartedly engaging with the small-scale trading sector. Simple cross-border shuttle trading quickly became one of the most visible forms of individual business activity right across post-Dayton B&H, requiring only a little cash up front from a microloan to buy or repair a vehicle and to buy some stock while abroad. Not surprisingly, however, the B&H trade balance began to suffer, inevitably diverting scarce foreign exchange from other more urgent areas, and thus damaging the overall prospects for economic growth and development. Of course, calculating quite how much of the negative trade balance has been *specifically* precipitated by the working out of the microfinance model requires deeper study. But even local analysts otherwise sympathetic to the microfinance model agree that the instant splurge of imports was deeply damaging to the B&H economy, and that it was partly attributable to the microfinance model because,'Microcredit often permanently institutionalises the smuggling of goods and the widespread (though legal) importation of simple, low value added goods that would and could be better produced locally' (Èièiæ and Šunje, 2002).

Destruction of local social capital

Social capital is now seen as a major factor in promoting successful local economic and social development, if indeed it is not the 'missing link' in development (Putnam, 1993). However, there is growing evidence in B&H to suggest that the microfinance model very actively *destroys* social capital. First, and more generally, by recasting individual survival as a function of individual entrepreneurial success, the bonds of solidarity, shared experience and trust that exist within poor communities are inevitably going to be undermined.

This is a truism. But more specifically, whenever community development and support activities are recast as commercial and strict cost-recovery operations – a central operating principle of the commercial microfinance model – the unavoidable consequence is a degeneration of the level of local solidarity, interpersonal communication, volunteerism, trust-based interaction and goodwill. In post-conflict B&H it is clear that the overarching emphasis upon individual survival strategies (as well as the accompanying inequality) has undermined the previous bonds of community and trust-based interaction that were pervasive throughout the country prior to 1991 and during the conflict itself (World Bank, 2002).

Consider also the effect of the evolving commercialization of most MFIs in B&H. The network of MFIs established by the international community after 1996 was initially warmly welcomed by most ordinary people. MFIs were said to be 'there to help' and to be 'showing their sympathy with the local population' by helping some of the very poorest to escape from their isolation and grinding poverty. However, once it became apparent that many MFIs were beginning to move out of the original market serving very poor and poor people, and into new markets serving the much less poor and the emerging middle class and new business elites, and also moving out of providing microloans for business purposes and into microloans for consumption goods (for example, cars and housing), attitudes began to change. They were just 'businesses' all along. The increasingly obvious concern they were demonstrating for their own survival, rather more than the survival of the local community into which they had been born, thus began to chip away at the MFIs' initially warm relationships with communities, key individuals and local politicians. The predictable outcome over time is that the commercialization inherent to the microfinance model in B&H will increasingly undermine any popular legitimacy and voluntary support from the local community. This development is in sharp contrast to the pre-communist and even communist-era community-based MFIs in B&H and in the wider Yugoslavia (for example, financial cooperatives) that generally evinced significant popular support and community involvement – that is, they actually *constructed* social capital.[10]

Second, the type of microenterprises associated with the microfinance model are, as we have seen above, overwhelmingly informal and largely displaying a limited ability to creatively interact with other businesses. Yet growing informality in B&H is clearly underpinning the already considerable lack of respect for legal process. It has also embedded a mistrust of government, and has encouraged the search for informal and sometimes illegal sources of protection (for example, criminal gangs) and power (for example, corrupt politicians) in order to continue to do business. The lack of regular inter-enterprise connections has been associated with secrecy, an unwillingness to trust, little sharing and few social connections that might substitute for legal process. Moreover, most microenterprises in B&H are also very weak and very typically involve insecurity and hyper self-exploitation (long hours, intense work, poor rewards, undignified working conditions, little security of income and so on). Such adverse conditions have inevitably generated alienation and antagonism towards the wider B&H society that is seemingly indifferent to the plight of those involved, with special enmity reserved for the tiny new business elite enjoying a stratospheric level of power and financial reward that is widely seen (with much justification) as having been illegally or unjustifiably accumulated.

All of these pretty regularly observed outcomes of the commercial microfinance model in B&H are unequivocally associated with the destruction of social capital (Bateman, 2006). The already fragile social foundations of B&H are, thus, further undermined and destroyed. Moreover, such an adverse social outcome in turn has served to further deter local savings, local investment, business cooperation and other key economic growth variables. All told, these very significant drawbacks to the commercial microfinance model in B&H were certainly not lost on B&H economists, including Èièiæ and Šunje (2002), who warned that, 'Very much as in Southern Italy, if the legitimacy of semi-legal, arbitrage-based occupational lifestyles is embedded within the local society and polity in B&H, it will eat away at the social capital upon which longer run business success will depend'.

Conclusion

While the commercial microfinance model established in B&H after 1996 is possibly associated with some short-run poverty reduction impacts, analysis of emerging trends and developments suggests that this immediate gain has been achieved at a very high price indeed. Very little evidence has emerged in B&H to suggest that the commercial microfinance model actually possesses the required 'transformative capacity' to secure genuinely *sustainable* poverty reduction, through genuinely *sustainable* local economic and social development. On the contrary, the commercial microfinance model is quite centrally implicated in the evolution of the disturbingly weak, unsophisticated, anti-social, disconnected and unfair economic and social structures we see in B&H today. Like a rapidly growing weed that hogs the nutrients and sunlight needed by the slower growing crops around it, the commercial microfinance model in B&H has absorbed significant international financial resources, high-level technical expertise, political commitment, valuable time and remaining accumulations of social capital, all in order to roll out a primitive 'bazaar economy' redolent of life in B&H 100 years ago.

Notes

1   That is, the World Bank and IMF, supported later on by their ideological affiliates, the EBRD and the OECD, through the multi-donor Investment Compact process.
2   Andor and Summers (1998) point out that the 'transition depression' that rocked all of Eastern Europe after 1990, particularly severely in Poland, was

not predicted by any of the IFIs, key western governments or their high profile economic advisors.

3   This point was articulated a number of times during discussions the author had with senior government personnel, academics and local employees of several international organizations during a research visit in 1998, and then also in February, 1999, on the sidelines of a major conference on the microfinance model held in Sarajevo.

4   For example, a 1996 World Bank survey (World Bank, 1997) of mainly industrial/production-based company owners found that their number one priority was to be able to access investment capital.

5   For example, see Weiss (1998) and Chang (2002).

6   One obvious post-conflict example that could have provided some useful lessons at this specific juncture (1996) was the recovery and re-industrialization of the Emilia Romagna region of central-northern Italy after 1945. Creatively utilizing what was left of its military-industrial sector in order to give birth to a raft of relatively technology-intensive small firms, the very pro-active regional and local governments and other support institutions were able to support into operation what was to become the core of a world-beating industrial SME sector (see Capecchi, 1990).

7   A more recent practical example referred to by Ellerman is that of the ARIA Project in Moldova, an innovative World Bank project that successfully gave birth to a raft of new small and dynamic enterprises within the collapsing hulk of an old state-owned industrial enterprise (see Ellerman and Kreaèiæ, 2002).

8   Alternative local financial models proposed by some of B&H's best economists were either ignored or blocked by the IFIs (see Bateman, 2003). It also didn't help that B&H's new private commercial banks were and remain extremely risk averse, for example 'investing' most of the capital they raise locally in German and UK bank accounts (see Èauševiæ, 2002).

9   Interviews by the author with ex-Energoinvest employees and former Energoinvest managers, summer 1997 and 1999, and 2002.

10 For the situation pre-WWII, see Tomaševic (1955); and for the situation under Yugoslav worker self-management, see Horvat (1976).

References

Amsden, A. (1994) 'Why isn't the whole world experimenting with the East Asian model to develop? A comment on the World Bank East Asia Miracle report', *World Development* 22(4): 615–70.

Amsden, A., Kochanowicz, J. and Taylor, L. (1994) *The Market Meets its Match: Restructuring the Economies of Eastern Europe*, Harvard University Press, Cambridge, MA.

Andor, L. and Summers, M. (1998) *Market Failure: Eastern Europe's 'Economic Miracle'*, Pluto Press, London.

Bateman, M. (2003) '"New Wave" micro-finance institutions in South-East Europe: Towards a more realistic assessment of impact', *Small Enterprise Development* 14(3): 56–65.

Bateman, M. (2006) 'The role of social capital in promoting sustainable poverty reduction in South East Europe', in UNDP (2006) (ed.) *Poverty Reduction in Bosnia and Herzegovina and the Role of MDG1*, UNDP, Sarajevo.

Brunner, H.-P. (1996) 'The Entrepreneurial sector and its role in industrial transformation', in Brezinski, H. and Fritsch, M. (eds) *The Economic Impact of New Firms in Post-Socialist Countries: Bottom-up Transformation in Eastern Europe*, Edward Elgar, Cheltenham.

Capecchi, V. (1990) 'A history of flexible specialisation and industrial districts in Emilia-Romagna', in Pyke, F., Becattini, G. and Sengenbeger, W. (eds) *Industrial Districts and Inter-firm Cooperation in Italy*, ILO, Geneva.

Chang, H.-J. (2002) *Kicking Away the Ladder: Development Strategy in Historical Perspective*, Anthem Press, London.

Èauševiæ, F. (2002) 'The effects of financial deregulation in Bosnia and Herzegovina – 1997–2001', in University of Sarajevo (ed.) *Jubilant Collection of Papers of the Economics Faculty of Sarajevo*, XXII, University of Sarajevo, Sarajevo.

Èièiæ, M. and Šunje, A. (2002) 'Microcredit in Transition economies: The case of Bosnia-Herzegovina', in Bartlett, W., Bateman, M. and Vehovec, M. (eds) *Small Enterprise Development in South-east Europe: Policies for Sustainable Growth*, Kluwer Academic Press, Boston, MA.

CIPE (Centre for International Private Enterprise) (2004) *Bosnia: Post-Industrial Society and the Authoritarian Temptation*, Executive Summary of a report by the European Stability Initiative (ESI), 18 January, Washington DC.

Dolan, K. (2005) 'Up from the rubble; Can $2,000 loans help revive a war-torn economy? Entrepreneurs in Bosnia and Herzegovina are putting microfinance to the test', *Forbes*, 18 April.

Dunn, E. (2005) *Impact of Microcredit on Clients in Bosnia and Herzegovina*, Impact LLC, Washington DC.

EBRD (European Bank for Reconstruction and Development) (2005) *The Business Environment and Enterprise Performance Survey (BEEPS) 2005*, report prepared by Synovate Consultants for the EBRD, Nicosia.

Ellerman, D. (2005) *Helping People Help Themselves: From the World Bank to an Alternative Philosophy of Development Assistance*, University of Michigan Press, Ann Arbor.

Ellerman, D. and Kreaèiæ, V. (2002) *Transforming the Old into a Foundation for the New: Lessons of the Moldova ARIA Project*, Policy Research Working Paper 2866, World Bank, Washington DC.

European Stability Initiative (2004) *Governance and Democracy in Bosnia and Herzegovina: Post-Industrial Society and the Authoritarian Temptation*, European Stability Initiative (ESI), Berlin.

Goronja, N. (1999) *The Evolution of Microfinance in a Successful Post-Conflict Transition: The Case Study for Bosnia-Herzegovina*, paper presented at the Joint

ILO/UNHCR Workshop: Microfinance in Post-Conflict Countries 15–17 September, ILO, Geneva.

Horvat, B. (1976) *The Yugoslav Economic System*, M.E. Sharpe, New York.

International Herald Tribune (2003) 'A nation unbuilt: Where did all the money go in Bosnia?', 18 February: 4.

Matul, M. and Tsilikounas, C. (2004) 'Role of Microfinance in Household Reconstruction Process in Bosnia and Herzegovina', *Journal of International Development*, 16(3): 429–66.

Ministry of Trade and Foreign Economic Relations (2005) *Small and Medium-Sized Enterprise Development Strategy in BiH: 2005–2007*, Draft for Public Debate: Short Version, Sarajevo.

Putnam, R. with Leonardi, R. and Nanetti, R. (1993) *Making Democracy Work: Civic Traditions in Modern Italy*, Princeton University Press, Princeton, NJ.

SAPRIN (Structural Adjustment Participatory Reviews International Network) (2001) *The Policy Roots of Economic Crisis and Poverty*, SAPRIN, Washington DC.

Taylor, L. (1994) 'The post-Socialist transition from a Development Economics Point of View', in Solimano, A., Sunkel, O. and Blejer, M. (eds) *Rebuilding Capitalism: Alternative Roads after Socialism and Dirigisme*, University of Michigan Press, Ann Arbor.

Tomaševic, S. (1955) *Peasants, Politics and Economic Change in Yugoslavia*, Stanford University Press, Stanford.

UNDP (United Nations Human Development Program) (2002) *Human Development Report 2002: Bosnia and Herzegovina*, UNDP, Sarajevo.

Weiss, L, (1988) Creating Capitalism: *The State and Small Business since 1945*, Blackwell, Oxford.

Weiss, L. (1998) *The Myth of the Powerless State: Governing the Economy in the Global Era*, Polity Press, Cambridge.

World Bank (1997) *New Foundations: Private Sector Development in Post-war Bosnia-Herzegovina*, World Bank, Sarajevo.

World Bank (1999) *Local Initiatives Project: Annual Report*, World Bank, Sarajevo.

World Bank (2002) *Bosnia and Herzegovina: Local Level Institutions and Social Capital*, ECSSD, World Bank, Washington DC.

World Bank (2004) *Labour Market Survey 2004*, World Bank, Sarajevo.

CHAPTER EIGHTEEN
Measuring the impact of microfinance

Richard L. Meyer

Abstract

Impact analysis has become one of the most controversial issues in the analysis of microfinance. This chapter focuses on quantitative studies of the impact of microloans. The first section summarizes the key methodological issues involved in conducting rigorous impact analysis. The second section reviews the key findings of two impact studies that have withstood most critical reviews. The third section highlights two new and very different directions being pursued in impact studies.

Measuring the impact of financial services has become one of the most controversial issues facing the microfinance industry. On the one hand, MFIs routinely advertise the positive impact of their small loans on poor people in developing countries. Their anecdotes typically involve poor women with starving children successfully climbing out of poverty after receiving a US$100 loan. The reader of these flowery accounts is surprised that these stores do not end with 'and they lived happily ever after'.

On the other hand, seasoned veterans of foreign aid argue that the gap between microcredit rhetoric and reality is widening, particularly following the hype and bloated claims associated with the UN 2005 Year of Microcredit (Dichter, 2006; Miller, 2006). The publicity surrounding the recent granting of the Noble Peace Prize to Professor Muhammed Yunus and the Grameen Bank has elevated the claims about the magic of small loans for poor people. However, recent stories reported in the popular media, such as in the *Economist* and *New York Times*, about the high rate of suicides by indebted farmers in India provide tragic evidence of the shame and despair of poor people who borrow but are unable to repay. Not everyone who borrows is able to repay, and the consequences can be tragic.

This chapter is divided into three sections. The first summarizes the problems faced by evaluators in objectively measuring the quantitative impact of microfinance. The second section highlights the results of impact studies with emphasis on two that have withstood most methodological criticisms. The third section reviews two new directions in microfinance impact analysis. The emphasis throughout the chapter is on studies of the impacts of lending programmes on individual clients or communities rather than impact studies of different financial products, processes or policies.

Methodological challenges in quantitative microfinance impact analysis[1]

The most common impact analysis involves estimating the quantitative benefits that clients of one or more MFIs experience by borrowing. Many problems have been identified in designing and conducting these types of studies. Some of the problems are similar to those faced in assessing the impact of any development project, while others represent problems unique to finance (David and Meyer, 1980; Von Pischke and Adams, 1980; Khandker, 1998; Coleman, 1999; Roche, 1999; Baker, 2000; Hulme, 2000; Karlan, 2001; Ravallion, 2001; Armendariz de Aghion and Morduch, 2005). They include issues of study design, data collection and statistical analysis. The ways they are addressed influences the robustness of the results obtained. It is easy to obtain results that exaggerate the benefits of borrowing. Since most studies focus on the impact of microcredit, rather than on savings or insurance, this chapter will likewise concentrate on microloan impact studies.

The key concepts and problems of quantitative impact analysis are summarized below:[2]

- *Poverty proxies*. Poverty proxies are used for two purposes. First, microfinance is intended to serve the poor so any impact study of a MFI must demonstrate that the poor actually receive the loans. Some type of poverty proxy is required to measure the poverty level of clients and, for comparative purposes, non-clients. MFIs often do not measure client poverty but establish specific targeting criteria, such as land ownership, income level or household characteristics, that they expect are highly correlated with poverty. Other MFIs simply offer only small high-interest loans and assume that richer people with access to other alternatives will not choose to become clients. But when client poverty is carefully measured, there is evidence that shows that, on the one hand, many non-poor use microfinance and, on the other hand, most MFIs do not serve large numbers of the very poor. Second, proxy indicators are used to measure the impacts or benefits realized by borrowers. Some benefits can be easily stated as concepts but difficult to measure in practice. For example, literally dozens of variables involving quantities and prices must be specified and estimated to determine if the annual income of a farm household changed because of borrowing. Benefits such as improved health are even more difficult to measure directly so measurable proxies must be selected, such as number of days of illness. Selecting appropriate proxies for broad concepts such as the empowerment of female borrowers is even more complicated and contentious.[3]

- *Counterfactual*. Impact analysis requires an estimation of what would have happened to MFI clients if they had not received the financial services (namely, the counterfactual) to compare with the actual outcome observed when the clients (that is, the treatment group) receive loans. Unlike in a physical experiment, the counterfactual can never be directly observed so an appropriate method is needed to estimate it. A robust method is critical for correctly measuring the impact 'caused' by the financial services. The treatment group must be representative of the clients for whom the results are to be generalized.

- *Control and comparison groups.* The counterfactual can be approximated by using control or comparison groups that did not receive the financial services. Control groups are selected at random from the same population as the MFI clients and are used in experimental research designs. In non-experimental designs, comparison groups consisting of non-MFI clients are chosen to compare with the treatment group. These groups must be as similar as possible to MFI clients in all attributes, including their level of poverty, except for the fact they did not receive MFI services. Meeting this standard is difficult under any circumstance, but especially so in places like Bangladesh or Bolivia where MFI coverage is intensive, making it difficult to identify potential control villages and persons not directly or indirectly affected by microfinance.

- *Displacement.* When some microentrepreneurs receive loans and others do not, it is possible that borrowers will grow and displace the economic activities undertaken by non-borrowers. Therefore the losses suffered by non-borrowers must be subtracted from the gains enjoyed by the borrowers in order to correctly estimate the net benefits of MFI lending. For example, MFI clients may use loans to expand their businesses and crowd out members of the control groups who are negatively affected because of the microfinance programme. One of the values of analysing control and comparison groups over time is that it may be possible to detect if displacement has occurred so the benefits estimated for the MFI can be adjusted downwards.

- *Current versus past clients.* Most analysts create treatment groups by sampling current MFI clients, excluding from the sample those who are no longer active. But MFI benefits may be underestimated if the inactive group includes many successful 'graduates'. Their number is expected to be fairly small, however, because it is difficult for even the most successful clients to graduate to commercial sources of finance. Moreover, the additional profits earned from borrowing during only a few loan cycles are likely to be too small to enable borrowers to self-finance their activities. It is more likely, therefore, that the largest share of inactives will be 'drop-outs' who withdrew or were pushed out of MFI membership. Some may have suffered setbacks so they could not repay or faced so much difficulty in repaying that they refused to take another loan. Others may have been forced out by their peers or loan officers as being poor credit risks. The results obtained from studying only active clients will overestimate the true impact of microfinance if drop-outs are significant in number and are mostly 'failures'.

- *Attrition.* Some impact studies are designed to interview treatment and control groups several times over a year or several years. Attrition occurs when persons or households drop out through migration and death, or simply refuse to continue furnishing data. Households grow in size through births and marriage, while others shrink. Households that are lost or experience major changes need to be analysed to determine if they are systematically different so their inclusion or exclusion in the overall analysis will bias the results.

- *Differential impact by poverty level.* The benefits realized by borrowers are influenced by the degree to which finance is a constraint for clients at different levels of poverty. There may be significant 'interaction' between access to finance and level of poverty so wealthier clients may realize greater benefits than very poor ones. When MFIs serve a wide range of clients, the impact study should contain a sufficient number of clients at different levels of poverty so the analysis can evaluate if level of client poverty systematically affects impact.

- *Causality and attribution.* If treatment and control groups truly differ only because one group received the treatment (that is, it borrowed) and the other did not, then any differences found in the impact measures between the two groups can be 'attributed' to the financial services; it can be argued that financial services 'caused' the difference. The amount of impact is represented by the magnitude of the differences. However, if there are other differences between the two groups, it is impossible to determine if the benefits were truly caused by finance, or by initial unobserved differences between the two groups, or by unobserved events that affected the treatment but not the control group. Likewise, if no differences are found between the two groups or if negative impacts are found, there is no way of determining if finance really made no impact or if its positive effects were overwhelmed by other factors producing negative impacts. Unobserved characteristics of clients compared to non-clients, such as their management ability or entrepreneurial spirit, may be more responsible for differences between the two groups than is credit.

- *Fungibility and additionality.* Money is fungible and loan funds can be used for many purposes so it is difficult to determine how they were actually used and what benefits were realized. For example, a MFI client may plan to expand her business through existing resources including personal savings, supplier's credits, or informal loans. If the MFI supplies a loan, the borrowed funds may 'substitute' for these other resources so they can then be used for other purposes, perhaps increasing consumption or sending a child to school. Therefore, the 'additionality' caused by the loan was not business expansion, which was already planned, but what the borrower actually did with the resources released. Likewise, funds supposedly borrowed for some purpose, such as business expansion, may be 'diverted' to another use, perhaps paying for an unexpected medical expense. It is difficult to estimate the additionality caused by a fungible resource like MFI loans without collecting tremendous amounts of data from both treatment and control groups on resources received and allocated.

- *Control variables.* Many factors other than microfinance, such as macroeconomic shocks, education, and participation in other poverty programmes, influence changes in household poverty. Information on these factors needs to be collected and 'controlled for' in both the treatment and control groups so that the only difference between the two groups is loans received.

- *Selection bias.* Two important biases have to be anticipated in designing impact studies. First, *selection of clients* is not likely to be completely random. For example, the first clients to enter a new microfinance programme may be more entrepreneurial or willing to take risks than the general population. Moreover, if clients are expected to form peer groups and exert pressure on fellow members who fall into arrears, they will choose group members who are expected to earn income and manage money prudently so loan payments will be made on a timely basis. Likewise, if loan officers influence the decisions about who should join groups and receive loans, they will likely select clients least likely to cause collection problems. If these differences between clients and non-clients can be observed and measured, they can be controlled for statistically. If not, the impact results will be biased, as the same unobservable characteristics that lead the poor to become clients will also affect the impact measures. Second, *programme placement* may not be random. MFIs may choose to locate operations in areas or villages with better communication and transportation infrastructure than found in randomly chosen villages. Therefore, the poor are more likely to receive microfinance if they live in a richer than in a poorer area. With these two types of selection biases, it is difficult to determine if differences between treatment and control groups are actually due to the financial services or to unrepresentative clients and/ or locations.

- *Identifying and measuring the treatment.* MFIs differ in the services offered. Some are minimalist and only supply loans with limited orientation to borrowers on matters such as disbursement and repayment procedures. Others provide obligatory or voluntary savings services. Still others provide training in nutrition or business planning. Some lend for any purpose while others attempt to direct loans to 'productive' purposes. Therefore, clients receive different 'treatments' including different loan sizes with different terms from the same MFI and different combinations of services by one or more household members simultaneously participating in two or more MFIs. Treatment must be measured in some way. Most studies simply look at loans. Sometimes treatment is crudely measured as participation in the loan programme, while other studies attempt to capture the intensity of participation by measuring the amount of loans and other services received and the time period they were received. Usually no attempt is made to disentangle the impact of receiving a loan vs. simply participating in a group, or receiving training as either an obligatory or voluntary component of the MFI's lending programme. When the clients from several MFIs are analysed without differentiating their services, the benefits generated by those producing the greatest impact will be masked by others producing fewer benefits.

- *Unit of assessment.* Financial services are normally provided to clients as individuals, but entire households may realize benefits. Therefore, data needs to be collected on all household members for both treatment and control groups to evaluate who benefits and by how much. This becomes difficult in studies designed to collect household data in repeated interviews because household composition changes whenever someone marries, dies or migrates. In group lending programmes, data may also need to be collected at the level of the groups to test the impact of group dynamics separate from the impact of finance. Data may need to be collected on enterprises to determine if enterprise-specific changes can be attributed to households that receive financial services. Some studies attempt to evaluate changes beyond households in financial markets and/or communities, such as whether on not the expansion of microfinance contributed to changes in terms and conditions of moneylender loans.[4]
- *Measurement errors and baseline data.* All studies must anticipate errors in the measurement of variables or in responses provided by persons interviewed. A frequent problem is that an assessment is conducted after a MFI has been operating for some time and no baseline data were collected at the beginning for the treatment or control groups. If a 'before and after' analysis is undertaken, members of the treatment and control groups are forced to 'recall' their situation prior to the time that they began to borrow. The interval could have been several years. The resulting measurement errors introduce unknown biases that may overestimate or underestimate the true impact of finance. It is logical to expect that the treatment group will perceive that the analysts will desire large benefits so they will exaggerate the data they report.
- *Collecting and analysing the data.* Independent analysts collect and analyse the data for most sophisticated and complex impact studies. They presumably have greater objectivity but face the challenge of obtaining correct data from members of treatment and control groups who do not know them. Some studies reduce this problem and the costs of impact studies by using MFI staff to collect and analyse data. Apart from the problem of having little time to perform this work, the staff may introduce distortions in the results because they have a vested interest in reporting favourable impacts. Their clients may also want to please them by giving 'desired' responses that skew the results.
- *Statistical analysis.* Many impact studies report only the average or mean differences calculated for the variables or indicators measured for the treatment and control groups. However, if no statistical tests are reported, there is no way of knowing if differences that appear large between the two groups are really 'not significant' because of the large variability recorded among the observations in the two groups. Econometric analysis is preferred to perform robust statistical tests, but these techniques require more specialized knowledge and skills than found among many persons who undertake impact assessments. Therefore, large results of microfinance impact may be touted when in fact they are not statistically significant.

Key findings of quantitative microfinance impact analysis

The methodological problems inherent in conducted impact studies have prevented the development of a clear general consensus about the industry. For example, in his major 1999 report, Morduch concluded 'there have been few impact evaluations with carefully chosen treatment and control groups (or with control groups of any sort), and those that exist yield a mixed picture of impact'. Several authors subsequently have surveyed the impact literature in search of generalizations. For example, Sharma and Buchenrieder (2002) summarized several impact studies that focussed on food security. They concluded that country- and programme-specific conditions have a large bearing on whether the impact of credit is positive, negligible or even negative. One important factor is the extent to which complementary production inputs are available to the borrowing farmer or entrepreneur. Loans received in the absence of complementary inputs will more likely be used for consumption smoothing and other insurance purposes that stimulate consumption in the short term but may even reduce it in the long term.

Morduch and Haley (2002) prepared a review in 2001 for the Canadian development agency CIDA, and the most recent review was published by Goldberg in 2005 for the Grameen Foundation. Goldberg concluded that microfinance 'can' increase incomes and lift families out of poverty. And it can contribute to other positive social outcomes such as improve children's nutrition and school enrolment. However because subtle differences between clients and comparison groups can affect the conclusions, the evidence is not quite good enough, and no incontrovertible study has yet been published. Surprisingly, a few years earlier Morduch and Haley wrote a more positive conclusion and stated that 'While the quality of many studies could be improved, there is an overwhelming amount of evidence substantiating a beneficial effect on increases in income and reduction in vulnerability' (2002). In 2005, however, Armendariz de Aghion and Morduch concluded that 'no study yet has achieved wide consensus as to its reliability', and they identified many methodological problems with existing studies.

A brief review of two of the most robust studies reveals the difficulties of arriving at general impact conclusions. They were chosen because the authors clearly recognized many of the methodological problems identified above and attempted to resolve them by careful design and analysis. The results, therefore, can be considered far more robust than many others, even though Armendariz de Aghion and Morduch found they also have limitations.

Impact study of village banking in Thailand

Coleman (1999) conducted a highly innovative study of member-owned village mini-banks in Northeast Thailand during 1995–96. Since the Bank for Agriculture and Agriculture Cooperatives (BAAC) in Thailand has high penetration in rural areas, there are fewer capital-constrained households to be served by specialized MFIs than in many developing countries.

Coleman's objective was to assess the impact of two NGOs promoting village banking in which women were organized into peer groups of 20–60 members. Individuals received the loans, but group members had to co-guarantee each other's loans. The first loan, usually for a term of six months, in the amount of about US$60 was the same for all members. For each subsequent loan, members could borrow an amount equal to the previous loan plus her accumulated savings in the village bank, up to a fixed maximum of about US$300, while the average size of BAAC loans in the survey region was over US$600. BAAC interest rates varied from 3–12 per cent, while the village banks charged 24 per cent per year.

Six of the 14 villages were treated as control villages because they had not benefited from a village bank, but would begin receiving village bank loans from the NGOs in 1996. A stratified random sample of households was selected in the villages. In total 445 households completed all four surveys conducted over the course of the year. The design involved a comparison of the 'old' members in the treatment villages with the 'new' members in the control villages. Participation was defined as months of village bank membership. Initially, loans are made with funds provided by the NGOs, but it is expected that the banks will mobilize enough funds to eventually self-finance all loans and repay the NGO. The NGOs reduced loan sizes after the first few loans in order to 'wean' the villages from external loans.

The results showed that loan size did not significantly increase with months of membership for three reasons. First, there was the weaning effect. Second, some members borrowed less than the maximum and, third, some women used the bank largely for savings rather than for borrowing. Borrowing increased with women's education level, with number of relatives in the village, with the village chief or assistant chief being in the household, and with the value of female-owned land.

The impact results showed that increasing the months of village bank membership made no significant impact on household physical assets, production, sales, expenses, labour time, or expenditures on health care and education. Surprisingly, membership appeared to increase the women's high-interest debt load and lending out at positive interest. Coleman explained these results by noting that several women had little to invest because they fell into a vicious circle of debt in which they borrowed from moneylenders at three per cent per day to repay their village bank loans, and then used their subsequent village bank loans to repay the moneylenders. Many women reported joining the bank largely for social reasons without having any specific investment plan. Still others borrowed from the bank at relatively low rates and lent out money at higher rates. The overall result was that there was no evidence that the loans were being directly invested in productive activities with a positive return.

Coleman argued that the lack of impact could be due to the relatively small loans made by the village banks. The average household wealth was about US$21,000, and average low-interest household debt was about US$1,250 of which women held US$370. Therefore, village bank loans of US$60–300 provided few additional resources to the households for productive activities. Instead these small loans may have been used largely for consumption smoothing rather than for investment purposes to increase household income and future consumption.

In a separate analysis, the author tested for impact on subgroups of borrowers (Coleman, 2006). He found that the probability of wealthier households self-selecting into the village bank was nearly twice that of poor villagers. Committee members (president, vice president, treasurer) were found to borrow significantly more than other members. Some borrowers used multiple names, such as those of family members living outside the village, to obtain larger loans. These persons tended to be influential committee members, who were wealthier, set policy and managed daily operations. Households reported that 35 per cent of the loan volume was borrowed by someone other than the persons listed in the bank records.

Impact was retested by separating committee members from 'rank and file members'. The results continued to be insignificant for number of months of membership by the rank and file. But months of committee membership were significant and positive for household wealth, savings, low-interest debt, household moneylending, women's self-employment sales, expenses and labour time, and educational expenses for boys in the household. Committee members may have been able to invest in larger, more capital-intensive projects by borrowing more from both the village banks and other low-interest sources.

Comprehensive World Bank impact study in Bangladesh

In Bangladesh, the World Bank conducted one of the most ambitious microfinance impact studies undertaken anywhere and the results were summarized by Khandker (1998). Data were collected from 87 villages and 1,798 randomly selected households. Of the households selected, 1,538 were target and 260 were non-target. The households were surveyed three times during the 1991–92 farming year, which marked the beginning of the great expansion of microfinance in the country.

Three microcredit programmes with similar approaches were studied. The first was the Grameen Bank, which provided loans with only limited skills training. The second was BRAC, a huge NGO that combined lending with training. Its borrowers typically received more hours of skills-based training than Grameen Bank borrowers. The third was the Rural Development Project-12 (RD-12) of the Bangladesh Rural Development Board, a semi-autonomous government agency charged with developing cooperatives for rural development. For RD-12, the board adopted the skills-based training approach of BRAC in addition to lending.

The three organizations made loans to individuals through joint-liability solidarity groups of typically five members. They emphasized membership for women and all borrowing groups are exclusively male or female. The three organizations targeted the poor, defined as persons holding less than half an acre of land. In addition, BRAC and RD-12 required that at least one household member work for wages. The groups were organized into five to eight group centers in Grameen Bank, into BRAC village organizations of 30–40 members, and into 15–35 member primary cooperatives in RD-12. Borrowers attended weekly meetings, made weekly loan payments and savings deposits, contributed to a non-refundable group fund, and paid nominal amounts for group insurance or cooperative shares. The maximum loan size was Tk10,000 (US$200), and the repayment was made in 50 weekly principal instalments with interest paid at the end. Nominal interest rates were 20 per cent for Grameen Bank and BRAC and 16 per cent for RD-12. Members were instructed in a code of conduct that encouraged thrift, discipline, good health and nutrition, and socially desirable behaviour.

The survey was designed to include eligible (target) and ineligible (non-target) households. The analysis measured the differences between eligible and ineligible households in programme and non-programme villages. After controlling for several other factors, the study expected that any differences found in comparing the two groups would be attributed to participation in one of the programmes.[5] Participation was measured as the deflated cumulative amount of borrowing over the five-year period before the survey was conducted. Impact was expected to vary among the participants because of differences in loan sizes, length of participation, receiving different mixes of services, and in member gender.

Borrowing by men and women had an expected positive impact on household per capita weekly expenditures. This result was significant for women in all three programmes but for men only for RD-12. The magnitude of increase for women was roughly the same for all three programmes but the increases for men were twice as great. However, borrowing by women produced either no or a much smaller positive effect on household net worth than borrowing by men, except that women's non-land assets rose with borrowing. These findings are consistent with the view that women allocate resources differently than men. Because of their family responsibilities, women may prefer to meet immediate welfare needs of the family while men may prefer to accumulate assets for longer-term gains. When women invest, they may prefer assets used for in-home enterprises rather than land.[6]

Microloans are expected to facilitate self-employment so borrowing may increase the time allocated to income-earning activities. The results showed that in fact women's borrowing increased their labour supply and the effects were slightly higher for Grameen Bank than the other two programmes, but both men's and women's borrowing reduced the labour supply of men. Since men had access to more wage labour prior to programme participation, borrowing may have induced men to choose more leisure.

Borrowing affected children's schooling but the impacts varied by gender of borrower, by child and by programme. For example, for Grameen Bank and RD-12, female borrowing seemed to benefit the school enrolment of boys more than girls. Boys' time is less likely to substitute for women's and girls' time so they are less likely to get drawn into self-employment activities. Women's borrowing was also more likely to make a significant impact on the nutritional well-being of both male and female children, a finding consistent with consumption expenditures discussed above.

The seasonality of the crop cycle affects labour use and income flows so microfinance may assist households to diversify into non-agricultural activities that will smooth consumption. Households with larger than average seasonal variation in consumption were more likely to participate in microfinance. However, no differences were found among the three programmes in their effect on seasonality of consumption or labour supply. Men and women both borrowed more from the credit programme during the peak season and reduced their market labour supply.

Several potential impacts were analysed beyond the household level because of the possible spillover effects into non-participating households. Production and income in programme villages were more than twice that in non-programme villages and higher non-farm production and income were an important source of the difference. The number of hours worked was also higher in programme villages. Participation in both Grameen Bank and BRAC tended to increase non-farm income, while RD-12 increased farm income. The presence of traditional banks also increased total household income largely through farm income. None of the programmes, however, made an important impact on village-level socio-economic indicators.

Finally, estimates were made of programme impact on poverty alleviation. The moderate poverty level was established at Tk 5,270 (US$105) per person per year. Actual per person expenditures of participating households amounted to Tk4,004 (US$80). Average cumulative borrowing for all three programmes was Tk5,499 (US$110) for women and Tk3,692 (US$74) for men. By estimating consumption before participation and using the observed relationship between borrowing and consumption, it was concluded that 5 per cent of the participant households rose above poverty each year.

These impact estimates were retested in a panel data set created by re-interviewing the same households. Over 1,600 of the households were interviewed again in 1998–99. Diminishing returns were found for borrowing as the greatest impact occurred for earlier loans and declined over time. Moreover, the estimated impacts on overall poverty were smaller than reported for the cross-section data. Microfinance was found to reduce moderate poverty levels by about a more modest 1.0 percentage point per year and extreme poverty by about 1.3 percentage points per year (Khandker, 2005).

These results point to some of the problems involved in trying to make generalizations about the impact of microloans. First, the mix of loans and other services received by clients should affect impact. Second, the opportunities and demands faced by clients affect how borrowed funds are used and contribute to the differences found in impact by gender. For example, a borrower who uses a MFI loan to repay a moneylender cannot experience a large monetary impact other than through better loan terms and conditions, such as paying a lower interest rate. Women often have the primary responsibility for supplying food in the family so it is not surprising to find that loans granted to women may affect consumption smoothing while loans to men may be more frequently invested to increase income and higher levels of future consumption. Third, depth of poverty should affect impact, because the marginal return to a small increase in capital for a very poor person with business opportunities may be quite high, while it may be much lower for a richer borrower who is already using a larger amount of capital in the business. Therefore, the impact of the first loan may be higher than subsequent loans if other constraints to improving business performance are not resolved. Fourth, even the relatively robust studies discussed above did not include an analysis of graduates or dropouts, so there is no way of knowing how their exclusion biased the results. Fifth, the differences in the results obtained from the Bangladesh panel vs. the cross-section study demonstrate how choice of technique can affect the results.

New directions in impact analysis

Dissatisfaction with the cost, complexity and lack of conclusive results has prompted two quite different new directions in impact analysis. First, randomized control procedures are emerging as a way to resolve some of difficult counterfactual problems in quantitative microfinance impact analysis (Karlan and Goldberg, 2006).[7] Although no randomized impact study of microfinance has yet been published, some related studies are underway that demonstrate how to improve analytical rigor. For example, Karlan and Valdivia (2006) randomly assigned clients in a FINCA group lending programme for women in Peru to test the impact of business training. During their weekly group meeting, treatment groups received entrepreneurship training while the control groups met but without training. The results revealed that training was associated with higher loan repayment, a 16 per cent improvement in client retention rates, improved business knowledge and practices, but surprisingly not to any measurable impact on business income or assets. In another example, Gine and Karlan (2006) report on an experiment conducted to test mechanism design in a Philippines bank that switched from group liability to individual lending. Half of the bank's 169 group liability centers were randomly selected for conversion, while the other half remained as a control group. The results showed that the conversion did not affect the repayment rate of existing borrowers, but led to higher growth in centre size through retaining more pre-existing borrowers and attracting new ones.

Incentives pose a practical problem when random assignment is considered for a quantitative impact analysis of a microfinance programme. By randomly selecting members to control and treatment groups, researchers hope that the unobserved attributes of clients that affect impact, such as entrepreneurial skills, will be randomly distributed in both groups. In this way, the treatment group is expected to differ from the control group only because of the treatment, not the unobserved variables. However, the problem for persons selected for the control group is that they must cooperate and provide impact data, sometimes frequently and over long periods, even though they do not receive the loans and other services received by the treatment group. For this reason, randomization seems to be limited to select circumstances where the control group is willing to wait to receive financial services in the future while participating in the study.

A second new direction in impact analysis represents an opposite response to the question of analytical rigor. MFIs have criticized the complexity, high cost and long intervals between start date and availability of conclusions for quantitative impact studies coupled with the limited benefits they perceive from participating in such studies. These problems have prompted a search for more user-friendly methods of impact analysis. An important initiative was the Ford Foundation support to the Imp-Act (Impact Assessment of Microfinance) action research programme involving several MFIs around the world. As part of this effort, Copestake et al (2002) argued for more emphasis on impact assessment that produces 'credible' results for use by MFIs in product development rather than providing statistical evidence to 'prove' impact. They proposed more qualitative analysis based on in-depth, semi-structured interviews to gain a more complete understanding of the causal pathways linking financial services to diverse effects.

The Imp-Act approach argues for using social performance assessment to improve social performance management (SPM) that is intended to affect both the social and financial performance of MFIs. Implementing SPM involves stating MFI goals (such as enhanced client welfare) then monitoring the breadth and depth of outreach, the number and reasons for drop-outs, and the effect of services on clients. This information is used to improve MFI services and information systems. Case studies for participating institutions are presented in Imp-Act publications to demonstrate that the improvements in MFI performance more than compensate for the cost of conducting SPM, thereby contributing to both financial and social performance. Woller (2005) extended the Imp-Act work by studying how 17 MFI members of the SEEP Network utilized various types of client assessment tools to evaluate their performance. One of the conclusions is that the members agreed that client assessment should be done to 'improve' rather than to 'prove' impact.

Conclusion

Does microcredit lift people out of poverty? Advocates of the industry strongly believe so but they have a vested interest in promoting positive images that assure a flow of funds into the industry. Independent analysts face great difficulties in employing robust techniques, partly due to the large methodological difficulties in undertaking impact analysis. Moreover, the fungibility of money makes it difficult to predict exactly where to look for impact within the households and businesses of borrowers.

On the one hand, granting small loans that may be equal in size to half the country's per capita income would logically seem to make an impact on the welfare of any poor household. On the other hand, since the money may be spent in many ways and the loans must be repaid, often with an interest rate high enough to cover MFI costs and risks, the net impacts of borrowing may be small, diffuse and unsustainable.

More robust analysis is needed so that donors can evaluate if microfinance is making the greatest impact on the poor relative to other poverty reducing strategies and investments. Using impact assessment to improve MFI products is an important step in making microfinance products and services more demand driven rather than the historic approach of 'one size fits all'. Designing products that are better suited to client needs should also improve their impact.

Notes

1   This section draws upon several ideas discussed in Meyer (2002).
2   A more technical treatment of many of these issues can be found in Ravallion (2001).
3   See Kabeer (2001) for a detailed discussion of the conflicting concepts and interpretations of research results concerning credit and female empowerment in Bangladesh.
4   The USAID project entitled AIMS (Assessing the Impact of Microenterprise Services) emphasized possible project impacts at several levels beginning with the individual up through the community.
5   Morduch (1999) subsequently criticized this approach on the grounds that the programmes did not strictly enforce the eligibility criteria so that as many as 30 per cent of the participants had more than the wealth level specified. He used the same survey data to reestimate the results using a different econometric approach, and came up with conclusions different from those published by the original authors in Pitt and Khandker (1998). However, to my knowledge, Morduch's work has not gone through peer review nor has it been published except as summarized by Armendariz de Aghion and Morduch (2005). Moreover, Pitt and Khandker have written a lengthy reply explaining why they think their approach is superior to that of Morduch.
6   However, Todd (1996) analysed women who were long-term clients of Grameen Bank and found that several used their loans and savings to acquire land as security for their old age.
7   Duflo and Kremer (2003) summarize arguments for the use of randomization in the evaluation of development effectiveness with a focus on education projects in developing countries.

References

Armendariz de Aghion, B. and Morduch, J. (2005) *Economics of Microfinance*, MIT Press, Cambridge, MA.

Baker, J. L. (2000) *Evaluating the Impact of Development Projects on Poverty: A Handbook for Practitioners*, World Bank, Washington DC.

Coleman, B. E. (1999) 'The impact of group lending in Northeast Thailand', *Journal of Development Economics* 60: 105–41.

Coleman, B. E. (2006) 'Microfinance in Northeast Thailand: Who benefits and how much?', *World Development* 34(9): 1612–38.

Copestake, J., Johnson, S. and Wright, K. (2002) *Impact Assessment of Microfinance: Towards a New Protocol for Collection and Analysis of Qualitative Data*, Working Paper No. 7, Imp-Act, www.Imp-Act.org

David, C. C. and Meyer, R. L. (1980) 'Measuring the farm level impact of agricultural loans', in Howell (ed.) *Borrowers and Lenders: Rural Financial Markets and Institutions in Developing Countries*, pp. 201–34, Overseas Development Institute, London.

Dichter, T. (2006) 'Hype and Hope: The Worrisome State of the Microcredit Movement', www.microfinancegateway.org/content/article/detail/31747.

Duflo, E. and Kremer, M. (2003) *Use of Randomization in the Evaluation of Development Effectiveness*, paper prepared for the World Bank Conference on Evaluation and Development Effectiveness, 15–16 July, Washington DC.

Gine, X. and Karlan, D. S. (2006) *Group versus Individual Liability: A Field Experiment in the Philippines*, Working Paper, Yale University, Department of Economics, http://aida.econ.yale.edu/karlan/papers.html

Goldberg, N. (2005) *Measuring the Impact of Microfinance: Taking Stock of What We Know*, Grameen Foundation, Washington DC.

Hulme, D. (2000) 'Impact assessment methodologies for microfinance: theory, experience and better practice', *World Development* 28(1): 79–98.

Kabeer, N. (2001) 'Conflicts over credit: Re-evaluating the empowerment potential of loans to women in rural Bangladesh', *World Development* 29(1): 63–84.

Karlan, D. S. (2001) 'Microfinance impact assessments: The perils of using new members as a control group', *Journal of Microfinance* 3(2): 75–85.

Karlan, D. and Goldberg, N. (2006) 'The Impact of Microfinance: A Review of Methodological Issues', unpublished paper, Yale University and Innovations for Poverty Action.

Karlan, D. and Valdivia, M. (2006) *Teaching Entrepreneurship: Impact of Business Training on Microfinance Clients and Institutions*, Working Paper, Yale University, Department of Economics, http://aida.econ.yale.edu/karlan/papers.html

Khandker, S. R. (1998) *Fighting Poverty with Microcredit: Experience in Bangladesh*, Oxford University Press, New York.

Khandker, S. R. (2005) 'Microfinance and poverty: Evidence using panel data from Bangladesh', *The World Bank Economic Review* 19(2): 263–86.

Meyer, R. L. (2002) *Track Record of Financial Institutions in Assisting the Poor in Asia*, Asian Development Bank Institute, Research Paper 49, Tokyo.

Miller, C. C. (2006) 'Microcredit is booming in India, but the loans don't often pull people out of poverty', *Forbes*, 27 November.

Morduch, J. (1999) 'The microfinance promise', *Journal of Economic Literature* 37: 1569–1614.

Morduch, J. and Haley, B. (2002) *Analysis of the Effects of Microfinance on Poverty Reduction*, NYU Wagner Working Paper No. 1014, New York University, New York.

Pitt, M. W. and Khandker, S. R. (1998) ' The impact of group-based credit programs on poor households in Bangladesh: Does the gender of participants matter?', *Journal of Political Economy* 106(5): 958–96.

Ravallion, M. (2001) 'The mystery of the vanishing benefits: An introduction to impact evaluation', *The World Bank Economic Review* 15(1): 115–40.

Roche, C. (1999) *Impact Assessment for Development Agencies*, Oxfam, Oxford.

Sharma, M. and Buchenrieder, G. (2002) 'Impact of microfinance on food security: A review and synthesis of empirical evidence', in Zeller, M. and Meyer, R. L. (eds) *The Triangle of Microfinance: Financial Sustainability, Outreach, and Impact*, pp. 221–40, The Johns Hopkins University Press, Baltimore.

Todd, H. (1996) *Women at the Center: Grameen Bank after One Decade*, The University Press Limited, Dhaka.

Von Pischke, J. D. and Adams, D. W. (1980) 'Fungibility and the design and evaluation of agricultural credit projects', *American Journal of Agricultural Economics* 62(4): 719–26.

Woller, G. (2005) *Building Successful Microfinance Institutions by Assessing Clients' Needs*, The SEEP Network, Washington DC.

CHAPTER NINETEEN
From microcredit to livelihood finance

Vijay Mahajan

Abstract

Five assumptions about microcredit are put forth in this chapter as seriously flawed. The author argues that credit is not the main financial service needed by the poor; credit does not translate into successful microenterprises; the poor do not all wish to be self-employed; targeting those above the poverty line is not mis-targeting; and not all MFIs can be self-sustaining. If we are to consider economic growth, then microcredit by itself is insufficient. It must become part of livelihood finance. Livelihood finance is a framework that includes financial services (savings, short- and long-term credit, several types of insurance, infrastructure finance, human capital development), agriculture and business development services and institutional development.

I was at the 1997 Microcredit Summit. The presence of many luminaries at the summit was an indication of the support it garnered. For example, from the speech of Hillary Clinton, it was obvious that she was sincerely involved in the field and had visited many microcredit institutions in developing countries. However, for many of the others, it was jumping on the bandwagon, and few raised any issues about the limitations of microcredit. After attending the Microcredit Summit in 1997, I had written a critical article titled *Is Microcredit the Answer to Poverty Eradication?*. My answer was a qualified no, but the article was largely ignored.

Since then, microcredit has become a global fad, to the point where all kinds of claims are being made in its name, as if it is the latest magic potion to resolve the problems of poverty in the world. In response, a range of others, from the *Wall Street Journal* to academic researchers like Jonathan Morduch have taken it upon themselves to question these claims and show that the impact of microcredit on the target households is exaggerated.

I want to explore the connection between microcredit and economic growth. I do this from the point of view of someone who has given 20 years of his life to this work, so I should not be seen as an outsider. But before I deal with microcredit and economic growth, let me repeat what I had said in my 1997 article on the limitations of microcredit even as a strategy for poverty eradication.

Limitations of microcredit: Five fatal assumptions

1. Assumption that credit is the main financial service needed by the poor. Actually it is not. The poor need and want to save much more than they want to borrow. They also want to cover themselves against risks through insurance. However, the field in general does not adequately emphasize other financial services, such as savings and insurance. Savings are particularly important, as these act as self-insurance in case of smaller contingencies: meeting sudden demands of cash such as due to illness in the family; acting as margin money or 'equity' for borrowing; and finally, to some extent acting as a collateral for repayment of loans, where savings are deposited with lenders. The experience of SEWA Bank in India, for example, shows that women value a safe place to keep their savings as an important service.

Insurance is another important financial service for the poor, given their vulnerability to livelihood risks. Here one is not talking so much of life insurance but of crop insurance and insurance for income earning assets such as livestock and irrigation pumpsets. For certain occupational groups such as sea-going fishermen and miners, life insurance is important. Money transfers are an increasingly important service, as a large proportion of poor households have one or more members of the family migrating for part of the year or several years at a time, in search of work. Thus to focus on microcredit alone and leave out microsavings, microinsurance and money transfers is myopic.

2. Assumption that credit can automatically translate into successful microenterprises. This is the familiar debate of 'minimalist credit' strategies versus the 'integrated' approach to microenterprise promotion. Others, (such as Mahajan and Dichter (1990)) argue that there is no one correct approach and that the strategy for microenterprise promotion should be contingent on the requirements of the situation, based on a systematic analysis.

Microcredit is a necessary but not a sufficient condition for microenterprise promotion. Other inputs are required, such as identification of livelihood opportunities, selection and motivation of the microentrepreneurs, business and technical training, establishing of market linkages for inputs and outputs, common infrastructure, and some times regulatory approvals. In the absence of these, microcredit by itself, works only for a limited set of activities – small farming, livestock rearing and petty trading, and even those where market linkages are in place. The Microcredit Summit Declaration did make a token recognition of this assumption when, in a shift from the draft to the final, they added 'other financial and business services' to credit.

3. Assumption that the poorest all wish to be self-employed and can be helped by microcredit. Most of the proponents of microcredit as *the* strategy for poverty eradication make the explicit assumption that the poor would all like to be self-employed. It is true that a certain proportion of poor people do like to take up small farming, livestock rearing, processing, manufacturing or trading activities, but usually they do so to supplement their income from wage-employment. A majority of poor people, particularly the poorest (such as landless labourers in India) want steady wage-employment, on- or off-farm.

Moreover, there is serious evidence that like all other 'single' interventions, microcredit works less well for the poorer clients. As Hulme and Mosley have shown (1969), the increase in income of microcredit borrowers is directly proportional to their starting level of income – the poorer they were to start with, the less the impact of the loan. One could live with this finding in an imperfect world, but what is really troubling is that a vast majority of those whose starting income was below the poverty line actually ended up with less incremental income after getting a microloan, as compared to a control group that did not get the loan. This should stop recent converts from offering microcredit as *the* solution for poverty eradication, since it can do more harm than good to the poorest.

4. *Assumption that those slightly above the poverty line do not need microcredit, and giving it to them amounts to mis-targeting.* Though several microcredit programmes, including the Grameen Bank and its replicators, have a vast majority of their clients who are poor, mainly landless women, this is not true of a large number of other microcredit programmes, including India's SHG-bank linkage programme. Most microcredit programmes mainly reach the upper layers among the poor and some, mainly those above the poverty line. Because the microcredit promise was to reach the poor, if not the poorest, this phenomenon is not well regarded.

Yet, access to credit by those who are not among the poorest is not very much better than for the poorest, and what is more, these people generate much needed wage employment opportunities for the poorest. In addition, it enables the microcredit channel to spread its costs over a larger base. To therefore treat any lending to those slightly above the poverty line as mis-targeting is naïve.

5. *Assumption that microcredit institutions can all become financially self-sustaining.* While one supports the overall move for financial self-sustainability, the assumption that this can be possible for all microcredit institutions, needs to be examined. Even the best cases take too long to get there (for example, Grameen Bank in its first 20 years) or have got there by shedding their NGO avatar that needed early subsidies (for example, PRODEM before it became Bancosol). India's SHG programme has grown big on the basis of external support to the one-time costs of group formation and on-going group-support costs. With political pressure to lower interest rates on loans to SHGs, even the variable costs are not being met in most places.

Recent studies by CGAP show that only about a 100 of the 10,000 odd MFIs round the world are financially self-sufficient. Thus the dual promise that microcredit is able to serve the very poor, and in a financially sustainable manner, is not borne out in practice. Experience shows that either one of these two mutually contradictory goals can be achieved, but rarely both together.

Risks of the 'microcredit by itself is enough' strategy

India has witnessed a large growth in microcredit over the last decade. Adopting and building on the work of a few pioneering NGOs like MYRADA, ASSEFA,

PRADAN and DHAN, NABARD has helped make the SHG-bank linkage model now perhaps the largest microcredit programme in the world, with an outreach to nearly 24 million poor women, who have cumulatively received loans of over Rs6,800 crore (nearly US$1.5 billion) from banks. This is an achievement that we can all – NGOs, MFIs, NABARD and the banks – be proud of.

But we should also not forget that the average loan size is around Rs2000 (about US$45), which is too little to even alleviate poverty, leave alone lift a family totally out of poverty, or trigger local economic growth. In many of the poorer states, it is still hard for SHGs to even open bank accounts, let alone get a loan. In other states, where a large number of groups have been financed, there is an attempt by various political parties to interfere with interest rates and other terms on which the groups work, to cultivate this new vote bank. Thus there is a real risk that in celebrating the SHG-bank linkage microcredit programme, attention is diverted from the larger problem of financial exclusion of the poor, and banks are let off the hook from their real job.

A second risk that the poor may suffer as a result of an over-emphasis on a microcredit strategy, is the reduction in government budgetary allocations for other efforts at poverty alleviation, such as the well-tried but less dramatic strategies of investment in human capital, for example, through primary health and primary education programmes. While there is no denying that such social sector programmes can be run more cost-efficiently and that they can be better targeted to the poor, the replacement of such programmes with microcredit programmes will be a double disaster for the poor. If the implicit subsidies to microcredit institutions are made explicit, then subsidizing microcredit programmes vs. subsidizing social sector programmes can become an informed policy choice, rather than be carried out under the mistaken notion that the former will require only temporary and diminishing subsidies. But the implicit subsidies to microcredit, legitimate as they may be, are not being described or analysed.

Thus there is the risk of reducing the overall resource allocation for poverty alleviation and social sector programmes. We need to recognize that by pointing to numbers like the Rs6,800 crore of bank credit to SHGs, politicians and the government can take attention off the fact that not enough resources are being put on more pressing needs such as nutrition, primary health and primary education. We have to thank the Indian Government's Eleventh National Plan Finance Commission (2000) for recognizing this and making additional allocations to the poorer states for precisely these things. But, as the mid-term review of the Tenth Five Year Plan shows, the progress on most of the Millennium Development Goals is tardy and no amount of microcredit is going to make up for that.

Microcredit and economic growth

What should then be done to make microcredit become a true instrument for poverty alleviation, and even further, for economic growth?

In an impact assessment study carried out by BASIX six years after inception, the MFI found that only 52 per cent of its three-year plus microcredit customers reported an increase in income, 23 per cent reported no change, while another 25 per cent actually reported a decline. What was the reason for this? Analysis showed that the reasons were: first, unmanaged risk, second, low productivity in crop cultivation and livestock rearing, and third, inability to get good prices from the input and output markets.

Based on this study, BASIX revised its strategy and now offers microcredit along with a whole suite of insurance products covering life, health, crops and livestock. For enhancing productivity, a whole range of agricultural and business development services are being offered to borrowers. For ensuring better prices, alternate market linkages are being facilitated both on the input and output side. Producers are encouraged to form groups and cooperatives, which are then given institutional development services to become more effective.

Since microcredit is able to address the livelihood problem only peripherally, we need to broaden the paradigm from microcredit to 'livelihood finance'. Let me explain the term first. Livelihood finance is a comprehensive approach to promoting sustainable livelihoods for the poor, which includes:

- Financial services:
  - Savings;
  - Credit, both short-term (for working capital and consumption) and long-term (for investment in natural resources such as land, water, trees, livestock, energy);
  - Insurance for the lives and livelihoods of the poor, covering health, crops and livestock;
  - Infrastructure finance: roads, power, market places, telecom, as needed;
  - Investment in human development including in nutrition, health, education and vocational training.
- Agricultural and business development services:
  - Productivity enhancement;
  - Risk mitigation, other than insurance (such as vaccination of livestock);
  - Local value addition;
  - Alternate market linkages.
- Institutional development services:
  - Forming and strengthening of various producer organizations such as SHGs, water users' associations, forest protection committees, credit and commodity cooperatives and *panchayats*;
  - Establishing systems for accounting, performance measurement, incentives, management information systems and so on.

Seen in the above context, microcredit pales into insignificance as a 'solution' for poverty alleviation and promotion of livelihoods. Microcredit by definition, is a single intervention: small loans, given for short durations, with repayments beginning as quickly and as frequently as possible. Moreover, whether given through SHGs, Grameen Bank-style groups, joint liability groups or directly to individuals, most microcredit eventually is loans to individuals, not to any collectives.

In contrast, livelihood finance will require large amounts; it may need more than just loans (it may need equity or risk funds and indeed some public subsidies); it will invariably be for long durations, at least five and maybe 20 years, and its use will almost always be for collective purposes. Thus microcredit and livelihood finance are fundamentally different.

I had tried to explain the difference in a lecture in January 2004, in the memory of my colleague, the late Jimmy Mascarenhas. To repeat, let me take you to a village called Rozkund in the Bijadandi block of the Mandla district of Madhya Pradesh, truly the heartland of India, known for the Kanha Tiger Reserve. The village is 16 km from a tarred road. The district was densely forested, though now the forest cover is denuded near inhabited areas. The rainfall is plentiful, between 1,200–1,400 mm per annum. The soil cover is still good. The inhabitants are mainly tribals – the Gonds, who till a generation ago lived off the forests and patches of valley land, irrigated by rivulets.

Anokhe Lal Gond, a resident of this village, has three acres of cultivable land and a separate patch of two acres on the hill slope. He has about 20 livestock, including a scrub buffalo, two cows, a pair of bullock and a dozen goats. He is married and has three children, and his mother also lives with him. Anokhe is unable to make a living from his land and goes to Jabalpur, about 100 km away for about six months every year. His wife joins him for part of the time, but comes back after every two weeks to look after the children and the cattle. With all this, we estimate Anokhe Lal's annual income to be Rs15,000 (about US$330), putting him squarely below the poverty line.

On first sight, Anokhe Lal looks like a potential candidate for microcredit. But I maintain microcredit will not benefit him much, if at all. Let us take the typical microcredit loan through the SHG route that his wife could get by being a member of an SHG. For this, she will have to join a SHG, which someone, perhaps an NGO or a government agency would have to form. No such agency is in sight. But even if a SHG were formed, and then its members met and saved regularly, it would take a bank at least 18 to 24 months before the SHG would qualify for a loan. By that time Anokhe's wife would have saved say, Rs20 per month or Rs360 (US$8) in 18 months, to eventually get an SHG loan of perhaps Rs1000 or Rs1500 (US$22–33). What would Anokhe and his wife do with this loan?

- They cannot level or terrace their three acres of farm land, to conserve soil cover and rainfall, since it requires at least Rs3,000 per acre or Rs9,000 in total (US$200).
- They cannot dig a well, which they need, since that requires Rs20,000 (US$440) and to prevent drying up it also requires treatment of the watershed.
- They cannot buy a diesel pumpset and pipeline to raise water from a nearby stream, since that needs another Rs15,000 (US$330). The stream also requires watershed treatment to prevent drying up.

- They cannot buy a buffalo, for that needs Rs9,000 (US$200) for even for the least expensive, and even if they do, without insurance, it can be a major risk. Once bought, it needs fodder, feed, veterinary care and the milk would have to be sold outside the village.
- They cannot plant trees on their two acres of sloping land, since that needs Rs5,000 (US$110) and the trees need protection from grazing for the first three years.
- They cannot get a road to their village or an electric line to their field, since the proportionate cost of each of these is Rs15,000 (US$340), or Rs30,000 for both a road and a power line.
- They cannot educate their elder daughter beyond the local school as that needs Rs12,000 (US$265) for her to pass a teacher's training course.

Yet, each of the above 'investment' opportunities has a positive rate of return, shown by numerous World Bank and NABARD studies to be in the range of 25–30 per cent and more. But all of them require larger, longer-term loans, with long moratoriums and no possibility of repayment for a number of years. And repayment would not only be after a long-term but also be rife with all kinds of uncertainties, since there are a number of externalities in the projects. This is the kind of situation that makes financial institutions shy away.

Even if we found a financial institution to give a loan for any or all of the above investment opportunities to Anokhe Lal, he alone cannot make much use of it, because almost all of these require collective action. Even digging a well on his own land, which looks like a simple, private thing to do, is no good, since unless the ridges and slopes overlooking the valley where his land is, are treated, the chances are that the water table will go down in a few years and his well will dry up.

Even if Anokhe gets water in his well, for him to make a return on investment on his well and pump, he will have to grow some cash crops such as vegetables and there is no way he can sell those, being 16 km away from a tarred road. In any case, drawing water from a well using a diesel engine is expensive, so unless he can get electricity, there is no point having a pump. Thus, if the productive base of the village has to go up, it cannot be just for Anokhe Lal alone, but for a much larger number of farmers, if not all of them. This necessarily means they have to be brought together in various groups – SHGs for savings and credit, watershed groups for land and water conservation, forest protection committees for regenerating the degraded patches, and so on.

Thus, in one shot of reality, we find that a Rs1,500 microcredit loan is at worst an apology for no access to formal credit, and at best a palliative to be used to smooth consumption in those months when Anokhe and his wife cannot even migrate to Jabalpur.

What Anokhe needs is not microcredit but livelihood finance. In that paradigm, the livelihood finance institution would begin with forming SHGs, not for disbursing credit but for encouraging savings and building a sense of solidarity. Other institutions – farmers' club, watershed committee, forest protection committee, dairy cooperative – in the village would also be formed or strengthened. Over a period of a few years, investment would be made on all the above projects, adding up to Rs100,000 (US$2,220) just for Anokhe Lal's household.

But we need to remind ourselves that livelihood finance is not only about finance. For the land treatment to work, the trees to grow on the land on the hill slope, and for the road to be built, functioning local institutions such as watershed committees, forest protection committees and *panchayats* are needed. To sell his vegetables or milk from his buffalo, in Jabalpur or Mandla, Anokhe needs to get together with other farmers, to transport the produce collectively. As we know, this rarely happens on its own. Some outside motivation and initial training is needed, from an NGO or a specialized agency such as a National Dairy Development Board team forming dairy cooperatives. Once formed, to function effectively, these groups/committees/cooperatives require regular hand-holding and ongoing institutional development. Intangible though that process is, it also requires an investment. Let us say this will need 25 per cent on top of the Rs100,000 of project investments we mentioned above.

After several more years, as the projects start yielding benefits, Anokhe would get a (back of the envelope) return of Rs25,000–30,000 (US$550–660) per annum and after paying interest and principal instalments, he would be able to increase his net annual income by at least 50–60 percent. He would also diversify his livelihood portfolio, reduce the risk due to rain failure after the crop is flowering and generate much needed work for his wife and his mother, while staying in their village. The investment would generate wage employment for landless families in the same village for an additional 60–120 person days. It would conserve land, water and increase the tree cover. Anokhe's eldest daughter could study and become a teacher, and the additional income would also enable the two younger children to finish school, and perhaps even pursue higher studies.

From microcredit to livelihood finance

So, to get out of poverty permanently, Anokhe Lal and 40 million households like his in India, each need Rs100,000 worth of direct investment, and another 2.5 per cent of that amount as institutional investment to make it work. Multiply and you arrive at a figure of Rs500,000 crore (about US$110 billion). This sounds like a large figure, almost 25 per cent of India's GDP. But is that too much investment to eradicate poverty, while rebuilding the natural and human resource base of the country?

Even if India were to spare 2.5 per cent of its GDP for livelihood finance on an annual basis, the task could be completed in a decade and we would still be in time for the 2015 deadline of the Millennium Development Goal of halving poverty. In any case, if we take into account that the Golden Quadrilateral and related highway works will cost the nation Rs100,000 crore, and that the proposed river linking system is supposed to cost Rs500,000 crore, livelihood finance is not such an expensive idea.

Thus, I wish I could say that microcredit can by itself promote economic growth. In reality, microcredit is barely adequate even as an instrument for poverty alleviation, let alone economic growth. To serve the purpose of economic growth, we need a new paradigm of livelihood finance, with much larger levels of resource allocation, both from public resources as well from capital markets.

So what's needed to adopt livelihood finance as a national strategy?

- Step one should be an intellectually rigorous analysis, careful crafting of the concept and then a wide and open debate on the idea of livelihood finance. The existing experience of both government and NGO projects in natural resource and human resource development should be thoroughly examined for lessons.

- Step two should be convincing the capital markets that livelihood finance is a good deal, and that the risk-adjusted returns in it are comparable to or better than well-accepted investments such as housing finance, which all banks are chasing with lower and lower spreads.

- Step three would be ushering institutional changes in the way our natural resources are owned and managed. New models will have to be developed that ensure a congruence of interest for the state, the community and for the investors.

- Step four is ensuring that high quality human resources are made available to work close to the ground in the districts, where all the implementation is done, in places like Bijadandi. Only highly capable and committed human beings working at the grassroots can make livelihood finance benefit people like Anokhe Lal and his family.

Microcredit and the SHG-bank linkage programme weres the right remedy for the ills of a banking system rendered hostile to the poor after the excesses of the Integrated Rural Development Program, under which they were forced to lend to a government generated list of poor households. Now it is time the proponents of narrow microcredit and the SHG-bank linkage programme move from this to the more holistic concept of livelihood finance.

References

Hulme, D. and Mosley, P. (1969) *Finance Against Poverty*, Routledge, London.

Mahajan, V. and Dichter, T. (1990) 'A contingency approach to small business and *enterprise development*', *Journal of Small Enterprise Development* 1(14).

CHAPTER TWENTY
Opportunity and evolution for microfinance

Mary Houghton and Ronald Grzywinski

Abstract

The scale, profitability and capacity for innovation of some microfinance institutions creates a platform to broaden the delivery of credit and to contribute to the economic development of many markets in developing countries. A more flexible view about types of capital that are of use, the range of financial and social returns that are attractive, the tools for evaluation of effective measurement is required, as is the recruitment/retention of talent equal to the task of managing more complex strategies.

When one of the writers was much younger she was privileged to hear Jane Jacobs, the legendary critical thinker about urban planning, economics and the environment, speak to a microcredit crowd in Canada. Jacobs started by observing the irony that such a brilliant financial innovation occurred in Bangladesh and other developing countries rather than in North America. American innovative development of new financial products is itself legendary but it is driven by lucrative financial incentives. The microfinance industry teaches that brilliant financial innovation can be created by individuals in developing countries with business instincts, but who are motivated primarily by the achievement of social returns.

The microfinance industry evolved by proving a concept on a small scale, applying management skill, and then launching successful rollouts. Accomplished professionals came to credit delivery from achievement in a different field and created the most successful institutions. The history is also a story of a global competition for transparency, efficiency and innovation. Remarkably this information sharing was as robust in the pre-Internet era of the 1980s as it is now. Today we watch the current gradual expansion of microfinance into fuller financial services. Some leaders today run world-class banking operations. What will the next 10 years bring?

- Will these social entrepreneurs innovate increasingly in related fields of development finance?
- To what extent will the conventional financial services industry serve this market, and to what extent will there be a continued need for development finance institutions that are permanent players with a rich market knowledge of and a commitment to reaching local, underserved populations?

- Will investor interest in microfinance for the purpose of poverty alleviation increase the financing options and resources available to institutions that strive to achieve social as well as financial returns?
- Will they attract needed additional entrepreneurial and management talent to the field of development finance?
- Will academic interest in microfinance lead to better methods of outcome assessment and support the concept of a measurable social return?
- Will the leading microfinance banking organizations innovate in related fields of development finance and thereby morph into something not yet known?

Following are some alternative possible evolutions in the field.

It is a given that most high performing microfinance institutions will operate as regulated banks. They will operate a regulated bank in order to mobilize and protect local savings credibly; savings in the local currency offer the most diversified, lowest cost and lowest risk funding for loan portfolios. Now imagine that these institutions are also successfully creating efficient housing and small business finance markets. These would now be full-service, market-disciplined, local development banks.

We believe that the conventional banking system will not fully take over the work of financing economic development activity at the 'bottom of the pyramid'. The largest banks must continue to find economies of scale through consolidation and non-locally-based systemization. Only institutions that know local markets deeply enough to underwrite risk at low loss rates, are willing to specialize in small transactions, and operate through a mix of organizational structures (for example, a for-profit bank combined with a non-profit enterprise development corporation) will fully meet the economic development needs of poor people.

One problem with this option is that MFIs may be unwilling or unable to develop a second or third profitable line of business for any one of several good reasons. They may justifiably prefer to focus on self-employment, the economic activity most accessible to very poor people. The organizational cultures of microfinance credit officers and small business credit officers and housing credit officers may be too different, making the management of the organization too difficult.

So another possibility for the future is that perhaps some MFIs will shift from a sole focus on microfinance to a sole focus on housing finance or small business finance. Although not yet adequately documented, access to housing finance and small business finance may have as much or more capacity as microfinance to improve the economic well-being of poor people in developing countries. Access to capital for small business and housing investment may help to create more personal assets and jobs than access to credit for self-employment does. Self-employment may increase household income but it rarely grows into a value-creating, job-creating business.

This transformation will not happen, however, unless accomplished social entrepreneurs, like those that were motivated to create and refine microcredit methodology, enter these other areas of finance and demonstrate that scaleable and profitable operation is possible. We know of only a few initiatives to refine small business lending methodologies so that they can reliably reach large and growing numbers of small business customers:

- Our employer, ShoreBank Corporation, has trained over a thousand bankers in 53 banks in 40 countries on the set up and management of small business loan departments; these departments have had low initial loan losses but have been small scale. Several of these banks have experimented successfully with tailored credit scoring to improve efficiency.
- BRAC Bank, sponsored by BRAC in Bangladesh, has advanced over 50,000 small business loans totaling nearly US$300 million, in its first five years in operation. (ShoreCap Exchange, an affiliate of ShoreBank Corporation, is currently working on a study of the effects of small business growth on the incomes of low-income small business owners and their employees by running a small pilot study at BRAC Bank.)
- ProCredit is managing a group of banks that tracks segments within micro and small business by loan size, performance and production data.

In housing finance there are larger scale successes and far larger market opportunities than in small business finance. Mortgage loans at high loan-to-value ratios and with the long-term tenors required to pay for a house out of annual incomes are not widely available in most developing countries. But strong borrower motivation will yield high repayment rates, just as it has in microfinance. Female customers of microfinance programmes work on self-employed ventures and repay microloans in order to earn more money to take care of family needs. In the USA there is no surer road to personal financial security than home ownership, as it provides a personal opportunity to benefit when real estate values appreciate. BRAC and Grameen have provided housing finance successfully for decades with this result. Early experimentation by other MFIs with three- to five-year loans for home acquisition or improvement demonstrates similar success, even when the lender has difficulty securing its collateral position.

Similarly there is little financing available for the construction and acquisition of rental housing for low-income residents. But there are a few examples that can be built on. For example, ShoreBank has been financing blue-collar African Americans and immigrants who buy, rehabilitate and manage rental properties in Chicago for 30 years. We have advanced US$950 million in loans in that period with average net loan losses from 2001–05 of 0.18 per cent of average loans outstanding. The Trust for Urban Housing Finance in Johannesburg has adapted our methodology and became profitable in the fiscal year that ended in March 2006 with just over R100 million (US$14 million) in assets, its third year of operation. It has approved over R250 million (US$35 million) on nearly 6,000 units of housing in 160 loans in Johannesburg; it plans to expand to other cities in South Africa.

But if there are to be profitable banks that specialize in these new forms of banking for the poor, additional constraints should be removed. These are constraints related to:

- Our tolerance for managing profit-making businesses alongside innovating affiliates that make strategic use of subsidies;
- The amount and type of capital available to development finance institutions;
- The methods of evaluation used by investors and donors to assess outcomes;
- Local legal and regulatory environments;
- The incentives required to attract needed talent to the field.

The phenomenal popularity of microfinance may help make this possible. Amazingly, after winning large grants for starting up operations, Grameen and BRAC insisted that their credit programmes attain profitability because only recurring profitability could assure scalability. If profitable, the credit programmes could attract investment as well as grants, mobilize savings as well as soft loans, and plough profits back into growth to continue to reach more customers. Interestingly, however, they both continued to develop other businesses and non-profit initiatives. Today BRAC also manages poultry, dairy, and seed businesses, runs a massive informal elementary education programme and university, and owns and operates banks and a mortgage company. Grameen runs cloth manufacturing, cell phone, cold storage and other businesses and is now entering cataract hospital development and nutritionally-fortified yogurt manufacturing. This desire and capacity to manage a multi-faceted institution stems from an understanding of the complex nature of poverty. This deep knowledge does not occur routinely in the microfinance industry. Only a few of the NGOs that have converted their credit programmes to regulated financial institutions, such as K-REP in Kenya, have maintained non-banking interventions through affiliated NGOs. BASIX in India started in the late 1990s as a family of both regulated financial institutions and NGOs. These four institutions – BRAC, Grameen, K-REP and BASIX – have taken on the task of managing both a profitable banking institution that does not require any subsidy after start-up with one set of managers and a range of other non-banking businesses and subsidized interventions with other sets of managers.

We have great empathy for this approach as it mirrors our own in the USA, where we attempt to deal with problems of poverty caused in great part by racial inequality. A bank is a powerful but usually reactive institution and the effects of racism in US urban neighborhoods will not be solved if bank loans are the only tool. In the authors' case we have used non-bank approaches most effectively to jump-start a housing market with large-scale, subsidized, affordable housing projects and to provide high-risk loans to young small businesses. ShoreBank collaborates with a small group of international institutions that espouse this approach called the Development Finance Forum. It published a paper entitled *Capital Plus*, available at www.dfforum.com, that fully articulates the case for this approach.

Unfortunately, in our experience, investors and donors prefer simpler solutions. It is infinitely easier to measure and appreciate financial returns than social returns. The norms of mainstream financial markets are almost universally considered inviolable. The instruments of finance may become ever more complex and differentiated, but the measures of success are simple and homogenous. Return is financial return and charity is charity.

One manifestation of this capital market demand for homogeneity and simplification is the lack of a language that makes necessary distinctions about customer segments and required product differentiation. The lack of a specific language is perhaps the most fundamental and telling indicator of how primitive the field of development finance remains. For example, we say SME as if both small businesses and medium-sized businesses are the same when we know that the age of the business, its revenues and its number of employees tell us numerous facts about required management capacity and the types of finance required. Sometimes we even use MSME (micro, small and medium enterprises) to describe all that is 'not big', further over-simplifying the kind of market we hope to reach. Similarly, there appear to be only two sources of equity for investment: conventional capital that expects a risk-adjusted market return above of 15 per cent, and philanthropic capital that it wants to subsidize by expecting the entities in which it invests to earn returns of 5 per cent or lower. But don't we live in a world that is more complicated?

Perhaps investing in regulated banks and corporate families that include banks in developing countries with uncompetitive banking markets is neither a high risk nor a high return business. Maybe bank businesses with some social outcomes could generate a variety of financial returns. Can we find a way to better match socially minded equity investors with the range of potential financial returns, be they 5, 9, 15 or 18 per cent? Some of this may be a matter of financial engineering – creating instruments that allow equity investors in the same entity to target different combinations of financial and social returns. But some require a better ability to match investor financial and social return appetites with the institutions most likely to achieve those results. The investor could choose which mixture or 'blend' of financial and social return he or she preferred.

Measuring the social returns will continue to be challenging. Luckily, academic interest in microfinance has grown significantly, especially among economists, including increased focus on the measurement of social outcomes. If there is an interest in creating permanent institutions that specialize in the delivery of finance of self-employment, housing and small business for the benefit of poor people, we need a variety of tools for internal and external evaluation at several levels:

- Innovating managers must measure and evaluate the effectiveness of new products;
- Management needs to routinely assess whether it is achieving planned social outcomes;
- Investors and funders need to be able to compare the effectiveness of institutions;
- Investors interested in more than a financial return need a way to evaluate the social return of an investment.

Economists interested in financial systems are both learning from and assisting innovators in product evaluation through randomized trial research. But our understanding of institutional effectiveness calls for much more nuanced tools for evaluation of our work. Social scientists have refined methodologies such as the logical frameworks and 'theory of change' approaches (both of which differentiate inputs, outputs, outcomes and impact), but these methods are imperfect when it comes to evaluating institutions that are responding to changing markets and needs. Business schools are supporting the application of business discipline to non-profit management and business school student interest in international development finance is growing. All this may help with the measurement of institutional social impact for use in financial markets, but most of those coming into the field continue to see business and non-profits as parallel worlds. The possibility of hybrid institutional forms is not yet part of organizational orthodoxy.

What could the best minds in our society achieve if, as Jane Jacobs observed, they were not so sharply focused on the affluent market? We can thank the achievements of the microfinance industry for turning the heads of a few academic departments and a few socially responsible investors. The agenda for the next several decades is rich and challenging, because there are so many more heads to be turned. Accomplishing this requires a managerially experienced, entrepreneurially, intellectually and socially strong and committed cadre of new leaders.

If the management challenges to an NGO of running an efficient microfinance business are daunting, the management challenges of running a multi-unit group of businesses and NGOs are many times more difficult. It requires that managers understand the reason that a complex strategy is required, have an instinctual collaborative style, and tolerate cultures and disciplines other than their own. If one could promise better compensation, longer tenure, more recognition in a competitive and innovative industry by academia and capital markets, and the opportunity to work in a reasonably sophisticated work environment, could we recruit managers with more business management experience to 'serious' but mission-focused banking institutions?

Poverty is a problem that should engage the best minds of our society but is very frequently relegated to second-class status as the work of undercapitalized NGOs. In a rush to applaud the large-scale innovation of microfinance that reaches poor people in developing countries, the tendency of investors to apply traditional definitions of risk, return and charity may well stifle further development of the field of poverty alleviation. But poverty alleviation and its cousin, economic development, could be important fields with a multiplicity of strategies and professional and investment opportunities, like education and health. Current world attention to the successes of microfinance provides the opportunity to move to new models of financially disciplined, scalable investment in the economic and social well-being of the world's poorest populations. It is an opportunity we can choose to seize.

Some final thoughts

Malcolm Harper

In October 2004, I visited Haripalala, a small cluster of villages some 200 km east of Hyderabad in India. As I was walking through one village I asked whether anyone had ever dropped out of a group. 'Yes', said my guide, 'that lady over there dropped out a year ago'. We went to talk to her and found that she had taken a small loan to pay for her sister's medical care. Then her husband became ill. She fell behind on her repayments, and after some time the other group members lost patience and locked her and her young daughters out of their hut. After living in the road for a few days she despaired and tried to throw herself and her children into the village well. Luckily she was stopped just in time, and someone pointed out that her savings with the group were actually enough to pay off her loan. Her account was cleared, but she was expelled from the group.

The next day, in a neighbouring hamlet, I asked the same question. The group to whom I was talking pointed to a young mother who was sitting disconsolately nearby with her child who was clearly unwell. A few months earlier her husband had been killed in an accident in a nearby town where he was pedaling a rickshaw. After some weeks his wife asked her group if she could have a loan to buy medicine for her sick child, but to her surprise they told her that she already had an outstanding loan. Unknown to her, the group had given a loan to her husband's family; what was worse, it was overdue and they demanded that she repay it. She left the group without paying, and had ever since been more or less ostracised by the whole village.

Those experiences, and others like them, prompted the writing of this book. Our purpose was not to suggest that the whole endeavour of microfinance is misplaced and should be abandoned. None of the authors believes that, but each of the contributions shows that something is wrong. They present a wide range of views, not all of which are mutually consistent, but they add up to a quite powerful answer to the original question posed in our title: there is quite a lot wrong with microfinance.

The most frequent criticism is not really a criticism of microfinance itself at all. Nobody would criticize an obstetrician for not being able to do open heart surgery, but if she, or her friends, claimed that she could do such a thing we might be justified in expressing some doubt. The one common thread that runs through all these papers is that too much is claimed for microfinance, and that expectations are grossly exaggerated. If too much is expected of a person, or of a movement, disappointment must inevitably follow. And, more seriously, other remedies may be neglected because the favourite occupies the institutional space, the time and the money that might have been devoted to different or additional cures.

There is an element of paradox in this. The chapters show not only that microfinance practitioners are over-ambitious in what they claim, but also that they are not ambitious enough in what they are trying to do. They neglect opportunities to develop techniques to reach further down the poverty scale, they fail to appreciate the need for products that can finance enterprises that will employ people rather than forcing them to be self-employed, and they continue to focus on credit and loans when their customers need savings and insurance far more urgently.

Over half the contributions specifically mention the lack of effective savings products. It is tempting to wonder whether anyone would have been awarded a Nobel Prize for developing and successfully disseminating a revolutionary new approach to savings mobilization for the poor. Probably not, but not because it would not have filled a gap that was at least as important as the need for credit. Loans are about transferring 'our' money to the poor, which is intrinsically more attractive than enabling them to accumulate their own money more safely and accessibly.

Several of the chapters also mention the fact that microfinance can 'crowd out' other initiatives. A senior civil servant in the Indian state of Kerala remarked at a seminar in Cochin that there was no longer any need to worry about primary health care or primary education for the remote hillside communities on the eastern part of the state, because 'they now have microfinance'. This may be an extreme view, but externally financed MFIs certainly have the effect of diverting attention and support from 'people's institutions', cooperatives, credit unions and similar ventures that are nowadays somewhat discredited but that laid the foundation for much of Europe's present financial infrastructure.

There is also some mention of the vexed topic of subsidy. It must be more clearly defined, and, perhaps more controversially, it is not always a bad thing. The institutions that dispense and receive the most subsidy are often those that criticize it most vocally, but the quest for 'sustainability', a classic development weasel word, has tended to discredit attempts by MFIs to reach down to poorer people that are unashamedly dependent on subsidy.

Many of these weaknesses are already being addressed; new savings products are being introduced and regulations are being changed to allow MFIs to offer them; some successful poverty alleviation interventions have been introduced; and a small number of institutions are trying both to broaden their offerings by including other forms of assistance, and to move 'up-market' in order to finance enterprises that create jobs rather than marginal forms of self-employment. Such initiatives are still few and far between, however, and they almost inevitably conflict with the need to be 'sustainable' and to squeeze out subsidies.

Less pervasive, but more serious, than exaggerated expectations is the damage that microfinance can do. At a national level it may distort a whole economy, and at the individual level it can destroy a person's self-respect and even their life. A banker to whom I told the sad stories from Haripalala responded by saying: 'you cannot make an omelette without breaking some eggs'. He may have been right, but it is surely unacceptable that an intervention that is intended to help the poor should injure any of them. If even a few of the many serious weaknesses are corrected, and if some of the exaggerated expectations are moderated, the book will have served its purpose well.

Index